OUR VISION OF EUROPE

Group of the European People's Party
(Christian Democrats) and European Democrats
in the European Parliament

OUR VISION OF EUROPE
Proximity,
Competitiveness
and Visibility

EPP-ED

2001

Garant

Published for: EPP-ED Group in the European Parliament
Chairman: Hans-Gert Poettering
Secretary-General: Klaus Welle

Responsible: Research-Documentation-Publications Service
                   Pascal Fontaine
                   Deputy Secretary-General
Coordinators: Emma Petroni & Jan-Willem Vlasman
Address: European Parliament
                   60 rue Wiertz
                   1047 Brussels
                   Belgium
Telephone: + 32/2/2842284
                   + 32/2/2846407
INTERNET: http://www.epp-ed.org
E-Mail: epp-ed@europarl.eu.int

The contributions in this book reflect the views of the authors and are not necessarily those of the EPP-ED Group in the European Parliament.

Group of the European People's Party (Christian Democrats)
and European Democrats in the European Parliament
"Our Vision of Europe"
Leuven-Apeldoorn, Garant 2001
255 pp. – 24 cm
D/2001/5779/80
ISBN 90-441-1180-9

Garant
Tiensesteenweg 91, 3010 Leuven – Kessel-Lo (Belgium)
Koninginnelaan 96, 7315 EB Apeldoorn (The Netherlands)

Contents

Introduction

Hans-Gert POETTERING
Chairman of the EPP-ED Group
in the European Parliament

The history of European integration is a story of unparalleled success. Countries that were once bitter rivals have become partners who are now united in the European Union. The quest for hegemony that took place in past centuries has been replaced by a co-operation between equals, based on trust. As a community based on the rule of law the Union has ensured peace and stability within our continent for the past fifty years. The co-operation over these five decades has reached a hitherto inconceivable breadth and depth. At the beginning it concentrated on the coal and steel industry, gradually expanding into other areas of commerce and industry. Today we have put into effect the European internal market, the Economic and Monetary Union and freedom of movement. In foreign and security policy, too, we are about to create more common ground and we are also committed to European rapid response forces for crisis management. From its origins as a purely economic union, the European Union is becoming a political union. It is about to take its first steps as a global player.

Over the decades integration has been more or less an end in itself. More common features, more activities undertaken as a community were seen as positive moves. However, today the process of bringing Europe together has reached the stage where it would seem to be advisable to stop and ask the question: What now? What are our current motives and aims for the integration process of the future? Do we continue with Jean Monnet's small step policy or has this policy outlived its usefulness and must we set off along a new path?

Now seems to me to be a good time to ask this question about the ultimate objective of Europe and try to find answers. But the time is also right for another reason: we are on the verge of the greatest expansion that the Union has ever experienced in its history. The increase by ten or more Central and Eastern European countries as well as Malta and Cyprus is, without a doubt, the greatest challenge and question for the future facing Europe at the beginning of the 21st century. The entry of those countries from Central and Eastern Europe that have done away with communism in an admirable, peaceful revolution is a moral, historic and political necessity. Expansion means peace and security in freedom for the European Union and the countries who are seeking membership, an increase in political and economic power for Europe in global competition, an expansion and strengthening of the internal market as well as historic justice and solidarity. In this context it is worth quoting Konrad Adenauer, who once maintained: 'We must look towards the East, too, when we think of Europe. Europe includes countries that have a rich European past. They, too, must be given the opportunity to join. Europe must be big, must have the strength and the influence to be able to look after its own interests in world politics.'

The Nice summit opened the door for expansion. But Nice did not produce the comprehensive reforms that an expanded Union needs in the 21st century. In particular, Nice retained governmental co-operation in the areas of foreign and security policy and in justice and home affairs, the so-called second and third pillars of the EU Treaty. This intergovernmental cooperation – the policy of the lowest common denominator – weakens the ability of the Union to act and is not subject to any democratic scrutiny or checks by the European Court of Justice. Hence, important areas of policy in the European Union do not comply with the demands of the rule of law and democracy. Nice did not answer the question of objectives either: questions on the structure of the Union, its institutions, its ability to act, the limitations of its authority towards the individual states, its democratic legitimacy and – last but not least – its responsibility towards its citizens.

The time has come for a constitutional debate. It must be wide-ranging. It must not be carried out over the heads of the citizens. Accordingly, the European People's Party (Christian Democrats) and European Democrats (EPP-ED) are arguing against the intergovernmental approach of the past and are calling for a conference along the lines of the Fundamental Rights Convention. In this the European Parliament and national representatives of the people as well as governmental representatives and the European Commission must play a leading role. The applicant states must also be able to put forward their ideas. This convention will put the imminent constitutional discussions on a broad foundation. A document drawn up here, that includes the Charter of Fundamental Rights, should then be used as a decision-making template for the intergovernmental conference planned for 2004. Perhaps we shall then succeed in finishing Robert Schuman's work which, with his plan of 9 May 1950, laid 'the first foundation stone of a European Federation that is essential for maintaining peace.'

The EPP-ED Group in the European Parliament deals not only with day-to-day policies but also with basic, conceptual questions of European policy. It is, therefore, in the logic of this tradition that the EPP-ED Group has – with this book – devoted itself to the future of the European integration process. We have reached a point in time when it is necessary to express clearly our vision of Europe in the 21st century. Only those who know their goals know the right path to take at the important crossroads. Only the visionary has a compass to show him the way through day-to-day politics. For this project it has managed to secure leading personalities from the European Parliament, national parliaments and governments as well as the European Commission. They all belong to the same European family. The authors, who have excellent knowledge and a wealth of experience, give their views on the most important issues that will affect Europe in the future.

I have already mentioned two of these issues: the constitutional question and the enlargement of the Union. Another critical theme for the future of the European Union is its competitiveness. The introduction of the euro is certainly the most spectacular step in all this. It will undoubtedly increase the competitiveness of our businesses, but it will also keep the European integration process firmly in the sights of each citizen. But other matters will also play a part in the question of the competitiveness of our businesses in the 21st century: for example, the development of the employment market, how we deal with the challenges of the Agricultural Policy and whether we succeed in playing a leading role in the new technologies.

I have pointed out above that the European Union is firmly on its way to becoming a global player. Foreign, security and defence policy matters are therefore becoming increasingly important. With the East-West conflict at an end, the European Union will be expected to take more responsibility for foreign policy. This applies first and foremost to its immediate neighbours. The European Union must succeed in further reducing tensions in the former Yugoslavia and strengthening co-operation with the countries bordering the Mediterranean as well as increasing the Europe-Arab/Islamic dialogue. The logic of the integration process includes taking on additional responsibility for foreign policy. The Union must be prepared to commit itself to the values it espouses. This applies above all to development policy.

But one of the most important tasks of this century is surely to bring the citizens closer to the European Union. The European idea must capture the hearts and minds of its citizens and become an integral part of them. I hope that this book can go some way towards achieving this aim.

1
PROXIMITY

EPP-ED

1.1 Bridging the gap

1.1.1 Transparency in the European context

Jean-Claude JUNCKER
Prime Minister of the Grand Duchy of Luxembourg

Maastricht – a turning point

The debate on the ratification of the Maastricht Treaty in 1992/93 constituted a *turning point* in European history. It put an abrupt end to the weak consensus which had surrounded the progress of European integration for most of the preceding decades. For a long time, an enlightened political elite, convinced of the need for European integration, had counted on the passive goodwill and tacit agreement of the people. The Danish 'no' in the referendum of 2 June 1992 unexpectedly signalled the appearance of the 'citizen', which was sensational in the Danish case, less dramatic elsewhere. It was all the more unexpected because strong parliamentary majorities in favour of the Treaty existed everywhere, including in Denmark and in France, where the referendum that was organised on President Mitterrand's initiative almost handed victory to the 'no' vote. The reality of a schism between a political class largely in complete support of the Treaty and a much more sceptical population was suddenly apparent. The negotiations had not anticipated this: at the time, the criticism that was levelled at the reform process emanated principally from pro-European fora, the 'European technocrats', who deplored the lack of ambition of the negotiating governments. As for the general public, it seemed to lose interest in an affair that was being conducted by an exclusive circle of initiates.

The atmosphere changed completely once the Treaty was signed. The actual scope of the new Treaty was certainly one of the reasons behind this phenomenon. The Treaty did in fact cover a certain number of areas that directly affected the interests of the citizens: currency, cross-border movements, and the right to vote in European and local elections. The political authorities were henceforth obliged to address the general public and explain the effects of the reforms that had been adopted. The reaction of the public was surprising. Curiously enough, it referred less to the content of the Maastricht Treaty than to the very foundations of European integration. The European project was less well assimilated and accepted by the people than had always been believed. To a section of the public, the project seemed remote, too ambitious and hermetic, imposed by politicians and bureaucrats far removed from the grass roots. The absence of transparency was first among the grievances levelled against the European integration process: transparency actually appeared to conceal the more than questionable legitimacy of the process, the system's inherent 'democratic deficit'.

As we shall see in the *first part*, the theme of transparency, has, therefore, logically held a central role in the reactions of European leaders to the upheaval caused by Maastricht. And yet, probably because the question of transparency was not understood in all its underlying complexity, the initiatives that were taken have not responded adequately to the citizens' questions. They have even had certain perverse effects.

In the *second part* we shall therefore seek to include the issue of transparency within the framework of a more coherent and comprehensive reflection on European integration. In this approach, transparency must be seen as a policy serving the development of a genuine area of European citizenship. Such a project requires, first of all, a redefinition of the objectives and means of the European project. It will also depend on our capacity to generate a genuine democratic debate on the future of Europe. Accordingly, as we shall suggest in the *third part*, we need to go beyond the prevailing limitations of the question of transparency in order to launch a debate on an active information and communication strategy to be pursued by all participants in 'European governance'.

An inadequate response: transparency as a panacea

The initial reaction to the citizens' rebellion was to take refuge in the search for greater transparency. The political leaders thought, or pretended to think, that improving access to documents and information was enough to redress the situation.

The Treaty itself already showed the way, albeit timidly: a declaration annexed to the Treaty stated that 'the transparency of the decision-making process reinforces the democratic character of the institutions, as well as the public's confidence in the administration'. As a result, the Commission was invited to submit to the Council, in 1993 at the latest, a report on the measures aimed at increasing public access to the information held by the institutions.

The conclusions of the European Councils of Birmingham and Edinburgh in

1992 followed suit by insisting on the need to ensure greater transparency in the work of the institutions. This invitation gave rise, soon after, to an interinstitutional agreement on transparency, democracy and subsidiarity, followed by codes of conduct in the various institutions devoted largely to access to documents. The 1997 Amsterdam Treaty elevated this right of access to documents to a constitutional principle (Article 255 of the Treaty, on the basis of which the Commission recently submitted a proposal designed to offer very extensive access to documents, while excluding internal documents that record individual reflections or exchanges of views or opinions expressed freely and without constraint in the context of internal consultations). At the same time, the Amsterdam Treaty was listing among the general principles of the Union the idea that decisions must be taken as close as possible to citizens, an idea that the recently adopted Charter of Fundamental Rights does not contradict. These *initiatives to promote transparency* did not remain strictly limited to access to documents: of particular note was the Commission's systematic effort to hold wide-ranging consultations before the presentation of legislative proposals as well as to simplify texts. In addition, the idea of opening up Council of Ministers' meetings to the public began to be accepted, albeit in a very restricted way.

All these initiatives possess their merit. However, they fell far short of finding a solution to the real problem. Influenced by various factors, which deserve proper identification, transparency understood as access to documents and the holding of meetings open to the public tended to become an objective in itself instead of being seen as part of a comprehensive reflection on the nature of European integration. The arrival of new Member States such as Sweden and Finland, which have an established tradition of transparency in public life, further reinforced this tendency. Because of the crisis of public confidence in the European project, there was a strong temptation to copy the Scandinavian methods, without thinking of adapting them to the Union context. Another factor played a parallel role in this context: in several European countries, the 90s witnessed operations to restore ethical standards in public life. Challenging the occult practices of the past and demanding total transparency in politicians' actions were the order of the day. Transparency became an instrument for giving an ethical dimension to political life. In this climate, eurosceptic circles deliberately drew a connection between political corruption and the 'opaque workings' of the Community institutions. Finally, a last factor, no less important though, was linked to the European Parliament's will to increase its political control over the Commission: transparency was raised to the rank of symbol of Europe's 'lurch' into democracy and instrument of power in the battle of influence between institutions.

In citing these factors, we are not seeking to minimise the importance of transparency. On the contrary, we are trying to pin down *the complexity of the issue of transparency* and to appeal to clarity. The reactions of the public to Maastricht reflect a profound unease which exceeds the framework of European integration. We are witnessing, and have been for some years now, a degree of scepticism towards representative democracy: people have less faith in their elected representatives to solve their problems. They often feel that they are losing their autonomy, that they are powerless in the face of new technology, globalisation and European integration. This explains the proliferation of local initiatives and requests for referendums.

This sentiment is exacerbated at European level because Brussels is more removed from the citizens and because the way the Community system works is not well understood. For a long time, insofar as citizens agreed with the general thrust, this was not a problem. The positive results of integration – reconciliation, peace and prosperity – legitimised the Community system. After Maastricht, questions about the general direction of integration led people to look more closely at the decision-making process and the way the system works. But for anyone who sees matters exclusively in national terms and seeks to understand the Union on the sole basis of the usual criteria for parliamentary democracy – the dominant model in Western Europe – the Union is viewed as lacking in legitimacy. The more fundamental criticism of the 'intrinsically undemocratic' nature of the Union has thus been added to criticism directed at opaque workings and the failure to take the citizens' wishes into account.

The charge of a lack of transparency covers, therefore, two very different things. Most of the initiatives taken over the last few years in the area of transparency have been concerned with the daily operations of the system and have neglected consideration of the actual nature of European integration.

This homing in on a very partial aspect of transparency is not without its *perverse effects*. We live in an era characterised by what can be termed a 'media frenzy': the speed and quantity of 'items of information' rate more highly than reflection and substance. Speaking sometimes seems more important than actually saying something. This situation rubs off on the transparency debate and leads to an approach that is more quantitative than qualitative. The current tendency to demand that the institutions, especially the Commission, publish all documents, whatever they may be, is excessive and, in the long run, counter-productive. Initially motivated by a concern to avoid potential mistakes made by the Commission, a 'not democratically elected' organ, it paradoxically weakens the credibility of the very parliamentary mechanisms laid down in the treaties to ensure democratic control of the Commission, by multiplying the fronts on which it must 'cover' itself. The Commission, like any institution, needs space in which to reflect freely. It is not natural to require it to publish internal memoranda that, as yet, commit noone but the author. There is a tendency to rank equally a junior official's note and a formal decision of the College of Commissioners. What really counts is that decisions, as well as implied motives, are explained in a completely transparent manner, and justified, by the institution. For years now the Commission, and on its own initiative, has been conducting very broad consultations with civil society before submitting its legislative proposals; it publishes Green and White Papers regularly, which enables everyone to evaluate its arguments and interests. We are justified in asking ourselves whether the total transparency demanded by some is not a way of enabling various lobbies, defending specific interests, to influence decision-making in a way that hardly conforms to democracy.

A second example concerns the debates in the Council open to the public. At the beginning of its mandate, each Presidency organises a debate open to the public in each of the Council's manifestations. It is hard to see how this tedious exercise, in which five Ministers and one Commissioner each reads out a statement lasting a few minutes, increases transparency. My impression is that it contributes instead to the cynical view of politics held by many citizens. Everyone knows that they are just going through the motions. The real discussions take place elsewhere. The issue of publicising the Council's work deserves a real debate. Several questions are raised in this context. Should there be a distinction between the legislative activities of the Council and its executive role? How can we avoid superficial transparency leading to a proliferation of secret consultations in the corridors, to the probable detriment of the small countries? If this debate is to bear fruit, however, it must be conducted in a context where the system of the Union is understood.

Transparency reinscribed within a comprehensive political reflection

Transparency cannot be the cure for all evil. It is not the solution to the problem of the intelligibility or the legitimacy of the Community system. It cannot be viewed in the abstract, separate from the fundamental substance and stakes involved. On the contrary, it has a crucial role to play in the context of a collective reflection on the future of the Union and as an instrument at the service of clearly defined objectives.

In the first place, *the objective of European integration* must be clarified, or clarified again. Preaching unity will not win the support of the people, jealous as they are of their heritage, for a process that calls for sacrifices and for efforts to understand the needs of others.

The primary objective of European integration has always been political: reconciliation in Europe and the preservation of peace. But, on the one hand, the chosen instruments – economic instruments – have contributed to a weakening of the visibility of that objective. On the other hand, for the generations that did not experience the war, these objectives are no longer perceived as the driving force of integration since they are considered to have been attained and to be self-evident. However, the current importance of the peace objective deserves to be recalled. The case of the former Yugoslavia should prompt us to do so. In this sense, the theme of enlargement brings us back, in a way, to the beginning. If the Community was once a peace effort, its enlargement towards the East and the South now has that role.

The Community was also built around the notion of solidarity. The reception given to the peoples of Central and Eastern Europe makes it possible, here too, to renew the debate about the objective of integration. Enlargement constitutes an opportunity to rethink this beautiful idea. Should solidarity not, henceforth, be placed at the centre of the European project, as a fundamental element of the European model of society: solidarity between regions, solidarity with future generations, solidarity in facing up to the effects of globalisation, and solidarity with developing countries? The Charter of Fundamental Rights – and this is one of its innovative aspects – encourages this by its very structure: dignity, freedoms, equality, solidarity, citizenship and justice.

Other objectives exist, focused on the notion of efficiency: expanding markets, maintaining our position in the global arena, and combating the threats to our security and pollution. They should not be neglected, but they do not suffice in themselves to legitimise the European project.

Let us dwell, precisely, on *legitimacy*. It is necessary here to get beyond the stage of chanting slogans about the 'democratic deficit' of the Union. That is a simplistic and dangerous view of reality in which the question of transparency tends to introduce an additional bias. The slogan is used by eurosceptics and europhiles alike. The former view national legitimacy as the only true legitimacy and consent, at most, to intergovernmental cooperation only. Here, the theme of transparency often serves to contest the legitimacy of the Community structure. The objections raised by the europhiles are of an altogether different nature. They are based on a conventional reading of the Community model, conventional in the sense of a parliamentary model. In this reading, the Union lacks legibility and legitimacy because the directly-elected European Parliament does not exercise legislative powers in the same way that a national parliament of a Member State does. This line of thought underlies the European Parliament's demands for more power. The European Parliament considers itself to be the exclusive depository, or at least the principal depository, of popular legitimacy. This approach underestimates the hybrid and distinctive nature of the European model, which has different legitimacies: parliamentary (the European Parliament, but also the national parliaments), state (the Council), as well as supranational and technocratic (the Commission). It is a model characterised by checks and balances, by power-sharing between different players reflecting various legitimacies.

Two questions arise in this context. The first concerns the nature of the system: is it appropriate to reinforce the parliamentary elements, as we have done since the Single Act and move towards a conventional model? Certainly, legibility would be improved, but this would profoundly modify the nature of the Union. In my opinion, the Union must remain a union of the people and a union of the States.

The second question concerns communication. If it is true that the current complexity has its reasons, it is also true that a real effort is required to explain and communicate. We shall come back to this in the final part.

The post-Nice debate will also cover the *demarcation of powers and responsibilities*. The citizens' negative reactions are partly explained by the tendency of the Union to creep into the furthest recesses of daily life while not making its presence felt in cases that clearly require intervention at European level. This question must be seriously addressed. I do not believe that a list of powers and responsibilities, carved in stone for all time in the Treaty, is the way to go. Had we acted in this way in the 50s, the Community would never have become what it is today. It should be recalled, in this context, that, during the negotiations for the Single Act, a simple reference in the Treaty to monetary ambitions caused a mighty rumpus. Six years later, the Union decided that a single currency should be created. The risk of setting the status quo in stone and making later developments impossible is more dangerous than maintaining a certain vagueness about what the future will look like.

Aiming for a progressive recentring of Union activities by political agreement seems a more promising approach to me. What does recentring mean? Concentrating on the important areas which, in all federations or confederations, are addressed centrally. For historical reasons, the Union has long done the opposite: while foreign policy, national security and currency were taboo subjects, or nearly so, Brussels made great progress with the management of sectoral policies, at the risk of being accused of nit-picking and bureaucratic interventionism. It is time to reverse the trend. The subsidiarity principle invites us to do so. Too often, we see it as an instrument to keep powers at or repatriate them to the national level; we forget that the subsidiarity principle demands action at a higher level when this is more rational and more efficient. To increase transparency, the annual budgetary debates in the Council and in the European Parliament should be accompanied by a multiannual programme approved by the three institutions.

The approach sketched out here does not necessarily call for treaty reforms. It is, at base, a question of political will and behavioural change. The Luxembourg European Council on employment and the Lisbon Council on the economy clearly demonstrate that action can be properly taken at grass roots level rather than starting with the institutional aspects. Union action would gain more legibility and therefore transparency. This is particularly important, in my view, with regard to foreign policy. We spend too much time focusing on the subtleties of common strategies, joint actions and common positions, instead of developing a real foreign policy. I think, in such an area, the desire to settle everything down to the very last detail reflects a worrying lack of ambition and political will. The real questions are elsewhere. Are we, yes or no, prepared to consider replacing the European members of the UN Security Council with the Union as a body? Is the Union prepared to assume its responsibilities in terms of external representation of the euro? Are our Member States prepared to bear the cost of a European defence system? With regard to external relations, do we aim to overcome tunnel vision and petty institutional battles? Analogous questions can be posed regarding the other big themes referred to above. I am sure that, by asking these types of question, we would fire the interest of the general public.

Transparency and communication

The best project is bound to fail if its promoters do not succeed in winning the communication war. The European project suffers from a communication deficit. The reasons are many and varied: the complexity of the system, the need to address fifteen different audiences and the constant search for compromise which leaves little room for simple and effective slogans. This is a case of real constraints that no press service reform could overcome. This is no excuse for the amateurish character of some of our communication efforts. All attempts to remedy this, to use the vector of television and new information technologies more effectively, are welcome. However, the real problem lies elsewhere.

It is often said that Europe must be 'sold' more effectively. I am wary of this type of slogan, which suggests a pretty product put together by experts that needs only to be packaged correctly in order to convince the public. Expressions such as 'Europe has to be brought closer to the citizen' also denote unsavoury paternalism. I am arguing for a more ambitious and more difficult approach: to make Europe into a project that is understood and supported by the people, a project that develops each day. The European Union is not just a happy state, created out of nothing 50 years ago, one 9 May, which protects itself and sings its own praises. It is also a clear vision, a stubborn will and an everyday conquest. Reinscribed within a comprehensive political reflection, the theme of transparency can exhibit all its richness; it is a question of implementing an active communication policy with the aim of achieving greater popular participation in the life of the Union. It is about something entirely different from ensuring access to documents, though this aspect does have its place. A caricature from the Maastricht days might illustrate the extent of the difference between access to documents and a real communication policy: certain governments, out of a laudable concern for transparency, sent a copy of the text approved by the intergovernmental conference to all their citizens. Since the text was set out in the form of amendments to former treaties, the result was inevitably disastrous. The poor voters did not understand a thing and felt that they were being led up the garden path by impenitent technocrats.

How do we develop an active communication policy resulting in true transparency? Three common sense conditions must be met: we must use a language of truth, accept the principle of European governance and generate a genuine European debate. I will briefly expand upon these different points.

The first requirement for success is to *use a language of truth*. The defenders of the European idea tend too often to promote only the positive aspects and cast a veil over the problems. Let us take the case of the euro. We cannot deny that it will require discipline, sometimes stringent discipline, and that it will demand more flexibility and more rigour. This is the price to be paid for a project with multiple advantages: claiming that there will be nothing to pay is dishonest. Likewise, establishing a real CFSP and ESDP, which we heartily desire, will not be possible at zero cost. If Europe wants to increase its defence capacity, for instance, it will have to agree to pay the price. Internal security, a widely-shared objective, has a price, in budgetary terms, but also in terms of a loss of sovereignty and national control. Another example is enlargement. I am sometimes embarrassed by the grandiose and solemn statements made for public consumption and the scepticism expressed in private. Why can we not have an open, honest debate about the advantages and the disadvantages of large-scale enlargement? We must not be afraid to say that this historical undertaking will incur costs and will entail threats to the cohesion and efficiency of the Union of the future. By concealing the difficulties, we run the risk of provoking, one day, a negative reaction on the part of the people, one which could deal a fatal blow to what is certainly the great historical challenge for the Union.

My second point is linked to the first. Using a language of truth also means recognising the existence in Europe of shared responsibilities and *a system of European governance*. The novelty of the European project resides precisely in the subtle equilibrium found between the various institutions, between the institutions and the Member States or regions, and between the Community elements and the intergovernmental elements. Everyone, at each level, must assume and fulfil their responsibilities. Constantly opposing 'Brussels' to the Member States is both dishonest and counter-productive. How can the citizen support the idea of Europe if all that is awkward and difficult is associated with 'Brussels'? The citizens' attitude towards the Union will not improve if we continue to use Brussels as the scapegoat for our difficulties, if we hide behind the procedural complexity to conceal our own responsibilities as governments. The governments' attitudes sometimes recall the behaviour of the child who, having killed its mother and father, says mournfully: 'have pity on a poor orphan'. The institutions have their role to play, but so do the States and the regions. It is easy to say that Brussels is responsible when there are problems. Brussels is all of us, that is the reality. When the Commission proposes a law, 'Brussels' has not decided anything yet. A proposal will be scrutinised by the (directly-elected) European Parliament and the Council (representing the governments of the Members States); they have the final say. When we point at 'Brussels' in response to popular dissatisfaction, implying that the citizen and even the national government can but endure and submit to the dark intentions of the anonymous eurocracy, we are in complete denial, as the psychiatrists say. I am arguing for reality to be reflected a little more in our communication. The institutional apparatus must be explained in as comprehensible terms as possible. We must spell it out: the Court of Justice has the judicial power, legislative power is shared between the European Parliament and the Council of Ministers, and the Commission proposes and implements legislation. It is clear that any initiative to simplify both the treaties and legislation can only be welcome. But one should not imagine that each citizen should or wishes to know the minute details of the codecision procedure; how many of our fellow citizens fully understand the internal workings of the national institutions? What is important is that the citizens know at which level of constitutional organisation – European, national, regional or local – the decisions that influence their daily lives are taken, and what means are at the citizens' disposal to influence these decisions, either by supporting a party manifesto or by sanctioning a policy. Such is not the case today, not sufficiently so.

In order to remove the taboos, in order for the Union to advance with and by the support of the people, it is not enough to work in the spotlight, diffusing to the wide world projects, counter-projects and non-papers. Those who drafted the Nice Treaty became aware of this necessity, since they felt the need to round off their work by *launching a vast democratic debate* on the Union of the future. I share the view of those who say that we cannot continue to use the Intergovernmental Conference as our only instrument. We have to move from diplomacy to democracy. The idea of proceeding in stages was suggested: I approve it. The year 2001 must be used for reflection involving the institutions, national parliaments and civil society. This will contribute to creating the unique democratic area and the sense of shared citizenship that are so desperately lacking at the present time. The debate will necessarily be adversarial and somewhat disorganised. We should not take offence: that is what democracy is all about. Let us stop crying 'crisis' every time adverse opinions are expressed or when a European Council meeting gives rise to a real discussion. As I said earlier, I do not think it is possible to define precisely the definitive shape of Europe. But I think the fundamental issues which I have described – the objectives to be pursued, the search for legitimacy, the nature of the system, and the recentring of policies – need to be discussed in depth. In a second stage, the Laeken European Council could decide to hold a Convention to work out the constituent elements of the future reform. The composition of such a Convention could be inspired by the Convention that drew up the Charter of Fundamental Rights. Transparency, the indispensable condition for objective contributions to this debate, will then find its true meaning.

Conclusion

The Maastricht turning point witnessed the abrupt entrance of the European citizen on to the European stage. For the Union, this is both a challenge and an opportunity. To cope with it, we must go beyond partial and overly timid reactions. Transparency, especially if seen from a narrow or even demagogic point of view, will not be the panacea. It can, however, become a crucial element in a thorough reflection on the nature of European integration and on a new European governance. Our objective must be to create a genuine European area of citizenship and democracy. These are the stakes of the post-Nice debate that will occupy us in the years to come.

1.1.2 Implementing subsidiarity in the right way

Dr Edmund STOIBER
Prime Minister of Bavaria

The process of European unification since the Second World War has been marked by reconciliation between peoples, reflection on Europe's common heritage and the values that sustain it, and an unparalleled economic upswing. Former enemies have become partners and firm friends. Europe today, for many people, is synonymous with hope for the future. This Europe is confronted by a whole new set of challenges: preserving peace throughout our continent, accommodating the influx of refugees, enlargement of the European Union towards the East, establishing Europe as a focus of business activity in a globalized world economy, combating international organized crime, promoting cross-border environmental protection and much more besides.

And so there are some crucial questions that have to be answered. What form do we want the Europe of the future to take? How is Europe to be organized, if it is to accomplish all these tasks as efficiently as possible? How can the European Union fulfil all its lofty aspirations? Do the Member States and regions still have sufficient freedom of action for the development of their own identities? Because the key to a successful Europe of the future cannot lie in centralism and uniformity, but only in the unity that arises out of diversity.

More than ever before, the central issue is to strike the right balance in dividing the tasks ahead between the EU, the Member States and the regions. Former Commission President Jacques Delors recently observed, *"The European Union gives the impression of wanting to intervene in everything, and is attracting justified criticism for doing so."*

It is a fact that, today, about half of all decisions that affect the domestic policies of the Member States are taken not in the national capitals but in Brussels. In the economic and agricultural sectors, the percentage is actually significantly higher. European policy is having an ever-growing impact on people's daily lives. It is increasingly coming to resemble a European domestic policy. In many cases, indeed, it is right that this should be so: the EU has brought many benefits to the citizens of Europe.

Even so, the question has to be asked: is the ever-increasing encroachment by European policy on the lives of the citizens necessary, justifiable and constructive in every case? It is obvious, after all, that decisions taken centrally in Brussels are necessarily more all-embracing, and may be less well adapted to specific local conditions, in other words less close to the citizen. Nor is it possible to avoid them being less clear to him: how they come about, and where the political responsibility lies, is very hard for him to comprehend.

There is a tendency towards expansion of the EU's areas of activity. The main reason for this is what has been called the "Monnet method" – an unending process of closer integration unsupported by any clear idea of where European unification is ultimately heading. This is made possible by rules on jurisdiction laid down in the Treaties – rules that in many cases are worded vaguely, in the style of blanket clauses or as mere declarations of intent. Yet the unlimited extension of the powers of the European Union would jeopardize its effectiveness and – no less important – public acceptance of European integration. The public would no longer understand the procedures applied or the decisions made. The citizen would no longer be able to identify where the responsibility lies, or where he should go for help with his problems. As a result, many people would criticize and reject the European apparatus. Doubt would thus be cast on the unique political success story of European integration, and on its eventual outcome.

To quote Jacques Delors again: *"I still wonder why Europe wants to concern itself with beaches and stretches of water where one can swim. And this is happening in the name of the citizens' Europe. I adhere to the principle of subsidiarity, which goes beyond the problem of the allocation of authority. It is not a simple principle concerned with administrative practice or policy, it is the expression of a specific notion of the individual, of personal freedom, of the responsibility of the grassroots groups. Society would work better if citizens were able to feel that they had a tighter grip on local matters, the matters that are close to their hearts, and that they had specific freedoms."*

Anyone who wants to see European integration succeed, then, must work towards the effective application of the principle of subsidiarity and the reorganization of the structure of authority within Europe. The principle of subsidiarity states that the European Union must act only if an objective cannot be satisfactorily achieved at Member State or regional level, so that European action is required if the goal is to be achieved. This is critical to the future viability of the European Union, especially an enlarged European Union.

I welcome the decision by the European Council in Nice to convene another Intergovernmental Conference in 2004, which will focus especially on the issues relating to a clear allocation of powers in Europe. I would like to see that conference deciding to broaden the principle of subsidiarity from its present status as a rule governing the *exercise* of powers within the EU to one governing the *allocation* of powers. When the next Intergovernmental Conference allocates tasks to the European Union, it should adhere to the fundamental rules of subsidiarity, and be guided especially by the following principles:

- ensuring that a greatly enlarged and much more diverse EU retains its efficiency and capacity to act;
- safeguarding diversity, independent responsibility and competition within Europe;
- transparency;
- clear attribution of political responsibility;
- democratic legitimacy;
- public acceptance.

The European Union must in future concentrate on those tasks that are genuinely European, meaning areas where a joint approach offers the only sure key to success. Anything where action at European level is not absolutely necessary, however, must be left in the hands of the Member States or regions, or transferred back to their jurisdiction. Then the functions of the EU must be critically scrutinized and redefined as clearly delimited, explicit powers.

This is the only way to ensure the efficiency and capacity to act of what will soon be a very large, diverse EU. It is the only way to ensure transparency and empower the citizen to allocate democratic responsibility for political decisions. Most of all, it is the only way to preserve that diversity of cultures, lifestyles and traditions that gives Europe its identity and its strength. And, finally, it is the only way to gain the consent of the public to the continuing process of European unification.

By contrast with this vision of a clear allocation of powers in line with the subsidiarity principle, there are those who argue in favour of "networking" concepts. These envisage the further europeanization of decision processes combined with the "networking" of all levels at which decisions are taken, with the involvement of what is referred to as "civil society" – in other words, the representatives of partial or individual interests. I take a sceptical view of ideas of this kind. The networking strategy would be more likely to exacerbate the present confusion of powers within Europe. Mixing up the various levels would bring a further lack of transparency and make the allocation of democratic responsibility very difficult.

Ultimately, the networking model would, in substance, sustain the present trend towards ever-increasing centralization of aspects of life at EU level. It amounts to no more, if you like, than business as usual under a new name. In the final analysis, the division of tasks would be that decisions are taken at EU level – albeit with the participation of various national authorities and representatives of interest groups – and implemented by the Member States and the regions, which would be relegated to the status of mere administrative bodies. And that would be the opposite of the distribution of tasks dictated by subsidiarity.

So what is to be done?

Firstly: The tasks of the EU must be redefined on the basis of the subsidiarity principle. That means transferring new powers to EU level as well as delegating present functions of the EU back to the Member States. The golden rule here must be that nothing is regulated at EU level unless Europe-wide regulation is actually necessary.

Foremost among those essential functions of the EU that can only be dealt with at Community level are the following:

– A joint approach to important issues of foreign and security policy.
– The preservation and full implementation of a single market with freedom of internal and external trade, and of a stable euro as an important factor in ensuring international competitiveness and inflation-free growth.
– A common approach to the EU's foreign trade interests, including a contribution to the development of a global organizational framework.
– The introduction of Community legislation on asylum and refugee policy, including a just distribution of the burdens involved.
– A Community visa policy, and the ensuring of high security standards at the external frontiers.
– An effective contribution to the campaign against cross-border crime.
– The agricultural market and pricing policy.
– Cross-border environmental protection.
– The promotion of top quality research.
– The prevention of unfair taxation practices.
– The strengthening of economic and social cohesion as an expression of European solidarity.

A more difficult question, politically, is to determine what should not – or should no longer – be regulated at European level. Difficult because it involves questioning vested rights and conducting audits of established structures. My view is that areas such as employment, social security, education, culture, the media, health, research, sport, tourism and regional planning should remain within the jurisdiction of the Member States – as should services of general interest, a much-debated area at present. It may well make sense for the EU to support action taken in these areas by the Member States, and to encourage cooperation between them, especially with a view to improving exchanges of experiences and information. But it should not be the function of the EU to impose specific targets and measures upon the Member States, or to dictate what their cooperation will cover and what form it will take. That is why the networking concept devised by the European Council in Lisbon, the new method of "open coordination", is unacceptable insofar as it aims to bypass the jurisdictional system laid down in the Treaties when imposing European requirements.

Secondly: Those powers that are to be exercised at European level in the future must be precisely defined. For example, it must be a function of the EU to preserve the internal market. But the implementation of the internal market must not be used as a pretext for legislation primarily designed to serve other objectives – such as those of health policy. To take another example, we need EU regulations on cross-border environmental protection, but the EU must not interpret that legislation as a mandate to impose requirements in such fields as regional planning or urban development.

Yet another example: the liberalization of services of general interest is releasing market forces beneficial to the interests of the economy and the public. But this must not be allowed to call into question the right of the Member States to determine for themselves what the content of such services should be and, especially, what considerations of public welfare should be linked to the provision of such services.

British Prime Minister Tony Blair recently summarized his view of Europe in the following terms: *"Integration where necessary, and decentralization where possible."* And he went on to lay out this vision of future European objectives: *"A Europe that does what it needs to do well; and what it doesn't need to do, it doesn't do at all. A Europe that matters by focusing on the things that matter [to Europe as a whole]."*

That is exactly what we shall have if the principle of subsidiarity is implemented in the right way.

1.1.3 Involving social structures and networks in policy-making

Marie-Thérèse HERMANGE
Vice-Chairman of the Committee on Employment
and Social Affairs in the European Parliament
Member of the EPP-ED Group
in the European Parliament

The contribution of organisations which are defending family life in policy making in the European Union.

How long and uncertain, through the chances of history, is the way to democracy, recognised today as the best mode of government possible for contemporary societies.... Starting on the fringes of early patriarchal societies, through its decisive development in the public places of Athens and Rome, its continuation in the great monastic orders during the periods of feudalism and monarchy, to its sudden resurgence in modern times and its formal recognition by the international community following the Second World War, the democratic model now stands unchallenged save by a minority of states or philosophical schools.

And yet our western societies, so eager after the Enlightenment, after the French Revolution, after de Tocqueville, after the grandiloquent speeches of the UN General Assemblies to champion the democratic ideal, today must have the courage and clearsightedness to recognise that this ideal is now in crisis. It has become a commonplace to point to the citizens' lack of interest in an ever more complex *res publica,* their scepticism over sterile programmes, their weariness with ponderous and faceless public services, their distrust of seemingly distant or compromised political leaders, in short, the universal underlying discontent at the feeling of being neither represented, nor understood, nor even really listened to.

I am convinced that these are just the growing pains of the democratic ideal: our social and political models, because they have shown their worth in the recent past, in a time of prosperity and collective grand designs, are struggling to reform in a context that has changed radically in the space of scarcely a few decades. The irony of history is that it is from the grassroots, the 'people' (δημοζ) that today new models of democracy may arise: in the wake of the medieval guilds and the impressive contemporary advances of the trade union movement have appeared numerous socio-economic partners, representative social structures or lobbies, interest or study groups, national or international networks, semi-public or private. Are these not today powerful guarantors, inasmuch as they are active and constructive as well as respected, of the continuance of a democratic model which finds in them the most direct expression of the hopes, visions and demands of the citizens, though the question arises of how truly representative our elected representatives are?

To illustrate my point, and because I have been invited to deal with this theme, I should like to take the specific example of the organisations and associations involved in the protection of family life in Europe of which my political responsibilities have given me a better understanding. For me this is the most typical example of local democracy in Europe, since the child and the family have the deepest and most immediate impact on the European citizen, whilst Europe as such is unaware, legally speaking, of these realities, choosing since its creation to focus its development on, among other things, economic, financial, legal and geopolitical questions. Is it any wonder that men and women living in Europe today have so little sense of being listened to and taken into consideration by the European institutions when all they hear about is the Europe of goods and what chiefly concerns them is the Europe of human beings: the Europe of their families and children? Here is an approach certain to bridge the gap between the governed and the governing, to bring Europe genuinely close to each and every individual.

A utopia? Yes, if by this you mean what Sir Thomas More meant: a dream that lifts reality to a higher level. There is a remarkable instance of this type of utopia: through one association's generous, untiring and constructive commitment political decisions were taken on behalf of the family – I should like to stay with this example for a moment. I am referring to the international movement *ATD – Quart Monde*, engaged since 1957 in the fight against extreme poverty in the so-called rich countries. Its hundreds of unpaid volunteers engaged each day on the ground have found that poverty affects not only individuals but whole families, confronted with illiteracy, long-term unemployment, shaky health and increasing marginalisation.

Faced with such situations of abject poverty, which in France spurred Abbé Pierre to sound his first alarm in the winter of 1956, the founder of ATD – Quart Monde, Father Joseph Wresinski, pluckily staged in November 1972 the first meeting between European Commissioner Albert Coppé and leading campaigners against poverty in Europe, not on the basis of a directive to be carried out, but simply on the initiative of representatives of civil society plus the personal acceptance of responsibility by European officials. The Commission, overstepping the mandate of the first Social Action Programme requested by the Summit of Heads of State and Government in October 1972 (adopted by the Council in February 1974), drew up an anti-poverty programme, the starting point for the Commission's whole involvement in this field. It was on the basis of a study commissioned from ATD – Quart Monde into the real lives of the very poor that Irish Commissioner Patrick Hillery conceived this programme (1976-1980).

The fight against illiteracy, for its part, typifies just how networks are involved in the procedure of political decision-making. In 1977, for its 20th anniversary, ATD – Quart Monde proclaimed the challenge of defeating illiteracy. The Commission, asked for its views, said it had no role in this area. Whereupon the European Parliament, fresh from its first elections by universal suffrage, agreed to take up the initiative, forming a parliamentary Intergroup christened *Comité Quart Monde européen*. This body called for a report on illiteracy in Europe, adopted in May 1982, the first official document on the subject, and pressed the Commission to entrust to the Movement a study into eight innovative experimental projects in Europe in that field. This report and study finally led the Council of Education Ministers to adopt a resolution on the fight to combat illiteracy in June 1984, and the illiteracy issue, we all know, is now covered by the majority of Member States.

I mention here three methodological aspects which I consider crucial: close consultation with associations on the ground, personal involvement of the political authorities, and a new genuine European awareness of the issues, putting these at the heart of all important decisions (producing an interservice group within the Commission, as well as an Observatory of policies to combat poverty). It is just such measures, which have been successful in tackling poverty (sadly, still very much with us), which need to be adopted today by all elected representatives willing to make children and the family a part of their political struggle.

This is the adventure I now share with some 30 MEPs who agreed to support the relaunch of an Intergroup on family and child protection: it means paying attention to family support associations, as diverse as possible in experience and inspiration, collecting their proposals, converting them into draft reports or resolutions and, finally, submitting them to a Commission which, invoking the subsidiarity principle, still acknowledges no responsibility in the matter. One day perhaps a new Albert Coppé, a new Patrick Hillery, will invite their Commission colleagues to seriously consider this fundamental issue. I am increasingly impressed by the scale of the resources deployed to resolve the mad cow crisis, when there is no meaningful Community concern to tackle children's problems. But the biggest crisis on our continent is not BSE: it is our society. And innumerable associations, networks and NGOs, but also experts from all disciplines, are constantly warning us that the origins of this sickness are largely to be found in the crisis of the family. Are they being listened to enough? Obviously not. I will now speak out and say, after years of effort on the ground and hearings of a diversity of personalities and experts, *the family is a new idea in Europe, and it therefore deserves a new examination.*

It is new for the sociologist, for it represents the best anchorage and stability for societies gone adrift. It is new for the lawyer, who, amid the proliferation of players and subjects of law, recognises it as the basic unit of society. It is new for the psychologist, because in it are unfolded the most fundamental stages of the child's awakening and development. It is new for the psychiatrist, because within it are worked out the masculine and feminine referents, the basis of all social equilibrium. It is new for the social worker, because it is the first support of the jobless or retired. It is new for the educator, for in it are learned solidarity, dialogue and reconciliation. It is new for the mayor, for in it are joined the private aspect of conjugal commitment and the public aspect of society's recognition and support. It is new for the historian, since he can study therein as never before the truly free commitment to love, unaffected by any external conditioning. It is new for the demographer, because it is the key – I need hardly mention! – to any rise in fertility in our 'Old Continent' never more deserving of the name. It is new for the parents themselves, as studies reveal that for various and – unfortunately compelling – reasons, the number of children they desire is, in Western Europe, less than the number they actually have. It is new for the economist, who now recognises the primacy of human capital in any business, as well as the investment and wealth creation value represented by the birth of a child. It is always new for the theologian, since he sees therein the image of the ever-renewed Alliance of love between the Creator and His creation. It is always new for the young, since there more than anywhere are their dreams and plans for the future rooted.

It is because the family is a new idea that many are coming forward, within the associations and in civil society, to share and develop this fundamental idea. But the approach is always incomplete, since it lacks financial and legal resources: many are concerned with the debt-ridden or broken families, or families with a handicapped child, or badly-housed families, or matters of custody or schooling, occupational guidance or medical care, etc. Provision of such a range of family support is much to the credit of the social players. But if their efforts are to be better rewarded, they need a coherent overall plan, since all aspects of family life are interlinked. I appeal to lawmakers, holders of power, and senior officials to heed the pleas of these social players, so that the family finally becomes, for them as well, a new idea.

Along this road, however, there are forces of resistance, if not of downright opposition. Family counselling is not supported in certain quarters of the major international institutions, nor even by governments of Member States of the European Union. Here is not the place to discuss this problem, which would need to be developed at length and could be represented in many ways. But one can at least – since this is most instructive – consider the treatment to be given, under the EU's enlargement process, to the legal provisions explicitly relating to family protection in the Constitutions of the Central and European countries. These Constitutions, which came into force in the aftermath of the fall of the Berlin Wall, contain for the most part all the guarantees required by families, in the heightened understanding rooted in 40 years of Communist dictatorship, that the family is the most solid foundation for democracy and freedom. Did you know that one of those countries, well-advanced on the road to European integration, had in October 2000 to withdraw its signature, in the course of discussions conducted by the UN's Economic Commission for Europe, from a 'consensus' text proposed by that Commission's 'Committee on Human Housing' on the grounds that reference to the family had dropped out of the final document? For us, the great strength of the association networks is that it can get at this type of often concealed information, and can spotlight it, in order to follow the arguments and developments in the full light of day. Another example of this was the Beijing Plus Five Conference in New York in June 2000, where associations were able to reveal to the public the scandalous pressures exerted by western delegates on the Polish delegation, pressures affecting the sensitive issues of protection of life and family which were not included in the mandates received by those delegates or in the official criteria adopted for the enlargement process.

Not to be overlooked in any consideration of family life and support is the specific case of families with a member affected by disability. Here too, the strength of the networks and associations has these past few years been impressive, as I was able to observe when drawing up my report on disability in Europe, with the extremely valuable support of the European Disability Forum. Here again, attention to the family as a focus for problem-solving is the most appropriate approach, if only because today in 37 million families across Europe, one of their members is directly affected by disability. Here too was confirmed the methodological principle, worked out by the anti-poverty associations: action to combat disability is undertaken, first, by listening to the families concerned, and then by actually involving them in the development and implementation of action programmes. The message now being sent to the political authorities – so often tempted by the model of technocratic and controlled efficiency – by these hundreds of disability support associations, and the millions of families they represent is this: 'Don't just act for us, act with us'.

I must instance here a brilliant success – the reader will forgive me another French example! – that of Téléthon. A handful of parents of children with muscular dystrophy, given up by the welfare services and the scientific research institutes, decided to start ambitious research and integration programmes themselves, counting only on the general public – appealed to in a marathon TV programme launched in 1987 – to provide the vital funds until then unavailable. It was an immediate success, which has grown year after year, backed by huge popular support. The French Association Against

Muscular Dystrophy (AFM), with its scientific council of international reputation, immediately embarked on research programmes into genetic diseases
which affect 25 million people in Europe, triggering, after the announcement
of initial results – the first human genome map was produced in the
Généthon laboratories in 1992 – the race between the leading American,
European and Japanese genetic engineering laboratories. The AFM was the
first association to sign with the French Government a bipartite genetic
research agreement and the French public authorities have always relied on
the considerable expertise generated by its tremendous development.

But the AFM does not forget its history nor its identity: it is first and foremost a parents' association and, as such, makes available to families a whole
network of services and multidisciplinary help. Today the AFM is taking the
fight to Europe with the creation of Eurodis, a European federation of associations fighting rare diseases, which are of little interest commercially and to
which it is trying to sensitise the European institutions – isn't it the duty of
the political decision-makers, in the democratic system, to offer their protection to the weakest and to encourage the fair allocation of resources?

In addition to this input into the field of genetic research – valuable experience indeed for European institutions that consult widely and have many
bioethics research groups – other family associations have long been stimu-
lating decision-making of a specifically more political character at European
level. Most notable is COFACE (Confederation of Family Organisations in
the European Union) which came into being at the very start of the Treaty of
Rome – the family associations immediately sensed the importance of this
event for their everyday life. Here, too, the purely economic character of the
EEC and its lack of jurisdiction in matters of family policy impelled family
organisations to seeks ways of influencing, for the benefit of families, the
political initiatives developed by the institutions. From the start of the 60s
they spearheaded the fight for the development by the EEC of a European
consumer protection policy, which would match the initiatives taken on
behalf of industry and commerce. Working closely with what was to become
the European Consumers' Organisation, and with the support of personalities such as Joseph Fontanet, French Government Minister, and
Commission Vice-President Sicco Mansholt, the family associations successfully pushed for the creation of the European Community Consumer
Organisations Contact Committee, which was joined by consumer coopera-
tives and trade unions. This was the Commission's first advisory consumer
body, still in existence today as the Consumer Committee. Another door
admitting family organisations into the strictly economic logic of the EEC
was the issue of relations between family life and the world of work, with particular reference to equal treatment between men and women, strongly
developed by the Community in the 1970s. For instance, in 1982-1983,
COFACE put all its weight behind the draft Directive on parental leave and

leave for family reasons, blocked unhappily by the Thatcher Government. Not until the Maastricht Treaty was the blockage removed thanks to collective negotiations at European level ahead of possible directives, but this time without bringing in family organisations, leaving the traditional social partners as the sole official negotiators. However, the same process of support for social issues at European level by family organisations scored other successes specifically in the area of disability, in the wake of pressure for integration through work, leading to a first European programme in 1980, prelude to the Helios, TIDE, HORIZON and EQUAL programmes, to name but a few.

As to family policy proper, the Confederation of Family Organisations in the European Union successfully secured, after years of engagement and collaboration with MEPs, the near-unanimous adoption in 1983 of a Resolution on European family policy, giving it for the first time an institutional profile and opening the door to funding for the family and, subsequently, children. Some years later, in 1989, pressure from COFACE led to the first Council of Family Ministers. This led in turn to the creation of the European Family Policy Observatory in Vienna and a Commission Interservices Group on the family dimension of the various policies, as well as institutionalisation of the Commission's DG V consultations with the European family organisations. But a shock was needed – the Dutroux case – before the words 'child' and 'family' finally appeared explicitly in our political debates at European level, leading to the adoption of specific budgetary lines for the DAPHNE and STOP programmes, adopted respectively to 'combat violence against children, adolescents and women' and to 'fight trafficking in human beings and the sexual exploitation of children'. It was in the context of the Dutroux case and these deliberations that I myself, in January 1999, secured the adoption by the European Parliament of my report on the protection of families and children which called for a number of measures including the strengthening of the European Family Policy Observatory, reactivation of the Commission's interservices group on questions relating to children, and regular meetings of a Council of Ministers responsible for family and children's affairs. I hope that in the run-up to the World Summit for Children in September 2001, this report, alongside other similar initiatives, will help raise European awareness so that one day the topic will finally appear in the Treaty on European Union.

This would be a fine tribute to all those who work unstintingly, often unnoticed, in the service of our children, and a strong sign that Europe is turning resolutely towards its future. A step was recently taken in this direction on 20 November 2000, with the meeting of all ministers responsible for children in the European Union, a meeting that I myself had long hoped and prayed for and which, I am happy to say, took up my repeated request: make 20 November of each year the European Day for Children's Rights.

I must also point out, with gratitude, that my report owes much to the many contributions sent to me by various European family associations, and to the information and pressure groups for children in Europe, such as the movement EURONET/Save the Children, 'the Children's European Network'. In the report I call specifically for the establishment of guidelines for children, to be drawn up with governmental partners, family associations and charitable associations that work directly or indirectly for a better social integration of the child in Europe. Lobbying? Yes, and it would be quite futile to regret this, since it is just one of the forms – not always in pursuit of profit – that a democratic system takes to help it express the aspirations of all citizens through the voice of its elected representatives. But with specific reference to issues of family and consequently of social options, the legislator must take extra special care, for the interests concerned are not 'simply' economic, but mainly ideological. He must therefore make sure that the interest groups whose opinions he agrees to listen to, and sometimes even to finance, are truly representative of the full diversity of situations for which they claim to provide remedies.

Involvement of social structures and the networks in political decision-making can be the best or the worst solution: the worst, if a pressure group obscure in its workings and having monopolistic tendencies gags civil society purely for the sake of its own ideological views and constituencies, at a time when the current debate on governance in Europe is focusing with great interest on the right of NGOs to participate in decision-making. Anyone who has closely followed the deliberations on the adoption of the budget by the European Parliament in December 2000 is sure to find food for thought.

But attention to the rank and file through grass roots associations can also be the best procedure for the politician, helping him or her to keep a sense of reality, of wholeness and stability amidst a disjointed, hurried and often superficial daily round. My biggest reason for gratefulness to the family support associations is that in the course of my successive political undertakings, I have strengthened my conviction – at variance with current dogma – that the future and happiness of our societies is to be found in the family, where a man and a woman make a commitment in love and through love. No, the 'traditional' or 'natural' family is not just one form of the contemporary family among others. It is the premier form and the reference model which families 'involved in accident' or 'hurt by life' attempt more or less consciously to rebuild for a fresh start. If the number of accidents increases, the first thing you do is not to change or denigrate the 'traditional' highway code, which has proved its worth, but to extend the road safety programmes and improve the effectiveness of the emergency services for the casualties. Contact with the many families has made me keep my eyes open, and keep in my heart this fundamental hope: the family is a new idea in Europe. And our Europe can hope for a profound renewal in this 21st century if it will but recognise this.

1.1.4   Does Europe need a Constitution?

Dr Angela MERKEL, MP
President of the German Christlich Demokratische
Union

More than half a century has gone by since the first steps towards European integration were taken in the wake of the Second World War. What was once a vision has turned into an everyday reality. With the introduction of euro notes and coins on 1 January 2002, 300 million citizens will daily experience the fact that the European Union is no longer merely a matter for politicians and experts, but forms their common destiny. The process of integration is already so well advanced and firmly rooted in the Union's institutions that the burning question at the start of the 21st century is no longer whether one is for or against European unification, but rather what shape Europe should take and how it should be constituted. In the light of this, the CDU fought the European election campaign in June 1999 using the slogan 'We have to get Europe right', winning the overwhelming support of voters in Germany. The CDU and CSU between them won 53 seats out of 99, giving them an absolute majority of MEPs from our country.

The main message as regards the future shape of Europe in the CDU's manifesto for the 1999 European elections was that we should seek to lay down a constitutional treaty. We made it clear that we did not mean by this a constitution in the conventional sense associated with international public law, as the purpose of the constitution was not to establish a European state. As long ago as in 1988, Helmut Kohl deliberately avoided referring to a 'United States of Europe', as many people associate this term with the 'United States of America' and the idea of a melting-pot of nations. We, as Christian Democrats, have no wish to merge the different characteristic regional and national features of Europe; on the contrary, against a background of globalisation, we actually want to further strengthen the regional and national diversity of our continent, so that people do not lose their bearings and their sense of where their roots lie, but can continue to feel they belong in their immediate home. In our view, it is the very cultural diversity of our continent which makes it so rich. We wish to reconcile regional and national traditions with technical, economic and social progress.

The approach taken to date of setting goals for further integration and creating the necessary powers at EU level in order to achieve those goals has led to more and more new powers being adopted in Brussels. An adverse consequence of this approach is over-regulation of the EU internal market, which restricts entrepreneurial freedom and results in a less dynamic European economy, unable to fulfil its growth potential. This is not only damaging from an economic point of view, but is also extremely negative in social terms, as it is not the prosperous who are affected the most as a result of a less dynamic economy but rather the weakest in our society, above all the unemployed and socially excluded. My reflections on a constitution for Europe are therefore concerned in part with the need to develop our approach based on the social market economy at a time of Europeanisation and globalisation.

In order to counter the creeping trend towards centralisation of powers in Europe and in order to prevent the establishment of a bureaucratic European 'super state', the CDU-led federal government succeeded in ensuring that Treaty negotiations at Maastricht dealt with laying down the subsidiarity principle, and those at Amsterdam dealt with the need to define the principle more precisely in a specific Protocol. The number of new draft directives relating to the European internal market declined. However, the basic problem remains that, in spite of the subsidiarity principle, almost any measure can generally be justified on the grounds of meeting the objective of completing the single market. At the European Council summit in Nice in December 2000, heads of state and government were also cautious about moving from unanimous decisions to more majority voting in the Council. That will remain the case until rules have been laid down regarding what measures may possibly be subject to majority voting in the future and what measures may not. In order to ensure certainty in this area, we need a constitution that clearly defines the powers of the European Union and its Member States. The decision taken at Nice to hold an intergovernmental conference in 2004 precisely for that purpose therefore represents a major success for the CDU. The intergovernmental conference must be properly prepared for. Wide public debate on a future constitution for Europe is therefore needed.

Our guiding principle with regard to the allocation of powers is the principle of subsidiarity. Calling for subsidiarity means giving precedence to the smaller unit over the next level of authority as regards taking responsibility and as regards scope for shaping measures. It is the task of the higher level authority to undertake what the lower level is unable to do itself. That means that the region only undertakes what the municipality is unable to do, the national state undertakes what the region is unable to do and, at European level, only those powers of regulation are assumed which the national state is unable to assume. A Europe developed on the basis of subsidiarity will therefore continue in future to be a Europe of municipalities, regions and national states. Only a Europe of this kind structured from the bottom up will be a

Europe close to the citizen.

Resolving the question of respective powers is the way to achieve a permanent solution to the remaining institutional issues. There needs to be a change in the system in the EU, away from participation by decentralised levels in the adoption of all decisions at the central level (cooperative federalism) toward a system of enumerated powers for the central level (federalism based on the division of labour).

Europe will be strongest if it confines itself to those areas of policy that really demand a European solution. The list of enumerated tasks produced will continue to be extensive and significant. Matters which should be regulated at European level above all concern the common foreign and security policy, internal security and rules on immigration in an area without internal border controls, ensuring competition within an internal market with a stable currency and social and ecological minimum standards and possibly a budget and a system of financial compensation.

In following the dictates of subsidiarity and seeking to ensure a clear division of powers, we must also get away from the idea that only those calling for wider and wider European powers are pro-European. To be precise, the principle of subsidiarity provides good grounds for transferring individual powers back to the national level. Those who defend decentralisation and subsidiarity do not have to be eurosceptics, but on the contrary may be particularly committed Europeans.

With a view to preparing for the 2004 intergovernmental conference, it is clear that Germany and France are the driving force behind European unification. We are pleased, therefore, that the debate on a European constitution has begun in France. Both the UDF and the RPR have put forward a draft constitution for Europe. In a speech before the Bundestag in June 2000, President Chirac advocated a European constitution with a clear definition of powers.

However, agreement in theory does not in itself suffice to move Europe forward. It is the task of the European People's Party to see to it that the issue of a constitution is debated at the European level. I expect concrete proposals pointing the way forward to be presented by the committee set up by the EPP Congress in Berlin and chaired jointly by Wilfried Martens and Wolfgang Schäuble. I support calls for the European Council to set up a convention comprising representatives of national governments and parliaments, including from countries applying for accession, as well as representatives of the European Parliament, in order to prepare for the 2004 intergovernmental conference. A similar convention performed very good work in drawing up a charter of fundamental rights of the European Union. I welcome the decision by the European Council at Nice to give the 2004 intergovernmental conference the task of determining the legal status of the charter. To me it is clear that the first articles of a European constitution must enshrine the fundamental rights of European citizens. I would therefore advocate that the charter of fundamental rights adopted unanimously by the European Council be incorporated in a legally binding manner into the EU Treaty.

A constitution will give the national states a permanent guarantee in respect of their continued existence. They will remain the bodies primarily responsible as regards the allocation of powers. At the same time, I am convinced that the state dimension of the EU will increase, notably in the key area of foreign and security policy.

With a view to laying down a constitution, we must therefore set ourselves the task of discussing freely, without any taboos, how the structures of the European Union should be democratically organised.

My vision of the future of Europe is of a more democratic, more efficient and more transparent EU.

We must therefore ensure above all that the growing state dimension of the European Union goes hand-in-hand with greater opportunities for citizens to exercise an influence.

The fundamental principle underlying any democracy is that voters determine the political course pursued by voting for or voting out governments, thereby indicating how satisfied or otherwise they are. However, many people feel powerless vis-à-vis the EU, as Socialist governments which are in a majority in the European Council of heads of state and government have pushed through a Socialist majority in the Commission contrary to the outcome of the popular vote in the European elections in June 1999. We should give citizens the same fundamental democratic right of determining through their vote the political course pursued at European level.

Let us therefore re-establish the chain of legitimation which starts with European citizens. A decision should be taken at the intergovernmental conference in 2004 that the European Parliament, which is directly elected by the citizens, be allowed to choose the Commission President, rather than merely approving a proposal from the heads of government. The other Members of the Commission should no longer be sent by the governments of the Member States, but should be selected by the Commission President.

Furthermore, we need to clearly separate again the legislature and the executive in the EU, and not allow important decision-making processes to become lost in a jungle of hundreds and hundreds of committees.

If we pursue such an approach, the EU will finally be represented effectively in external affairs. At present, the Council Presidency, which is rotated every six months, the Commissioner responsible for external relations and the High Representative for the Common Foreign and Security Policy argue over who is authorised to perform what task. That is clearly a recipe for dramatically reducing efficiency. We need to swiftly improve this situation in order to enable us to fulfil the goal which we, as Europeans, have set ourselves of achieving a more equal transatlantic partnership.

I am aware that a great deal of perseverance will be needed. That is always the case when genuine reform is being sought. However, Europe is the cradle of democracy, and all those who would resist making the necessary changes in the European Union need to be reminded of that. I would urge the European People's Party and its members, by taking a committed stand and using their powers, to lend their weight to efforts to achieve as quickly as possible the essential goal: making the EU fully democratic on the basis of a European constitution.

1.1.5   Towards a European Constitution

Michel BARNIER
European Commissioner responsible for regional
policy and intergovernmental conference

For some time now, the simple fact of referring to a European constitution
has been tantamount to breaking a taboo. Advocates of European construction themselves avoid the use of this expression wherever possible, for fear of
arousing public concern.

These days the term has lost much of its intimidating connotations. For over
a year while discussions on the future of the European Union and its objectives have been revived, many European leaders have been referring, in turn,
to a 'constitution' or a 'constitutional treaty'. The taboo has been lifted, but
at an individual level we are no clearer as to what the expression means.

Does the European Union need a constitution? This cannot be an end in itself. It
all depends on what this European constitution would be and what 'added
value' its adoption would provide for the construction of Europe and the
people of the European Union.

* * *

Clearly it is not the word 'constitution' itself that is important. In some
languages, the expression 'fundamental law' is used, which enables its true
meaning to be more readily grasped. Besides, the International Labour
Organisation, created by the Treaty of Versailles, was given a basic text called
a 'constitution', even though it is a conventional international organisation.
The words thus have their own importance but let us confine ourselves here to
their content. What would a 'European constitution' entail?

First of all, what is a constitution? It usually refers to the fundamental law of
a state, which is at a higher level than all other laws, which concisely sets out
the ground rules for the political organisation of the country in question, as
well as the fundamental liberties and rights of its citizens, and which can
only be modified by following a specific procedure.

* * *

Would adoption of a constitution turn Europe into a state? Certainly not.
The European Union is not a state, and never will be.

Throughout history there have been different models for the political integration of peoples and territories. In modern times the model of the 'Nation State' has emerged, a basic element in the political structuring of the world. In the nineteenth and even the twentieth century, the voluntary or forcible union of territories which formerly constituted separate states could only be done by integrating them in an existing state, creating a new state (the current federal model) or, where the political relationship between these territories was unequal, through creating colonial empires.

Since the end of the Second World War, other methods of political integration of peoples and territories have emerged throughout the world – but in the clearest and most straightforward way in Europe – and not involving the creation or expansion of a state.

These new methods, generally known as forms of regional integration, aim at conferring a permanent structure on co-operation between certain states in a given region of the world, without these states disappearing. These structures are generally created by an international treaty concluded between the participating states.

Of all these forms of regional integration, the European Union is undoubtedly the most developed and the most successful.

One particular aspect of the European Union which is not unique in principle, but is unique in its size, is that it has benefited from transfers of competences from its Member States. At both an internal and an international level, the European Union thus assumes certain responsibilities which have been traditionally reserved for states, such as enacting rules that are directly applicable to individuals or even concluding international agreements.

Is the European Union 'supranational'? *The fact is that it does not replace its Member States but is an adjunct to them.* It constitutes a form of integration at a different level and of a different legal nature from that of the States themselves. It does not replace them in the same way that the expansion of the regions, at a subnational level, does not threaten their survival.

In other words, it is not a question of transforming the European Union into a 'superstate', and the adoption of a European constitution would change nothing in this respect.

* * *

So why does the European Union need a 'fundamental law' if it is not to become a state?

The European Union is currently based on the Treaty on European Union (the Maastricht Treaty of 1992) and the Treaties establishing the European Communities (the Paris Treaty of 1951 and the Treaties of Rome of 1957).

These Treaties have, of course, been repeatedly amended (most recently by the Treaties of Amsterdam and Nice).

The Court of Justice of the European Communities has recognised the fundamental nature of these treaties. It has even described the EC Treaty in many of its judgments as the 'basic constitutional charter'.

Does the European Union not already have a constitution with these Treaties? I do not believe so, for at least three reasons.

They do not constitute a brief and concise text containing all and only the basic rules of the European Union.

They do not contain a list of fundamental rights of individuals.

They cannot be modified through a constitutional procedure.

These are three reasons why these Treaties cannot be for the European Union what a constitution is for a state; and three lacunae to be filled for it to be otherwise.

A concise basic text

Currently what is referred to as the 'primary law' of the European Union, in other words the Treaties and texts of equivalent standing (such as protocols), constitutes a huge and complex mass of provisions: *four basic treaties (in total more than 700 articles), four membership treaties, plus a number of protocols appended to these treaties*, and countless declarations.

It is difficult to pretend that they all form part of the 'basic constitutional charter' to which the Court of Justice was referring, but nonetheless it has to be realised that these provisions are superior to acts originating from the Community legislature and that they can only be amended (except in a few rare, specific cases) by a new treaty.

Even if we confine ourselves to the two most important treaties, the Treaty on European Union and the Treaty establishing the European Community (which, following the amendments introduced by the Treaty of Nice, alone contain 381 articles), the analysis is puzzlingly inconclusive. An uninformed reader would have absolutely no chance of deducing from this the fundamental aspects for European construction.

This also fails to take into account that these treaties combine provisions of unequal levels of importance. Who would seriously suggest that any potential constitution of the European Union should, as a matter of course, include provisions such as Article 74 of the EC Treaty, which provides that 'any measures taken within the framework of this Treaty in respect of transport rates and conditions shall take account of the economic circumstances of carriers' (obvious though it may seem) or even Article 142 of the same Treaty, which provides that 'Member States shall endeavour to maintain the existing equivalence between paid holiday schemes' (a laudable but pious sentiment, dating from a period when economic and social conditions were very different)?

Added to the difficulties posed by the length and complexity of these basic treaties are those originating from the very wording of these provisions. As the fruits of political compromises sometimes agreed at the eleventh hour, they are not all crystal clear and comprehensible at first reading. Incidentally, do not for one moment assume that those drafting these Byzantine arrangements took pleasure in doing so. Through complex, and sometimes confused, texts they have managed to reconcile respect for certain national situations and the progress of European construction. A certain amount of complexity is the price to be paid for avoiding a uniform Europe.

But one conclusion has been unavoidable for some time: *the Treaties are becoming less and less readable and comprehensible.*

Fundamentally no-one doubts the value to be gained from coherently and concisely assembling into a single basic text all the provisions that are truly fundamental for the European Union: not only those relating to the composition and functions of the institutions of the European Union but also the key elements of the policies they pursue, to the exclusion of all other provisions of a subsidiary nature.

But many doubted that it would be possible to draft such a basic text, in such a concise manner. This is why the Commission asked the Robert Schuman Centre at the European University Institute in Florence to examine this question.

The report presented to the Commission on 15 May 2000[1] concluded quite clearly that the drafting of a basic text is not only feasible but even possible 'under constant law', in other words without the need to make changes to the core text. The Florence Institute has proved this by drafting a model fundamental treaty for the European Union[2] which consists of only 95 articles.

This does not mean that none of the choices made by the authors of that report merits discussion. Besides, the Commission has adopted a communication on this subject containing a number of comments[3].

But in the wake of the Florence Institute's report, it is no longer possible to use the pretext of difficulties of a technical or legal nature to claim that it is impossible to assemble the fundamental provisions in a basic text which is comprehensible and concise. This is one gap that it would be possible to fill.

---

1. http://europa.eu.int/comm/archives/igc2000/offdoc/repoflo_fr.pdf
2. http://europa.eu.int/comm/archives/igc2000/offdoc/draftreaty_fr.pdf
3. A basic Treaty for the European Union (COM (2000) 434 of 12 July 2000,
   http://europa.eu.int/comm/archives/igc2000/offdoc/com434_fr.pdf

A basic text containing a catalogue of the fundamental rights of individuals

It is difficult to imagine the constitution of a democratic state not containing a declaration of the fundamental freedoms and rights of individuals. Yet the basic treaties of the European Union do not contain such a statement.

Article 6 of the Treaty on European Union goes no further than affirming that 'the Union shall respect fundamental rights, as guaranteed by the European Convention for the Protection of Human Rights and Fundamental Freedoms signed in Rome on 4 November 1950 and as they result from the constitutional traditions common to the Member States, as general principles of Community law'.

Certainly, there is no real gap in the legal protection of individuals. The Court of Justice of the European Communities ensures respect for fundamental rights by the European institutions and by the Member States when they have to apply Community law. However, as stated in Article 6, the sources of this protection are diverse and, above all, external to the European Union.

How can we continue to explain that the European Union which – quite rightly – in relations with third countries, emphasises observance of fundamental rights, which makes this fact an essential condition of accession for new members, and which even has a procedure for punishing Member States in the event of serious and persistent violation of these rights, does not even have a text of its own in which these rights are stated? And that the 'basic' treaties only mention these rights by reference to other texts?

This was a situation which was increasingly intolerable in terms of the political development of the European Union.

The European Council of Cologne in June 1999 requested that a Charter of Fundamental Rights be drawn up, in order to give due prominence to the exceptional importance and significance of fundamental rights in a way that was visible to all individuals.

The *Charter of Fundamental Rights of the European Union* was drafted by a Convention, a group of representatives of the European Parliament, of national parliaments, of governments of the Member States and of the Commission. It was formally proclaimed by the European institutions in Nice on 7 December 2000.

Although the drafting of the Charter was more a task of codification than of innovation, it presents real added value in relation to the profusion of existing legal and political texts.

The added value stems in particular from the inclusion in the Charter, alongside traditional civil and political rights, of fundamental economic and social rights, as well as the establishment of certain 'new' rights which had not hitherto been explicitly established, despite the values they are intended to protect – such as the protection of personal data, principles of bio-ethics or even the right to efficient administration.

But the Charter of Fundamental Rights of the European Union constitutes above all a work of codification in which the very essence of European experience is embodied in terms of fundamental rights.

The Charter has only been proclaimed. This deliberate choice was the only way of avoiding its drafting being held up by a prior debate on its legal significance. But this issue, like that of its inclusion in the Treaties, still remains.

It would not necessarily be difficult to deal with, so long as specific solutions are provided to a number of precise and rather delicate issues: that of the relationship between the Court of Justice of the Communities in Luxembourg and the Court of Human Rights in Strasbourg and, above all, that of the possible role of the European institutions (especially the Commission and the Court of Justice) in monitoring compliance with the provisions of the Charter by the Member States.

These questions are delicate. But they are not insurmountable. *In fact it is the very absence of a common political aim which prevented the Treaty of Nice from including the Charter in the various treaties.*

But it is not a simple report: if the European Union adopts a concise basic text in the way I described earlier, the Charter of Fundamental Rights should quite naturally find its place within it. In this way the second gap differentiating current treaties from a constitution will be filled.

The revision of the Treaties in accordance with procedures other than that of international law

Revising a constitution is more difficult than amending a law. The fundamental significance of a constitution for the fundamental rights of individuals, for the functioning of institutions, for spelling out the competences of public authorities, requires in fact that it cannot be changed overnight by a chance majority, for the sake of short-term objectives.

Each State therefore has specific procedures for amending its constitution: special majorities in parliament, a constituent assembly larger in composition than the parliament, a period of reflection, the opinion of a constitutional court or even the possibility of a constitutional referendum, etc.

Although it is – much – harder to change a constitution than a law, constitutions are not immutable. Special procedures guarantee that they are not treated as a 'scrap of paper', but enable them to be changed, without the changes necessarily meeting the approval of everyone. They can be changed by majority decision, without the need for unanimity.

Amending the Treaties requires the unanimous agreement of the Member States.

Article 48 of the Treaty on European Union provides that the Treaties can be amended by a conference of representatives of the governments of the Member States. The changes determined by common accord by this conference (which take the form of a new treaty, as was recently the case with the Treaty of Nice), shall enter into force 'after being ratified by all the Member States in accordance with their respective constitutional requirements', in other words after approval by the national parliaments or, if necessary, by a referendum. The absence of ratification on the part of a single Member State, for whatever reason, prevents the entry into force of the amendments.

In principle, such a procedure is fully justified. A treaty is viewed as a contract (between the signatory states), comparable to a private 'contract'. It is therefore logical that this 'contract' cannot be amended without the agreement of all the 'contracting parties'.

But this principle is less obvious when the treaty creates an international organisation: the rule of unanimity can in fact lead to paralysis. Accordingly, the founding text of most international organisations can be changed without the agreement of all its members. Thus, amendments to the Charter of the United Nations come into force when they are ratified by two-thirds of the member states, including all the permanent members of the Security Council.

The European Union does not have such a rule, probably because, unlike most organisations, it benefits from significant transfers of competences from its Member States and it can have an immediate impact on the lives of its citizens. It would, in fact, be unacceptable for sovereign states to submit to transfers of competences without their express agreement.

It is therefore understandable that, except in some rare specific cases (such as, for example, an increase in the number of judges in the Court of Justice), the Treaties should not be changed except through the formal procedure involving ratification of amendments by all the Member States.

While this situation is very understandable, there is the increasingly pervasive question of ascertaining whether it will be possible to maintain the requirement of unanimity and ratification by all the Member States in the context of a Union of twenty-seven (or more) Member States when paralysis will then be not simply a risk but a reality. And it not only threatens really fundamental texts, but also texts relating to what is referred to as 'primary law'.

This is a much harder problem to resolve than the two previous problems.

Although it is easy to imagine treaties being amended through more flexible procedures not requiring the agreement of everyone, basically the objection is still there: is it possible to take a decision on the transfer of competences without the agreement of the Member State concerned?

More fundamentally, the problem raises the question of knowing what is the 'constituent power' of the European Union. So long as the answer to this question is 'Member States alone', the problem of amending the Treaties by a majority decision will remain insoluble.

But this is different if we accept that other sources of legitimacy can form the basis of the European Union, including the citizens of the European Union themselves.

A new system could be constructed around several procedures adapted to the nature of the standards needing to be amended or introduced.

New transfers of competences would remain subject to unanimous approval, and ratification by all parliaments.

On the other hand, for the other provisions, a different procedure could be established, with an appropriately modified level of formality.

For provisions of a fundamental nature, corresponding to the basic Treaties, the procedure for amendment would remain formal. For example, unanimity would be required of the Council, with an opinion from the European Parliament, and if necessary a 'period of reflection' enabling the governments of the Member States to inform or consult their national parliaments.

For 'primary law', this procedure could be simplified, with a decision by the Council by qualified majority, accompanied by a positive opinion from the European Parliament.

* * *

In adopting both the Treaty of Nice and a declaration on the future of the European Union involving the holding of a new intergovernmental conference preceded by a major debate on the future of the European Union, the Heads of State or government clearly sought to make up for what had been perceived as a lack of ambition in the face of difficult but essential reforms.

But they have also opened up the prospect of studying new areas, not only those referred to in the declaration (some of which constitute a potentially retrograde step, which is something I cannot ignore).

More generally, the debate on the future of the European Union, and the more structured task that this will entail – hopefully in the framework of a convention inspired by the Charter of fundamental rights – should enable us to fill all three gaps: the absence of a concise basic text, the absence from that text of the fundamental rights of citizens of the European Union, and the absence of procedures specific to the European Union, and distinct from those applied under international law for amending the Treaties.

In this way, at the end of a constitutional process with which the European Parliament and the European Commission are both in favour, we will be in a position to provide the European Union with a constitution liable to be read – and understood – one day by all the citizens of a greater Europe.

1.2 From the bottom up

1.2.1 The development of Europe from an industrial society to a knowledge and information society

Viviane REDING
European Commissioner responsible for
education and culture

The role of the European Community in the transition to the knowledge and information society is a subject of the utmost importance. This process of development calls for changes in the field of education and learning, to ensure that every citizen can be provided with the information needed to keep abreast of this development in the future. And that, of course, will change the role of education policy – and the role of 'Europe' in shaping that policy!

In general, responsibility for education lies with the Member States. But in Germany and its federal states, for example, as in other Member States of the European Community, education policy is closely associated with national and regional culture, identity and democracy. The European Treaties give the European institutions a part to play in the advancement of quality and cross-border mobility. But there is no centralized European remit to impose educational syllabuses on the individual Member States – to determine what is to be taught, what is to be learned, and how that knowledge is to be imparted by teachers to students. As the principle of subsidiarity requires, these issues lie within the jurisdiction of the individual Member States.

The transition to the knowledge and information society:
the challenges for Europe

What are the most important challenges that Europe has to confront in making this transition to the knowledge and information society?

The first fundamental challenge is the question of lifelong learning. As the pace of technological change increases and 'new knowledge' accumulates, so the knowledge, skills and qualifications of the individual become *perishable goods.* The individual has to *continuously update his knowledge and skills,* which makes it clear that the responsibility and challenge of adapting to the information society cannot be left to our schools and universities alone but are a constant theme of our lives, from cradle to grave. This adaptation is a generalized challenge to society as a whole, and all members of that society who are involved in providing the wide range of services that make up formal, informal and non-formal education and training have an important part to play in meeting that challenge.

The Commission has produced a European *Memorandum on lifelong learning,* which addressed a number of fundamental questions relating to specific ways in which the concept of lifelong learning can be put into practice. Although we hear the phrase 'lifelong learning' everywhere today, it is still a very abstract concept for many people and for the majority of countries.

We are going through the stage where lifelong learning is just a romantic dream. Now we have to move on to the practical phase. We know that lifelong learning is a necessity, and the phrase conjures up in our minds the pleasant vision of a *'renaissance of the mind',* in which we can all sit around reading books and learning new things to our hearts' content. The reality, though, is rather different. For one thing, the concept of lifelong learning depends on a couple of basic conditions: that people want to learn, and that they have time to do so – but, in the real world, do they have that inclination and time? Most people have enough trouble as it is in facing up to and meeting the demands made on them by their jobs and families, and reconciling the two. We cannot simply add the extra burden of learning, unless we can construct some kind of triangular relationship between living, working and learning. Lifelong learning also calls for a shift in perspective, especially as regards the way in which people determine and organize their priorities for their future lives.

But lifelong learning calls for other decisions as well. In particular, how are we to *organize the learning process, and how are we to renew teaching methods* so that learning is made both attractive and accessible? We must think about *how we are going to recognize, certify and review the quality of what is learnt within informal and non-formal structures.*

We need to discuss the roles that we are going to allocate to regional and local communities. The local and regional authorities and institutions are closer to the citizen; they are better placed to identify what the citizen needs to learn, and to consult with employers on the best way to react to that demand.

The Memorandum on lifelong learning raises all those questions, and many more besides. Its aim is to further a widely-structured discussion in all the Member States on the essential question of what decisions must be made and what approaches adopted to make lifelong learning a reality. The results of these discussions will be available to us in the summer, and the Commission plans to follow up by launching an initiative for the further advancement of lifelong learning from autumn this year.

The second fundamental challenge is this: *what basic knowledge and qualifications should the learners acquire* to enable them to play their full part in this knowledge and information society?

Interestingly enough, some studies suggest that eighty per cent of the abilities needed to master the information and communications technologies are social and interpersonal skills: the ability to communicate, cooperate and interact with others, to structure and manage information, to distinguish between important and unimportant information, and to work within the multicultural environments that the Internet is making a reality for us all.

On the other hand, it can only be a good thing that the technology itself is becoming much more user-friendly. The day may come when information and communications technologies are taken for granted as part of the essentials of life, like electricity and water today. In other words, before we rush to revise our entire curriculum we should pause for reflection, and make quite sure that we are looking at things in the right way. Only then should we make changes – and the changes must be in proportion.

At present, a debate is under way in all the Member States regarding the new basic knowledge and skills. The time has come for answers to be found to these problems, and I regard that as a very fundamental challenge to the European Union. To be able to find those answers, we have to *travel forward in time*. We have to consider what kind of a society we want, and what knowledge and qualifications our citizens should acquire if they are to *sustain and improve upon our 'European model of society'*. There is more to this than learning how to use a computer keyboard – even more important are social skills, entrepreneurial skills, the ability to speak other languages, to name but a few. In ten or twenty years' time the whole architecture of knowledge will look very different, and the time has already come for us to begin to imagine that new architecture and to anticipate it.

At the special meeting of the European Council in Lisbon on 23 and 24 March 2000, the heads of state and government called for a draft of a *European framework plan for the new basic skills* in the knowledge-based society. Clearly, the Member States believe that this discussion is a matter of urgency – and that the European institutions have an important part to play in it. Since Lisbon, the Commission has put forward further proposals. One example is the proposed creation of a task force to suggest ways of eliminating the *existing shortage of technical qualifications in the labour market*. Employers will play a key role in these initiatives, as will civil society and all those responsible for decisions on educational and training policy.

We have to make a start on addressing both of these basic issues, but there are also a few direct problems that call for direct solutions. So we face a dual task: *outlining long-term approaches to solutions and finding short-term answers*.

The transition to the knowledge and information society: the role of Europe

E-learning is only one example of what Europe can do *to create a common agenda and mobilize the Member States to implement it*. We can set ourselves specific objectives and deadlines at European level, so emphasizing both the urgency of the matter and our joint responsibility for moving forward to the knowledge and information society.

We have to be clear in our own minds that these problems cannot be solved by a policy of *'less Europe'* – what is needed is *'a better Europe'*. That is precisely the message I also get from the young people I meet. They have no interest in turning back the wheel of history: they want to move forward in a Europe that lives up to their hopes and expectations and offers them very specific advantages.

We have to be clear in our own minds that the pace of globalization is increasing, and that the process of European unification is not one in which we will lose our national roots or our sense of belonging, but one in which we can extend those roots deeper – as a response to globalization – in a broader community of values.

In actual fact, I feel sure that our national economies are developing into something like 'national climates', which in a way is itself a contradiction in terms. The national economy is only one of the portals in a giant network of links and interdependencies, in which a minor change in one country can have a very much more powerful knock-on effect in another: *the euro rates, international currency speculation, the increasingly transnational stock exchanges, restructuring and relocation by big multinational companies, international trade agreements, oil prices, the new virtual Internet economy, and so on.*

Just as our economies cannot escape the effects of changing modern technology, nor can our 'value systems', whether national or European. The Internet offers us a rich potential for information and communication. But, at the same time, we must not forget that the Internet too has its disadvantages.

The fact is that the Internet is also able to circumvent many codes and values to which we attach great importance within our societies. The Internet does not always respect privacy, or intellectual property rights; people are seduced by various means into violating principles of this kind, and the necessary mechanisms of constraints and penalties are not universally available. Not only that, but interpersonal contacts could increasingly come to be replaced by virtual contacts – contacts between customer and supplier, between the state and its citizens, between employer and employee. And so it may well come to pass that the Internet changes the concept of 'community' and the 'art of coexistence' – so undermining one of the cornerstones of any modern democracy.

We have to appreciate that there are certain tendencies that may have repercussions on various fundamental aspects of our societies. The function of education here is to impart the intellectual skills that will enable us to come to terms with these changes. *As H. G. Wells presciently said, human history becomes more and more a race between education and catastrophe.*

That message has been received by the political leaders of Europe, and at the European Council meeting in Lisbon on 23 and 24 March last year they drew the appropriate conclusions.

The Lisbon summit marked the start of a *quiet revolution*. As I said at the outset of my remarks, it has had two effects:

– it assigns a more important role to *education in Europe*, and
– it assigns a more important role to *Europe in education*.

Both these points call for some explanation.

First, education is the 'new frontier', the frontier of the next decade. In Lisbon it was finally brought home to us that the heads of state and government are not concerned only with economics and finance but are shifting the main focus of their attention to the fundamental aspects of growth and cohesion in our society: the information society and the part education has to play in it.

In Lisbon, the Union set itself a new strategic target for the next decade: *the target of making the Union the world's most competitive and dynamic knowledge-based economic area – an economic area capable of combining sustained economic growth with the provision of more and better jobs and greater social cohesion.*

This is a strategic aim that is just as important as the completion of the single market, the introduction of the euro and the enlargement of the Union. And the means we need to achieve these aims are to a large extent education-based. Let me briefly list some of them:

– We must define common objectives for our educational systems.
– Per capita investment in human resources must be increased substantially *every year*.
– The percentage of school pupils who leave school early, having completed a lower secondary education at best and so obtained no higher qualifications

(currently standing at 21%), must be cut by half over the next ten years.
- A European framework must be established to define the new basic skills for the implementation of lifelong learning.
- A European diploma in basic ICT skills must be introduced.
- We need a European model for the writing of CVs.
- Students, teachers and researchers must be offered incentives to increase their mobility.
- We have to develop local learning centres that are open to all.

Common objectives, European standard models, diplomas and framework regulations ... are we moving towards a European educational system?

Secondly: Europe's role in education. We attach the utmost importance to the principle of subsidiarity and the legal basis enshrined in the European Treaties. As you know, the European Commission is ultimately the *guardian of the Treaties*, and it is an essential part of its work to respect them and defend them.

The Lisbon presidency conclusions should not be seen as an incursion by European politics into national educational policies. An interesting point about the conclusions, though, is that this is the first time in our history that we have felt the need to discuss the *common aspects* of education: in the past, we always focused – almost automatically, as if programmed to do so – on *diversity*. This is an important *'paradigm shift'* taking place as part of this quiet revolution. We acknowledge that, despite the enormous differences between our educational systems, the challenges we face and some of our aims are similar, if not indeed identical.

For this reason, the Member States have embarked upon a new road of cooperation. The new *open method of coordination* that was adopted in Lisbon preserves the principle of subsidiarity while at the same time endeavouring to exhaust all the options available under that overriding principle.

The question is not whether or not we observe the principle of subsidiarity – because yes, we do observe it. I believe that, basically, this is just the old argument about whether the glass is half-empty or half-full.

The Member States, and the European institutions too, have always tended over the last forty years to regard the European education glass as a half-empty one.

Since Lisbon, we are more inclined to view the glass as half-full.

So the *open method of coordination* is really designed to help the Member States with the progressive development of their own strategies. And each of those strategies may include one or all of the following aspects:

- The definition of *guidelines* for the Union, to be combined with specific time-tables for the implementation of the short-, medium- and long-term aims.

- The development of suitable *quantitative and qualitative indicators and benchmarks*, which reflect the world's highest standards, are tailored to the needs of the various Member States and sectors, and offer an instrument for best-practice comparison.
- The translation of these European guidelines into *national and regional strategies by defining specific targets* and taking appropriate action, with due respect for national and regional differences.
- *Regular monitoring, evaluation and peer reviews*, organized so that each of us can learn from the others.

As I have said, this open method of coordination preserves the principle of subsidiarity. We need it as a way of breaking free from the customary practice of 'declarations of intent' (in the best case) and withdrawal into dogmatism (in the worst). With this open method of coordination *we are placing our efforts on a more sustainable footing* and trying to measure and monitor how much progress we have made towards the goals we have set ourselves.

If the Union, as I said earlier, has set itself the strategic target of becoming one of the world's most competitive knowledge-based economies, and if all Member States feel a commitment to that objective, and if it is acknowledged that the development of the necessary human resources is a key factor in achieving that aim, *then every Member State is also responsible for taking the appropriate action*, within its educational and vocational training systems, to release these forces of innovation, change and creativity.

This idea of reciprocal accountability is an enrichment of educational policy in Europe. It does not mean that the Member States can be called to account by the European Commission; what it does mean is that a Member State feels a sense of commitment to accountability towards the 'community' of the other Member States. A comparable process of observation and mutual scrutiny is also developing at present in the field of employment policy – and I think it has already produced some gratifying results.

I am convinced that we must never lose sight of the context of the data, and that we must beware of confusing quantity with quality. Nor should we allow ourselves to be misled into trying to classify countries in some kind of order of merit. That could bring about a mood swing in education policy, which in turn would adversely affect the new, constructive dynamic that we are just in the process of building in the aftermath of the Lisbon summit.

On the other hand, we should be careful not to throw out the baby with the bathwater. Quantitative indicators can be very useful when it comes to putting political aims into practice and observing and measuring our progress in doing so. The important thing here is that the Member States should themselves define their objectives, and that they should do so by a 'bottom-up', participative process, not a 'top-down' one imposed by the European

Commission. That is a very important principle to me, and one that I will always defend.

Nice and future developments

Let me conclude by saying something about Nice, and looking forward briefly to future developments. Much has already been said about the inter-governmental conference in Nice. Some of it has been critical, including some of the things said by the Commission. But in the context of our talks today we should also single out some of the plus points of the European Council meeting, the part of the Nice summit that took place before the debate on the amendments to the Treaty.

There are four points I think which are particularly worth making.

1) First, the European Council meeting in Nice adopted the *European social policy agenda*. This is a major achievement in the interests of the balanced and sustainable development of the knowledge and information society. The modernization and enhancement of the model of European social order to which this agenda relates is a necessary enterprise that must form the basis for the transition to a knowledge-based economy. If we want to ensure that this new economy comes into being without exacerbating the existing social problems of unemployment, social marginalization and poverty, it will be essential to invest in people and to develop an active and dynamic welfare state. The European social policy agenda has a clear message here, referring very openly to the need for life-long learning, the mobility of both teachers and students, and the combating of all forms of discrimination and marginalization.

2) Secondly, the European Council of Nice incorporated the *structural indicators* against which the year-on-year progress of the European Union on its journey to the knowledge and information society is to be measured. I am glad that these indicators were taken into account, because they include important educational indicators, such as the per capita sums invested in human resources, the school dropout rates and adult participation in lifelong learning. With the help of these indicators, we now have it down in black and white that the progress of the Union must also be progress in meeting the needs of educational policy.

3) The Nice European Council also adopted a *resolution to support the action plan for mobility* for teachers, students and researchers. The action plan for mobility, which was developed under the French presidency, is a highly flexible *'toolbox'* from which the Member States can select the tools they think will be best suited to enable them to promote mobility between our countries. I am currently concerned with the question of

how the Commission might use this toolbox, within the powers and re-sources available to us, although the main users should be the Member States themselves: they need these tools because most of the obstacles to cross-border mobility lie within the jurisdiction of national legisla-tion and procedures.

4) Finally, the Nice European Council adopted the new *employment package*: this, to my great satisfaction, has made further advances and also deals with the significance of education and vocational training in the context of lifelong learning. The employment package testifies that the develop-ment of human resources and the continuous updating of skills and qualifications are indispensable for the development of more and better jobs and ensuring less unemployment and a higher employment rate for all citizens: men and women, young and old alike.

***

We have a following wind, and we know the course we are steering. The development of Europe into a knowledge and information society should release the forces of innovation and growth with which this continent is so richly endowed. But everyone should be involved in this transition; no one can be left behind. Lifelong learning, a renewed and reinforced social agenda: these are structural, long-term projects that must be backed up by quick-acting solutions and means to narrow the gaps that exist in the area of digital development between the two sides of the Atlantic.

We must combine short-term action with long-term and forge an unbreak-able link between economic development and social cohesion. And we must do it together: like fifteen oarsmen rowing a boat over a stormy sea. The waters may be rough but – I have no doubt at all of this – we can have com-plete confidence in our eventual landfall.

I wish every success to the learners and teachers among you. Everything we do is intended to benefit you, the citizens. Because, ultimately, it will be you who shape and accomplish the transition to the information and knowledge society.

1.2.2   Civil society: a European partnership

Marianne THYSSEN
Member of the
EPP-ED Group in the
European Parliament

Chris TAES
Former
Secretary-General
of the Belgian
Christelijke Volkspartij

A key concept

For Christian Democrats, "civil society" is a key concept in their political analysis. Unlike liberals, Christian Democrats think that individual freedom is a basic condition, but not a sufficient goal in the organisation of society. Unlike socialists and ecologists, Christian Democrats think that public authorities should offer a basic guarantee for just social relations and a durable environment, but not that these authorities can substitute for true human relationships and creative, authentic freedom.

Civil society manifests itself in an extensive and pluriform variety of social organisations and networks, each with their proper missions, ideas and goals, based on voluntary commitment and independent of public authorities or market mechanisms.

Subsidiarity

Christian Democrats believe in the principle of subsidiarity, which means on the one hand that a competence should be exercised at the most efficient decision level (vertical subsidiarity), and on the other hand that public authorities should not try to copy or replace private initiative, but should rather promote responsibility and solidarity in civil society (horizontal subsidiarity).

Freedom and responsibility inspire our political principles. In recognising freedom of association, social organisations are held to be of essential importance, as they can be the bearers of standards and values and can create a framework for the realisation of solidarity and respect. In the European People's Party, emphasis is clearly placed on the value and significance of social organisations, as they are partners in a growing process of horizontal subsidiarity. This principle should be further elaborated and consolidated in European decision-making.

In Community law, the state-market school of thought prevails, although references are made to the roles social organisations can fulfil. Although the European Convention on human rights and fundamental freedoms offers guarantees for the rights of association, the principle acknowledging social organisations' autonomy (horizontal subsidiarity) could be included explicitly in the Treaty. Such a provision would create opportunities for a more significant and structured presence of social organisations.

Co-operation and self-regulation

The EU should promote co-operation with civil society as much as possible. Community law should provide more opportunities for social organisations, allowing them to regulate their own concerns autonomously. We should increase self-regulation and diminish bureaucracy and centralism. Increased attention should be paid to the relationship between the criteria of judicial review regarding the free movement of people, goods, services and capital, and the recognition of the social, cultural and environmental dimensions of European integration. In this way, the right path is taken towards a European social order which takes into account the sense of responsibility of European civil society and which implements the concepts of solidarity and sustainable growth.

Apart from the many regulations and EU policies, social organisations bear a great deal of responsibility themselves in terms of co-operation and the development of international initiatives. In an increasingly integrated Europe where cross-border regions are being formed and where the movement towards internationalisation is quickening in pace, private and social organisations have a vital role to play.

Europe is more than a public institution

Analyses on the future of Europe usually concentrate on the role of European institutions or the functioning of the market. Society, however, is much too complex for such narrow analyses. A whole conglomerate of social organisations exists, giving colour to European society. These organisations establish a barrier against excessive state interference and reduce the predominance of the market. They offer a framework within which citizens can operate and they serve to transmit standards and values, contributing to the promotion of social responsibility. In an era in which there seems to be a reduction of community spirit in favour of individual or national interests, economic regionalism and cultural isolationism, social organisations can contribute to a true European integration. A community with a purely economic orientation cannot survive, because it does not carry any social significance. It is clear that Europe needs social organisation and networks which strengthen the foundations of the European Union.

Interdependent levels

In many Member States, national authorities limit intervention. Because of this, social organisations assume an important role in the process of European integration. In Europe, the public authorities, business, organisations and citizens are increasingly interdependent. This results in an inter-active society where social organisations can and do contribute generously to the development of society.

Employer and employee organisations, trade associations, inter-university associations, parents' councils, associations of technological institutes, professional organisations, organisations for regional development, small business organisations, environmental and peace movements, Eurocities – all stress the significance of social organisations. Many of these networks are very active; others are in their initial phase. There are advantages to be gained through European-level exchanges and by re-inventing a cultural dimension which has been in the background for much too long.

Research has shown that the European Parliament is very responsive to signals from these organisations, whereas the Council often tends to turn a blind eye. Why should we not encourage the Council to develop a closer co-operation with European civil society? Europe cannot be governed against or without European citizens and organisations.

Social organisations are the expression of the principle that society must be able to organise itself freely. The state's role is to respect this freedom. Citizens are responsible people who are part of a series of interdependent social spheres, which, in turn, are custodians of standards and values, and which offer a framework where mutual responsibilities can be expressed. The European People's Party underlines these notions and includes a provision which affirms that the state must acknowledge the relative autonomy of social organisations in its programme of principles. These basic notions can then be applied to concrete issues such as legal frameworks, the system of consultations and informal consultations, the promotion of private co-operation and self-regulation.

Government or the market?

In the political debate, discussions commonly take place in terms of government and the market. There are exhortations for strengthening the primacy of politics, which entails a guiding role for government, or in favour of the market: "More market, less government".

The market is considered responsible for the dissemination and distribution of goods and services, while the government is considered responsible for the creation of legislative frameworks for social development. As such, the government has the right to establish rules. When inflexibility sets in, and hence "excessive regulation", and the government becomes an overwhelming financial and administrative burden, solutions are sought in a more efficient market. In this context, deregulation and privatisation are requested.

Truly recognizing civil society

Society, however, does not only consist of "government and the market". A rich variety of social organisations and institutions exists alongside the public sector and the market. These social or private initiatives stimulate and improve the functioning of society. This conclusion is reached on the basis of analytical considerations. The subject, however, also has an important legislative component.

For Christian Democrats, non-governmental social organisations are not simply arbitrary groups of citizens, consumers, or manufacturers who wish to safeguard specific interests. Social organisations indicate the people's sense of responsibility. This type of voluntary commitment should be encouraged and strengthened. Therefore, self-regulation is of essential importance to Christian Democrats as an expression of social responsibility. Civil society acts as a framework for the transfer of fundamental human values. This opinion on social organisations is closely related to the Christian view on man not simply as an individual being, struggling independently and exclusively for his personal interests, nor as someone completely absorbed by state collectivity, but as a unique person who finds his destiny and his happiness in real encounters with fellow-human beings and in a responsive and responsible inter-active exchange with the community in which he lives. Man in society is considered a responsible person, not only for himself, but also for his fellow-human beings, for nature and for the development of society. Civil society is important for Europe, not only because of its social significance, but also because it serves as a countervailing power to the predominance of state and market.

Shared responsibility

For Christian Democrats, this shared responsibility between public authority, the market and civil society, determines the *desired structure* of society: not a society administered from the centre, nor a society where only autonomous initiatives by the individual citizen count, but a society which needs and requires the responsibility of citizens and their organisations in various sectors of life, a society where those wielding power are responsible for the use of this power towards those who depend on it.

Solidarity refers to the bond existing between human beings, a relationship where strong and weak members sustain and support each other. Solidarity appeals to the responsibility of the stronger members in favour of marginal groups and persons who are "outsiders". Solidarity expresses itself on a national and international scale. Nationally, it concerns the development of fiscal and social welfare systems; internationally, it concerns the development of relationships – the transfer of information and know-how, commerce, foreign aid – between Western countries and countries of Central and Eastern Europe, between the north and the south.

A human environment

Christian Democrats respect the world they live in and the natural resources they have inherited from former generations. This respect differs from the liberal and from the ecological approach. Unlike liberals, Christian Democrats do not put economic interests first. Unlike green parties, Christian Democrats do not put ecological interests first. Christian Democrats put human interests first in a human environment and a human economy. This implies that they reject ecological radicalism as well as uncontrolled and polluting economic obsession. Respect for a truly human environment also implies an ethical judgment, with a careful and skilful use of talents and gifts in the fields of science, technology, culture and the division of labour.

Not just talking

Social organisations are active meeting places where citizens unite on the basis of common views, values and objectives, and where people – as a group – can assume their specific responsibilities. The specific goals of social organisations do not prevent them from co-operating in the perspective of broader social, cultural, economic or ecological perspectives.

Social organisations are not just "organisations where discussions take place" but primarily "organisations where actions take place" to the benefit of the development of society.

Christian Democrats believe in:

– A responsible individual: each individual carries not only a personal responsibility, but also a responsibility for those who depend on him (family,

friends, neighbours). There is also a more general responsibility towards the development of society, which is of vital importance for full citizenship.
– A responsible society: a society in which organisations and institutions act in a socially and environmentally responsible way; a society in which pluralism of lifestyles, philosophies and ideals is mutually acknowledged and respected.

Positive integration instead of centralisation

During the Eighties, in many European countries there was a demand to limit the role of the state. This demand coincided with the emergence of supply-side economic theories along with demands for deregulation and privatisation. The central role of the state was questioned and alternatives were sought regarding state management of society.

At the European institutional level, there seemed to be an opposite trend. The possibility of extending the powers of the Council, the European Commission and the European Parliament was examined along with a search for a clearer position of these institutions in European society. This resulted in more and stronger guidelines and EU attention towards national authorities with an increased "administrative centralisation".

In the process of European integration, emphasis is placed on strengthening market mechanisms and on increased economic liberalisation. Christian Democrats believe that these aspects are important, but insufficient. We need a broader, more comprehensive view on the future of Europe. A two-tier Europe, actively involving civil society, may offer the possibility of more positive integration.

Grass-roots integration

The image of continuing European integration through Economic and Monetary Union and European Political Union, with administrative responsibilities and decision-making powers transferred to European institutions, is beginning to show the first signs of disintegration. Perhaps it is time to provide new stimuli for European integration. Despite the political and administrative vicissitudes, the Europeanisation of social life proceeds at an unstoppable pace: trade, mobility, production, telecommunications, tourism. The process of integration should develop from the grass-roots (bottom-up), with a legal, political and administrative organisation that is logically based on the principle of subsidiarity. This also means: a process of integration whereby cultural pluralism is fully protected and where the market system's increased importance is balanced by strong political institutions and by a powerful civil society.

This balance influences the Christian Democratic view on the prospects for the European Union. It is clear that if discussions on Europe's future were limited to political and administrative issues, the consequences could be negative. Private social organisations – however different their positions in the European states may be – constitute the true fabric of society. They are extremely important to guarantee the proper functioning of society. If this fundamental concept is denied, there is the risk of overestimating the roles of the state and the market. Christian Democrats highlight the role of non-governmental social organisations and of private initiative.

Social, philosophical and cultural diversity

The recognition of social organisations also implies the acknowledgement of social, philosophical and cultural pluralism. Europe is rich in cultural and spiritual traditions. Damage would be enormous if pluralism were errone-ously subordinated to a uniform system of regulations and policies. These threats are related to the inadequacies of EU development. Social organi-sations face new challenges: private institutions which are involved in international activities must find some kind of international self-regulation, or risk losing their influence. They will have to work towards more intense trans-frontier cooperation with their foreign counterparts and convince them to adhere to self-regulation agreements. From a Christian Democratic point of view, governments should support this internationalisation of self-regulation in view of a pluralistic Europe where public authorities – at all levels – assume a subsidiary role. After all, organised social life must be able to articulate itself in a relatively independent manner (from economic and political forces) and in different forms of self-management (schools, chari-ties, trade unions).

The European People's Party, representing European Christian Democratic parties, aims at providing a perspective for tomorrow's Europe which takes into account the position of social organisations. These organisations should get the recognition they deserve on the basis of authentic Christian Democratic notions such as subsidiarity and responsibility.

EPP Congresses in Athens and Berlin

A fair balance between the political, social and economic aspects of EU development was already sought in the document "A Federal Constitution for the European Union" presented at the EPP Congress of November 15 and 16, 1990.

The role of social organisations was outlined specifically in the draft Basic Programme of the EPP, which was used as the key document at the EPP

Congress in Athens in 1992. The EPP political programme on the role of civil society derives from the basic principles contained in this document.

The EPP Congress in Berlin, which took place on January 13, 2001, went even further. It recognized the importance of collective social agreements between associations of employers and employees in a new type of European social model and it stated explicitly that "(for people) an essential part of freedom and responsibility is the possibility to live and to organise themselves in a civil society according to their beliefs and convictions".

The EPP fully acknowledges the role of social organisations and networks and recognises their specific contribution towards European unification and towards European social and political development. The EPP calls for the support of private organisations and the promotion of dialogue between social partners. The constitution – as yet unwritten – of European Political Union should include this concern.

Conclusion

The process of European integration is not only a question of politics, economics and institutions. It is, foremost, a question of people sharing the same commitment and the same ideals. Therefore, it is vital for the EPP to recognise, promote and support the non-governmental dimension of European integration. This concern should be linked to the political notion of "horizontal subsidiarity", respecting the different socio-cultural, historical and legal positions of social organisations in European countries and regions.

Europe should develop an active partnership with civil society. With public authorities and social organisations working together, Europe is certain to gain a stronger public and democratic support. *Plus est en nous*. It is a question of vision and daring. It is a question of connecting with a large potential of positive energy. Let's dare to.

Note: In writing this chapter, we are very much indebted to Luc Martens (MP in the Flemish Parliament), Peter Burssens, Peter Poulussen and the Dutch CDA.

1.2.3 Citizens: the heart of Europe
Citizenship and Europe

Maria MARTENS
Member of the EPP-ED Group
in the European Parliament

The European Union began with an ideal. After the Second World War, people like Schuman, Monnet and De Gasperi came together to reflect on how wars on the European continent could be prevented in the future. They had a vision of a Europe of peace, justice and solidarity. Starting from this vision, they embarked on a process of co-operation: an ambitious initiative which proved to be successful. It is unthinkable now that EU Member States would go to war against each other; the free movement of people, goods and services has made many things easier and all countries have made economic progress on that basis.

The process was not confined to co-operation but grew still further into a process of unification. A great deal of work is still needed on this, for the result is far from a foregone conclusion. The commitment and involvement of many people is needed. The European Union will only grow succesfully if new generations of citizens are prepared to commit themselves to that. It is up to the Member States, but also up to the EU itself, to interest and motivate new generations and to prepare them for this project. To that end it is important to involve citizens as much as possible in the further development of the European ideal.

This task is now all the greater since it appears that citizens' interest in politics is dwindling: not only in European politics, but also in politics at national, regional and local level. This is clear, among other things, from the turnout at elections. In some countries, the turnout at the last European elections was no higher than 30%. The falling turnout at elections in nearly all countries of the European Union points to a decline in active citizenship. The classic concept of citizenship in Europe was one of active partnership between the administration and those administered, between the government and the governed. That is increasingly a thing of the past, and politicians are faced with a great challenge: how to make politics perceptibly relevant and attractive to citizens. Politicians, and in particular political parties, have the task of making people interested in the organization of society, in the work of politics. That naturally also means that people must be given a real opportunity to take on responsibility. Education and training are particularly important in this respect.

The survey of European values is also giving cause for concern. Every three years a poll is carried out amongst some 500 m people in Europe (including Russia and the Ukraine) by researchers at European universities, and from this some general trends emerge. The most recent such study was held in the second half of 2000. Its results show similar trends in both Eastern and Western Europe: more individualism, greater secularism, more tolerance, and more pessimism about a number of issues. This is important data, for politicians too. Politics calls for different values, such as a sense of community, involvement, and confidence in the future. This is all the more important now that the European process is not only about co-operation; it is also about working towards unification, towards a Europe as a community of people. A feeling of responsibility for each other, commitment to the common interest and confidence in the future are crucial to that end.

This dimension has long been neglected. Since the European Union was founded, the accent has been placed mainly on co-operation in the economic field. This was understandable, as it was easiest to see a common interest in that area. However, people are not only economic beings, they also live in a community. They are not just individuals but above all social creatures. When community is at issue, questions about diversity of cultures, traditions, religions and languages arise. That may make the question more complicated, but not less important.

If Europe wants to be a stable and strong community, it must not only have economic matters well under control, there must also be room and respect for diversity, and consideration must be given to how this diversity can actually be perceived and experienced, respected and valued as a unity. I am reminded of the picture conjured up by the American Amitai Etzioni, a supporter of community-based pluralism, who speaks of society as a mosaic. 'A composition of stones of differing shapes and colours, held together by a basis of cement and a framework.' By the cement he meant basic values, which bind everyone together and are binding on them, such as the recognition of the democratic system and the rule of law: tolerance in practice, a common language.

The EPP too is aware of the importance of shared values for the proper functioning of Europe, precisely from the perspective of Europe as a community of people. In its statement 'A Union of Values' in January 2001, the EPP set out the values it considers important as a basis for political action: freedom and responsibility, the worth of the human being, solidarity, justice, the rule of law, democracy and subsidiarity. The EPP states that it is the people who are most important, people and their welfare. This links up with the vision of the Christian faith, where 'serving God' always implies 'serving one's fellow men'. Hence Chapter 1 of the statement begins with the words 'Every person counts'. That must not be an empty slogan, it must really be the starting point for our political action. A 'Europe of Values' must not only be strong in financial terms, it must also be a social Europe, geared towards quality and humanity. Europe must be not less creative in inventing structures for the protection of the weak and most vulnerable in society.

The EPP is devoted to democracy because the democratic system guarantees the involvement of citizens in political choices, and gives to the governed the opportunity to select and control those who govern them. An authentic democracy, however, is only possible in a state based on the rule of law and founded on values which guide political activities. Otherwise ideas and convictions could easily be used as instruments to gain power. A properly functioning democracy therefore calls for a coherent vision of the general welfare, a balanced hierarchy of values and a detailed understanding of human values and rights.

If we really want to pursue the building of Europe on the ideals of peace, justice and solidarity and within a democratic state based on the rule of law, this calls for people who are prepared to work on the basis of these ideals and values, not only now but in future too. A vital and democratic state based on the rule of law presupposes citizens who are aware of their personal and social responsibility and freedom. It must be based on active participation of as great a number as possible of citizens and their associations. It is the task both of the authorities and of individual initiatives to support and promote this participation.

It is not for nothing that the Treaty of Amsterdam also speaks of the European Union's task to work towards the development of active citizenship. Not only in the area of 'citizens' rights' but also and especially building on the ideal of a 'Europe close to the citizen'. When the European Community was set up, the rights of citizens to travel and stay in the territory of the Member States were described: the right to vote and stand for election, the protection of diplomatic bodies and the right to submit petitions. Active citizenship, however, covers more than just these rights; in particular it means active involvement and participation in the further integration of Europe. Europe is not a completed project, and new problems and developments will face Europe with ever more challenges and demand new political choices.

The question is how politics, and in particular political parties, can keep people interested in it and motivated to work to this end. Who are the possible partners? How can we encourage young people to develop into active citizens in society? What place and what responsibility is offered to young people? Where can young people be made to feel that their commitment is relevant? What is needed in the field of training and education, whether intellectual, ethical, emotional, creative or communicative? How can we train the powers of a new generation so that they are in a position to find the right answers to new questions?

It is not just a question of theoretical knowledge but of opportunities to gain experience. The experience of a specific living community may be an extraordinarily important experience for young people.

In this connection I should like to refer to the importance of the 'intermediate structures' of civil society, of citizens' organisations and associations. In the past, such organisations were active in many areas, such as health care, education, women's rights, culture, etc. One only needs to think of the farmers', employees', employers' and women's organisations, sports associations and old people's clubs, or of smaller citizens' associations, e.g. those in voluntary work. They bore great responsibilities and did a great deal towards making Europe what it is. They are rightly called the social capital of society. For many years they have inspired society, and challenged politicians with regard to new social and economic developments. They were often the first to seek solutions to new problems in society. These organisations are also an important training ground for people to learn to take responsibility. In the Netherlands, and in other countries, they undeniably played a great role in the construction of society in the last century.

These organisations have a long tradition in Western Europe. With a view to enlargement, it is a good idea to remember that there is very little experience of these kinds of associations in Central and Eastern Europe. The candidate countries for membership of the European Union are mainly in Central and Eastern Europe, where people lived for many years behind the Iron Curtain under a communist dictatorship. For a long time there was no intention of letting them organise themselves into their own associations, and they were not allowed to take their own responsibility for the general interest. If citizens are now expected to do this, there will be a problem in these countries. While in Western Europe there is apathy as a result of growing away from politics, in Central and Eastern Europe there is a serious lack of familiarity with the bearing of responsibility for matters in the general interest. They have no tradition in this area. Even if the distance from politics in the various parts of Europe is perhaps to a great extent the same, the solutions to this problem will probably have to be different in Central and Eastern Europe from those in Western Europe. Enlargement thus presents the European Union with another challenge, to consider the relevance and underlying assumptions of active citizenship. What does the European Union expect of its citizens? How does it intend to prepare citizens for taking responsibility? How does it intend to work towards a Europe 'close to the citizen'?

At present there are a number of programmes aimed at the younger generation seeking to interest them in the European ideal. For example, the Youth for Europe programme is clearly a useful instrument to that end. Exchanges, temporary study, work or training in another European country seem to be a good way of experiencing and learning to value the wealth of various cultures, societies and languages in Europe. This is important in the interest of a stable Europe. Growing mobility, the free movement of persons, goods and services and increasing migratory flows require ever more knowledge of and respect for the diversity of cultures.

New developments, such as financial and cultural globalisation, multi-culturalism, environmental issues, new technology, and increasing violence in society, all call for new responses. It will be a great challenge to ensure that these programmes not only consider the theoretical and financial aspects of such responses, but always take the person as their starting point. The 'Soul of Europe' programme offers good opportunities for this. Unfortunately this programme is disappearing from sight. It was a programme for citizens' groups aimed at active European citizenship. This is something which needs to be considered in view of the increasing flows of migrants. Many migrants come from countries not noted for their democracy and not governed by the rule of law. If they stay in Europe it is very important that programmes should exist to familiarise them with the European way of thinking, with rights and values which are the essential foundation and cement of the further construction of Europe, so that Europe will be truly a union of values, a community of peace, justice and solidarity.

In my opinion Europe is not doing enough in this regard. As long as there is still twice as much money being spent on subsidies for tobacco growing as on the total budget of the Committee on Culture, Youth, Education, the Media and Sport, the balance between the economic, social and cultural construction of Europe is not right. Then the proper proportions are skewed and too little is being done to prepare the new generation for its responsibilities in the further construction of Europe.

Summary

We have a European Union which deserves to be developed further. The EU was founded on an ideal of peace, justice and solidarity. For the future of Europe it remains important to keep these ideals in mind, particularly since in view of new developments such as enlargement, new technology, increased mobility and European co-operation has hitherto been primarily economic in nature. However, if the EU wants to remain a strong concept in future, this calls for citizens who are familiar with, and devoted to, the ideal of peace, justice and solidarity, and the underlying values of democracy, the rule of law and subsidiarity. Europe must therefore invest a great deal in the future generation and thus not only prepare them for working life but also for active citizenship. My contribution sets out this position in more detail.

1.2.4　Europe: a community of values

Ruth HIERONYMI
Member of the EPP-ED Group in the
European Parliament

Any analysis of the framework conditions for civic education in the European Union after the Nice IGC will produce mixed results.

On the one hand, it was not made easier, but more difficult, for the Member States to take unanimous decisions in the Council of Ministers. The European Parliament, directly elected by the citizens, gained no discernible advantages. On the other hand, however, the Charter of Fundamental Rights of the European Union was adopted after a record period of nine months.

The EU Charter of Fundamental Rights shows that Europe is founded on a canon of shared values. Now every citizen has access to a short, concise presentation of the values underlying united Europe. The Charter of Fundamental Rights is thus a decisive step forward as regards furthering European political education. The catalogue of Fundamental Rights covers the rights to freedom and equality, economic and social rights as well as procedural principles governed by legal criteria. Nor was the EU Charter drafted in an IGC but in a convention composed of representatives of the 15 Member States' governments, 16 European Parliament representatives, a European Commission representative and 30 representatives of the Members States' parliaments. Their task was not to draft a new catalogue of fundamental rights for the EU, but to reach a consensus, drawing on all the constitutional traditions of the 15 Member States of the European Union. In this way Europe's shared canon of values took shape for the first time.

Are people in Europe aware of this canon of values? What part does it play in everyday life? Twentieth century history has shown that values such as democracy and human rights should not be taken for granted, that there is often only a thin veneer of civilisation staving off the return to dictatorship and intolerance. Extremist acts of violence against foreigners and people with different ideologies are contemporary examples showing that Europe's civilising values must be constantly upheld.

The Enlightenment that established reason as the touchstone for government was a European movement. It heralded the notion that the State could not encroach on the freedom of the individual. The rule of law, democracy and human rights were the spiritual ideals that Europe 'exported' through-out the world. They still contain an explosive potential feared by dictators. Nor would our self-image as Europeans be complete without the value of solidarity, the strong protecting the weak. The European People's Party, in particular, drawing on Christian ideology, considers freedom, solidarity and justice to be our shared ideological heritage and the benchmark for political action.

Europe's political unification is based upon this foundation of common values. But what do values such as democracy, human rights, solidarity and a sense of community really mean to the people of Europe?

How does the European community of values affect the everyday lives of people in Europe?

Democracy and human rights are firmly established in Europe and have become a given. Freedom to travel and freedom of establishment are part of everyday life. It is quite natural for pupils and students to participate in exchange programmes. Europe has long since entered our everyday lives, not only in an economic context and through regulations, but also through the pervasive influence of common values. The success story, spanning more than 50 years, of peaceful coexistence in Europe, enjoying freedom and social stability after two terrible wars, could not have come about without political conciliation.

But it is startling and frightening to witness how limited an understanding we have of this historic marvel Europe. People do not think as Europeans. European institutions are still being developed but Europe is not yet part of our perception. Political events and contemporary history are still coloured by a nationalist perspective. How is this development to be explained?

When the French Foreign Minister Robert Schuman outlined his plan for establishing the European Coal and Steel Community on 9 May 1950, the added value of Europe was clear. There were two deciding factors then: the memory of recent horrors and, soon after, the common threat of communist dictatorship.

Today, these memories have faded, partly obliterated. Indeed, all Europeans want freedom, human rights, democracy and the rule of law. Whether this mere 10% of the global population can continue leading lives in the light of these concepts has less to do with will-power than with the fact that no ordinary nation state can protect these rights single-handedly any longer. Therefore the real, unchanged purpose of European integration is to ensure we can continue to live out our shared vision of European values and concepts of freedom, human dignity and democracy in the future as well.

The ongoing extension of competences, significantly encouraged by the project of establishing the internal market, and the increasing differentiation in EU decision-making procedures as well as the complex interplay between regional, national and European levels make it nearly impossible for citizens to identify and critically appraise decision processes and responsibilities. Along with growing political reticence, this has fed a general feeling of insecurity and dissatisfaction. European topics, such as the euro debate and the debate on enlargement, have shown how political polarisation can develop in the population but also between the governors and the governed. This is why the positive aspects of the European union are currently easily overshadowed.

The venture of European political education also faces new challenges in this context. The keystones of the traditional canon – learning about the institutions, the history of European unification – are still relevant. However, issues of European integration can no longer be treated in isolation as 'EU topics', but must be dealt with, first and foremost, in the context of general political themes. This applies to the topics of unemployment, education, and environmental and social policy but also to the Common Foreign and Security Policy. In view of the current state of European integration, the transition from domestic policy to EU policy has been smooth. Political education must respond to this altered and highly complex state of affairs and help the public increase their knowledge and powers of judgement, to assess 'Europe's added value'.

However, there is clearly a need for direction and it is doubtful whether the success story of European integration can continue with neither vision nor a plan to foster solidarity.

In view of the enlargement of the European Union to a union encompassing 20 countries or more, it will surely become increasingly difficult to agree on common goals, e.g. in the form of a European constitutional treaty.

Political education must bring Europe closer to the people

Civic education cannot replace the political decisions that are necessary but political education must, and can, reinforce people's awareness of 'Europe's added value'. Political education centred on Europe must prevent ignorance from turning to lack of interest, in turn breeding further ignorance.

School education is, and remains, the focal point for conveying this basic knowledge of Europe. What we need most is for education to take on a consistent European dimension. History, geography, social studies and politics must systematically integrate European components. Europe should not be relegated to a dry chapter in social studies on the history of institutions. It is important to know about the institutions, as too many people, the decision-makers among them, are ignorant of who decided what and when. But that is only a fraction of the Europe to be grasped.

We need to be informed and to understand why so many issues in Europe regarding environmental protection, domestic and foreign security, consumer protection, shared economic activities and employment can no longer be settled on a purely national level. At the same time it must also be understood that joint action amounts to more than simply the lowest common denominator between Member States. The fundamental be-all and end-all of added value Europe is, crucially, to teach the younger generations that the history of the European Union is a success story, which has brought us peace, freedom and social stability.

A key prerequisite is, however, the willingness of the Member States and their Education Ministers to tackle the European dimension in education in a bold, resolved manner. This cannot and must not mean harmonisation à la Brussels, with regulations prescribing school textbooks.

Education policies clearly come under the responsibilities of the Member States and must continue to do so, to safeguard Europe's cultural diversity. However, this task should entail the commitment for each national body responsible for education policies to implement the European dimension in education. This is, moreover, the EU project that has been most supported by the people of the European Union. In the current 'Eurobarometer 2000' an average of 83% supported the demand for schools to teach how the EU works, with approval ranging from 69% in the United Kingdom to 91% in France, Italy and Sweden.

The highly successful EU education programmes ERASMUS for student exchanges, COMENIUS for the European school partnerships and LEONARDO for vocational training are significant for teaching young Europeans active citizenship. The ERASMUS programme has allowed hundreds of thousands of young people to gain a sense of the shared continent and thus has made a considerable contribution towards 'Europe – the peace project.' Young people's personal encounters help to permanently deconstruct common prejudices.

However, Europe's political foundations also need to do more to encourage transnational civic education. The exchange of experience and information between foundations must become a vital component of political education, helping citizens to find out more about each other and the common tasks to be solved. There should be more opportunities for transnational encounters and the EU should also specifically encourage cooperation in European networks.

The role of the media

Political education does not end in the classroom or the lecture theatre. We gather most of our political information from the media. Here, however, Europe is all too often confined to special programmes outside prime-time viewing. The media must finally develop a European dimension.

Europe is not a free-floating entity somewhere in Brussels. The media, too, should acknowledge their responsibility for political education in Europe. The experts from Strasbourg or Brussels must be questioned more often on European topics, not only the movers and shakers from Berlin or Paris, who loftily tend to shift the blame onto 'the people in Brussels'. The European Union must put names to faces for the citizens. It is inappropriate for the media only to take an interest at times when spectacular conflicts are raging in Brussels. Yet the media must also recognise that they are not a substitute for politics. When it comes to identifying the European protagonists, there is a need, as yet unfulfilled, for the clear, unequivocal allocation of competences between the European institutions.

Conclusion

People are still far from understanding the European Union's common structures and values. The purpose of a civic education in the European sense is to provide information and to dismantle prejudice. The European dimension is crucial in education in schools and outside the school sector. It is primarily the duty of the Member States who are responsible for their education policies. The Ministers for Education in our Member States must acknowledge and overcome the challenge posed by people's scepticism and insecurity about Europe.

However, civic education through schooling, adult education and media information cannot replace the discourse on Europe's future. The overview of the Nice IGC shows that Robert Schuman, Jean Monnet, Konrad Adenauer and De Gasperi sought to convince people of their political vision. Today, it is still a political duty to answer citizens' questions about the future of Europe and for deeds to follow the words. While the common values were successfully enshrined in the Charter of Fundamental Rights, on the strength of a broad consensus, the Heads of Government have still not answered questions about the future of EU institutions and their democratic basis. The Treaty of Nice was supposed to bring greater efficiency, transparency and proximity to the citizens.

The outcome is well known: the problems were not solved. The future voting procedure in the Council has been encumbered, not simplified. Efficiency and transparency have not been enhanced, but undermined.

The European Parliament was not given the right to equal participation.

The result deals European political education a serious blow. Against this background there will be even fewer possibilities for civic education to increase citizens' awareness of the shared European community and its democratic structure.

Therefore, all efforts must concentrate on the 'post-Nice Process', which the European Parliament particularly supports. The public's readiness to take an interest in these processes will only grow if the bodies responsible for taking decisions for Europe become more informative and transparent. Only on this basis can civic education contribute towards strengthening the shared sense of a social and cultural European community.

1.3 Recent member states and candidate states

1.3.1 Lessons for the future: the experiences of Sweden

Gunilla CARLSSON
Member of the EPP-ED Group in the
European Parliament

In 1648 Sweden was established as a major European power. In the German cities of Osnabrück and Münster negotiators signed a treaty that would end thirty years of war in Europe. The Peace of Westphalia was welcomed by the people of Central Europe, most of whom had never experienced any condition of society except for the brutality of war. The peace treaty meant that Sweden for decades to come took an active part in European politics, with German provinces and representation in the Reichstag.

347 years later, in 1995, Sweden once again entered into the epicentre of European politics, this time without armies threatening Vienna, looting Prague, ravaging Germany or laying Poland to waste. Sweden became a member of the European Union; a project for freedom, democracy, peace and prosperity. Membership ended a period of what can be described as self-chosen political isolation, an isolation that originated in a Social Democratic belief that a policy of non-alignment, or rather ideological indifference, was the only means for Sweden to avoid being involved in war in the cold war era.

For the Moderate Party, and for me personally, Swedish membership was a dream come true. The struggle for membership started in 1962; it was periodically toned down due to a cutting political wind on the domestic scene, but culminated in the light of the events of 1989. I remember well how I campaigned, along with other young Moderates, for membership – in the face of an unsympathetic political establishment. To take a stand for Swedish membership of the European Community was not "comme il faut". Indeed, it was considered an oddity.

The fall of the Berlin wall and the collapse of the Soviet empire changed everything. Suddenly Swedish politicians realised that a new Europe was being shaped, without Swedish participation. It was obvious that the already well-established communion of Western European democracies would be at the centre of this dynamic process. Sweden would be left behind if drastic measures were not taken. Overnight the political establishment, the ruling social democrats, decided that Europe was not such a bad idea after all.

The years that followed, until 1995, constituted a turbulent period in modern Swedish history. During a painful economic recession a government led by the Moderate Party, under Prime Minister Carl Bildt, concluded negotiations for membership. The necessary adjustment of laws and regulations took many Swedes by surprise, and the consequences of structural problems of a domestic nature, created during a long period of Social Democratic rule, were blamed on the process of adjustment. When a referendum was finally held in late 1994, enthusiasm for membership had faded and the majority in favour of membership was narrow.

This is an important explanation as to why public opinion in Sweden has been, and still is, sceptical towards the European Union and Swedish membership. This is in combination with, once again, a self-chosen semi-isolation. The Social Democrats, returning to power in 1994, hesitated in following the other member states on their path to a common European currency. Lack of political leadership contributed to negative public opinion concerning the euro. I fear that we Swedes for years to come will be stuck with a small and unstable national currency.

Another reason why Swedish enthusiasm for Europe is limited is probably disappointment with the current course of the Union. Many Swedes feel that the Union deals with issues that would be better dealt with domestically. Others fear that we now are creating a "Fortress Europe" with less openness. For me, and the other young Moderates who campaigned for membership, liberalisation was – next to peace and the protection of democracy – the key issue. Sweden would, as a member, take part in a great project of liberalisation. The tearing down of border controls, the abolition of customs and the single market were what we believed would be the main tasks for the European Union. Our membership would result in deregulation and broadened space for the market economy, and more opportunities for our citizens. Later, developments in the Balkans clarified the need for a deepened common foreign and security policy, and military co-operation.

I, too, am somewhat disappointed. Membership has, in some fields, meant reregulation, rather than deregulation; less market economy, rather than more of the kind; not always focusing on the four freedoms and an open and transparent union. It is not only the people who say "no" who are critical of the lack of openness and the old bureaucracy, especially in the Commission.

One of the most obvious examples is the agricultural sector, which was almost totally deregulated in Sweden. Now this sector is once more an arena of regulations and subsidies which are so extensive that they are threatening, or at least delaying, what must be the first priority of the Union – enlargement: a process that is the logical result of the political changes that took place in 1989, and a project that most Swedes endorse.

Unfortunately, with a Socialist and Social Democratic hegemony in the Council, the European Union tends to expand into branches of society and political issues which the principle of subsidiarity clearly states it should not be involved in, thus directing our focus away from the really important tasks of the Union. I fear this diversified agenda will further alienate the Swedish public from the Union and from the basic and fundamental task we politicians have been assigned to execute: to keep the peace, to open up borders and to build prosperity by clearing a path for the market economy. It also places the enlargement in jeopardy as there are limits to the adjustments it is reasonable to demand of future members of the Union.

The European Union is in need of a new political leadership, a leadership with visions for the future, replacing a leadership that is struggling to protect existing structures by embracing ideas of the past. The path to the future is not the path of Socialism, the ideology that is responsible for the creation of most of the problems European countries are facing today. It did not take much of an effort to state in Lisbon that the economy of the European Union within ten years will be the most dynamic in the world. Words and grand declarations come easily but are not always as easy to fulfil. Without major political reforms within the welfare systems of Europe, without further deregulation and without focusing on the essential tasks of the European Union, Europe – and the economy of Europe – will not be more dynamic in ten years from now than it is today.

The European Union of the future must be a slim but strong union. It is important to limit the influence of the Union to those fields of politics where decisions cannot be made better at any other level. I think this is the only possible way to make the Union function. When the enlargement has been completed, with more states and citizens, the people of Europe will ask for more "self-governance", the means to rule their own lives and to influence everyday politics.

It is quite simple. To regain people's confidence in the European Union as a project of freedom and peace, the Union must concentrate on its core issues. What the EU embraces must be dealt with properly and this is the only way to win back people's belief in supranational co-operation.

This definitely does not mean that the European Union should be stripped of power, rather the reverse. In some fields European co-operation must be broadened and a somewhat weak structure of decision-making must be given strength to face problems and to overcome obstacles. The development of a military capacity is promising; the European Union must be capable of handling conflicts on the European continent. It would be a mistake to rely on American intervention in a future crisis in our own European neighbour-hood. However, the link to NATO will of course still be of the utmost importance.

The experiences of the cold war prove that democracies must co-operate in order to keep the peace and to secure democracy itself. This is the same for all democratic states, not only those within the European Union. During the post-war era, Sweden chose a policy of non-alignment and neutrality in the event of war. This was not only a mistake which could have cost us dearly but it was also morally wrong. Like other countries in Western Europe we had a responsibility to stand up for freedom and democratic values.

Without doubt, enlargement of the European Union is the most important means we have to secure peace and freedom in Europe. The importance of enlargement should not be underestimated and we cannot allow a delay in the process of accepting new members to the European Union. For me, who was born during the cold war and can still be considered a "young" politician, it is extremely important that we fulfil and live up to the will of our founding fathers. To delay enlargement would be to let down their commitment and their efforts to make our continent more peaceful. We must move on in the same direction and not lose sight of their vision. If enlargement fails, we will bear a great political and historical responsibility.

We often assume that candidate countries will patiently wait for member-ship, but looking back at the negotiating process that led to Swedish membership I am not so sure that we should take their patience and willing-ness to join the European Union for granted. Therefore, in the present Union, we must ask ourselves what the alternative is, and what the human and economic costs are.

It would be wise of us to do everything within our power to simplify the process. If a candidate state is not able to live up to a regulation, or if the implementation of a law would do a candidate state great harm, the European Union must be willing to make concessions. We must never forget that most of the nations that are standing on our doorstep, knocking on our door, have experienced half a century of Communism and oppression. This was not a situation chosen by the Eastern and Central European countries, it was forced upon them. Therefore we, who were more fortunate, have a responsibility to help them on their way back to the European family of nations by obtaining full membership of the European Union.

The need for reforms within the European Union is of course not only a necessity for enlargement, it is also a matter of self-preservation. A union without a clear structure of decision-making, without aims and without a distinct set of goals, is a vulnerable union. Europeans will lose faith in the Union if they do not see it as a tool for improving their conditions and for the maintenance of peace and security on the continent they share. If the Union expands its ambitions to fields better handled by the member states, to social policies or to taxation, it will expose itself to public discontent. That would be a potentially disastrous path to go down. To prevent such a development, Europe will need a constitution, a constitution that clearly states what the Union should do and should not do.

The greatest obstacle in Sweden's way to the European Union was what most Swedes considered an inability among European decision-makers to let things alone. That was six years ago, and unfortunately regulations have not been reduced in number, and nor have subsidies to the agricultural sector and to regional policies been cut. When many Swedes saw Europe as a project of liberalisation, of increased freedom for individuals, the enthusiasm was astounding, but when they realised that the political package they were about to buy contained much more (more of the policies and regulations they were trying to escape), many hesitated and quite a few turned sceptic. Following the same pattern the initial enthusiasm of Central and Eastern Europeans is now less significant. The message being sent to the European Union could not be much more evident.

Let there be no doubt of my commitment to and respect for co-operation between countries within the European Union. I once campaigned for Swedish membership and I have continued to campaign for the ideals that constitute the foundation of the European Union. There is simply no alternative. But the objective must always be, as stated in the Treaty of Rome, "...pooling their resources to preserve and strengthen peace and liberty, and calling upon the other peoples of Europe who share their ideal to join in their efforts".

1.3.2 Preparation of Bulgaria's citizens for enlargement

Ivan KOSTOV
Prime Minister of Bulgaria[1]

> *New opinions are always suspected,*
> *and usually opposed, without any other reason but*
> *because they are not already common.*
>
> *John Locke*

The last ten years of the past millennium saw rapid fundamental change in the development of our continent. No doubt the project of re-establishing the historical boundaries of Europe is the leading one.

Today, at the very beginning of the 21st century, it can be ascertained that the processes occurring in Europe are irreversible. Today the discussion is not whether Europe would admit countries aspiring for membership but when. With reference to John Locke who came to this understanding after the Glorious Revolution of 1688, real progress can be said to have been made when new ideas and projects become a generally accepted mode of conduct and of action in a society.

I feel tempted to note that when I am writing about the Bulgarian citizens' preparation for enlargement, this preparation must be considered also as part of the common European process, which occurs with the societies and politicians of the EU Member States.

Translating the above in modern terms and refracting it primarily through the prism of Bulgaria's achievements in the EU accession process, I think that the most difficult part of the distance was covered between 1997 when the Allied Democratic Forces came into office and now. In the course of these four years something very important occurred in Bulgaria: the "wrong way" syndrome was overcome, the government recovered from a marginal position and Bulgarians regained confidence in its government institutions. Within those four years Bulgaria made a very long trek from the chaos of

---

1. May 1997-July 2001

crisis and ruined statehood to the security and stability of a respected candidate for EU membership and from the anxiety of whether it will be able to cross the threshold to guaranteed membership in our European family.

Bulgaria has now its 10 seats in the Council of Ministers and 17 seats in the European Parliament. The European prospect is nearer and touchable. Nice chose Bulgaria.

Four years ago Bulgaria unhesitatingly opted for Europe by way of supporting the Allied Democratic Forces agenda. A single national platform for negotiations with the EU was formulated for the first time in the country's recent history. That platform became the key to the preparation of Bulgarian citizens to think in European terms about the country's place and to take their share of responsibility for the course to take. It is difficult to achieve consensus in a ruined and robbed state; it is painful to regain confidence in one's own potential. It needs a tremendous effort to pull out of national nihilism after living with it for 50 years and understandably it is impossible to effect a change overnight or over a year. To prepare for a new condition needs knowledge of the parameters and projections of this new condition. The ADF's agenda was precisely such an action plan with specific objectives and tasks. It was a plan that required mobilization of the national potential, setting the whole society in motion, taking responsibility and addressing ourselves. What is it that makes an agenda of government an engine that enables its priorities and guidelines to materialize? These are the real results achieved that become the most important correction of the agenda itself. It is in the absence of such an agenda that the policy of a government becomes marginal, devoid of content and trapped in the vicious circle of unattainable wishes.

The Bulgarian Government took responsibility for carrying out the hard and painful reforms. The Bulgarian economy started a healthy growth. Though directly and badly hit by the Kosovo crisis in 1999, the economic performance invites optimistic forecasts of growth. The private sector in Bulgaria stands a real chance of becoming independent of the State.

Macroeconomic stabilization, which is a target of Programme 2001, has been achieved. The 1999 real GDP growth was 2.4%. In 2000 it was 5.1% and thus for a third year there is positive growth. The economic growth projected for 2001-2003 is over 5% each year.

The Government's overall economic policy is designed to generate a sound business environment. The completion of the structural reform in the industrial and financial sector contributes to competition in the economy.

A modern administration system with clear rules of operation and interface has been put in place. 56% of employees in the central administration and 45% of employees in the regional and municipal administration have the status of civil servants.

Today the Government is having a public debate on the issues of maintaining macroeconomic stability, confining inflation to controllable levels, and generating higher GDP growth in real terms. Bulgaria is no longer a passive party in negotiations with international financial institutions. The year 2000 was the first year when external factors impacted to a far lesser extent on the Bulgarian economy, which became much more adaptive. While the Government continued to stick to the basic parameters of the philosophy of its economic policy, it reordered its priorities. Emphasis has been laid on the microeconomic parameters, that is the factors that will have a direct impact on the welfare of the Bulgarian citizens, on Bulgarian producers and on the economic actors in the country.

Summarizing what has been done in the context of preparation for EU membership, I will note that today Bulgarian citizens have a vision and prospects. Preconditions have been generated for the national potential to be further activated. Those four years changed the agenda of the public debate, made the debate open and concrete and put the issue of the country's European future in the spotlights. The mentality of the political class in Bulgaria changed as did the conduct of government institutions. The next Government's agenda will contain not platitudes and hollow promises but facts, figures and results achieved on the basis of which the strategy for the coming years will be developed and the targets to meet by 2004, the date that the present Bulgarian Government has set for the conclusion of the EU membership negotiations, will be met. Continuity, one of the main parameters of political stability in state government, will be back in the vocabulary of political analysts. Translated into the language of the ordinary citizen, this means security, stability, the real feeling of moving forward to the materialization of the wish that a rich and prospering Bulgaria will be an EU member.

An event in late 2000 was of tremendous importance for the Bulgarian public and for individual Bulgarians. The decision of the Council of Ministers of Justice and Home Affairs to unconditionally eliminate the visa requirements gave courage to Bulgaria and gave it back its European dignity. The course taken by the Bulgarian Government and by the Bulgarian citizens to comply with requirements for lifting the visa regime proves firmly that when unity of action is the dominating component in relations between citizens and the Government, success is a logical outcome. This fact should also be looked at from a different angle, namely, the responsibility that the Government of Bulgaria took to meet the EU requirements for border control, passport regime, identity papers, etc. We were successful because the Bulgarians were mature, grasped their Government's message and took their share of work and responsibility primarily upon themselves.

A couple of days later the EU announced it stands ready in a high measure for further enlargement. In Nice Europe demonstrated its political will to unite. Those two developments gave substance to a process that the

Bulgarian Government and all government institutions initiated four years ago – it was the process of making the concept of national conduct an equivalent of European conduct. For the first time the Bulgarians could see themselves in the projection of dynamic processes of European enlargement and could consider themselves as an important element of the general integral mechanism of implementing the 20th century's greatest project, United Europe.

The mentioned developments are a natural outcome of the overall foreign policy in the past years. These developments provide incontestable proof of the ADF's correct foreign policy line of securing a geopolitical position for Bulgaria. Seen through the prism of the Bulgarians' preparation for enlargement, this line of conduct performed a very important function – that of focusing the public debate on the national identity issue and on what gives a nation its dignity. The Bulgarians' set of values was reordered. Today the national interest is not an abstract notion or a passive reflection of some processes in which we are not involved but must comply with because Bulgaria is a small country and is not present on the map of geopolitical developments.

After being absent for half a century from international relations and not being a real player in them, today, at the beginning of the 21st century, Bulgaria is a recognized member and an active player in the processes that are to make Europe an indivisible whole consisting of prospering democratic nations.

The reflection of the success scored in foreign policy on ordinary people and on Bulgarian politicians is a process that must perform important functions in the future related to the interpretation of Bulgaria's rights and responsibilities in the sense that was indicated above, as an active member and player in the ongoing events. The importance of the country in foreign policy terms and of the commitments it has taken to justify the confidence that the European Union has offered in advance gives the preconditions for a real debate on enlargement in real time and with real messages. The litmustest of public opinion becomes much more sensitive and precise in the evaluation of the Government's policy. And so it should be. The Bulgarian Government counts on public opinion to correct the policy that it pursues.

The new economic policy that the Government advanced at the end of 2000 is such a process of setting the new parameters of the debate and of updating it in the context of achievement and forthcoming action. The debate has two milestones. The first is the faster economic reform that as a result of the changed circumstances will be designed to improve the standard of living of each Bulgarian, economic actors, farmers and all who generate the national product. The second is EU negotiations that even this year will start dealing with more active and difficult matters and touch areas on which any nation is sensitive. What has to pool and synergize the efforts of Bulgarian citizens and Bulgarian politicians is the awareness of the objective nature of processes, of the need to take our share of responsibilities and obligations that we have requested having once applied to be an EU member.

At the end of our term of office, which will remain in the annals of new Bulgarian history as the first full four-year term of a government, it is indeed difficult to remember the chaos and ruin that brought the Bulgarian people to utter despair in 1996. It is difficult to give a clear account of what occurred during those four years. It takes time to assimilate it. What can be said for sure though is that had it not been for the support of its citizens, the Bulgarian Government would not have achieved what it has achieved. A government can be said to have achieved results with its priorities if it can quote public support figures before its term expires. Today 87% of Bulgarians support the country's EU membership. In practical terms this means that public opinion in Bulgaria and the course of reform chosen become interdependent. It is up to us to accelerate our movement forward and meet the target dates as set.

The preparation of Bulgarian citizens must be discussed as part of the preparation of politicians and citizens of the EU member countries for the future enlargement and for their readiness to let the candidate countries join them. The message from Nice of the EU's readiness for enlargement has a very positive impact on the Bulgarian public. Indeed the debate on the future EU format continued for a long time because of the important issues underlying the member countries' decisions. A formula was devised for achieving the common goal – the United Europe project – and crowning it with the shared efforts and the responsibilities and obligations that the member countries and candidate countries take.

The conclusions of Nice opened up a new vista for Bulgaria's preparation for membership to be much more specific and in tune with the paradigm of the European institutions for enlargement. I am sure the wisdom of this vision for the member countries and the candidate countries to work in a team in building their common home will reflect positively on the final aspect of this home.

The concern of our European partners has objective justification in history. The candidate countries have a great responsibility but the member countries have no less responsibility as do their politicians to change the relatively high rate of euroscepticism among their citizens. This certainly worries us as in the long run the acceptance of the candidate countries as equals by the member countries will be complete when a Bulgarian citizen and a European citizen become synonymous phrases. In other words, when the ideas underlying the European enlargement find a common source of energy to materialize – the common wish and responsibility for making Europe an economically prospering and competitive continent in the globalizing world, and a common set of values and standards of conduct.

For Bulgaria and for the Bulgarian citizens 2000 was the year when the European Union gave a very important signal that the course chosen is the right one. The debate on future enlargement will reach depth and substance in the years ahead and enable the potential of the ideas that underpin the grand project of United Europe to materialize. The Programme of the present Swedish Presidency gives grounds to believe so. Enlargement, the first of the "three Es", is a top priority. The successful start of a new stage in negotiations, including a number of sensitive areas and the aspiration to open as many chapters as possible, will be in the focus of the EU's attention.

With the full responsibility of a politician and as Prime Minister of Bulgaria I will note that the beginning of 2001 saw an event which is unprecedented in the country's new history – the overlapping of the priorities of the Bulgarian Government for EU membership and of the priorities of the 15 EU Member States.

This can be interpreted to mean that from now onwards the extent of preparation of Bulgarian society for enlargement will be the indicator which indicates much more definitely the professionalism of Bulgarian politicians and of the Government to meet the commitments taken primarily for their citizens – the commitments of making all the preparations for joining the family of European nations.

1.3.3   The readiness of the Baltic States to undertake a role in the European Union

Andris ŠĶĒLE
Chairman, Latvian People's Party,
and former Prime Minister

The post-independence period – a period of transformation in the Baltic States

The fall of the Berlin Wall and the subsequent restoration of independence in Central and Eastern European countries changed the map of Europe once again. We hope that this time it has been changed for good. The three Baltic States – Latvia, Lithuania and Estonia – regained their independence after 50 years of Soviet occupation. This happened shortly after the fall of the Berlin Wall, and it was a turning point in the collapse of the Soviet empire, as well as in the rebirth of democracy in Russia.

The restoration of independence and the establishment of statehood occurred differently in the Baltic States than in other Central and Eastern European countries. The process of change was more complicated in terms of domestic and foreign policy. Many people in Russia have longed to keep the Baltic States within Russia's sphere of influence, even years after independence was restored. Since 1990, the Baltic States have undergone a very intensive period of transformation. The most important achievement has been a shift in the scale of values in society. Protection of human rights and establishment of democracy – these were the cornerstones of the emergence of the new countries. The Baltic States were once countries that were hidden and locked away behind the Iron Curtain, but today they have formed open societies. These are societies which respect the values of the civilised world and are prepared to make their own contributions to the global effort to establish peace, justice and welfare.

There have also been critical changes in terms of economic restructuring in the Baltic States. During the Soviet period, trade among the three republics was minimal – trade mostly took place between Russia and the individual Baltic republics. This meant that the economies of Latvia, Lithuania and Estonia developed in separate ways, and the mutual and comparative advantages which could have existed did not. Since 1990, however, trade among the Baltic States has increased very significantly, as has the integration of the three economies. The economies of Latvia, Lithuania and Estonia have successfully transformed into open market economies, and they are now competing against the economies of other countries in the world.

Increasing processes of globalisation and integration are presenting the Baltic States with new challenges and opportunities. These are opportunities which can only be described with the word "historic".

EU enlargement – a historic "window of opportunity" for the Baltic States to return to the European club of countries

The enlargement of the European Union represents a historic opportunity for the Baltic States to return to the community of European countries to which Latvia, Lithuania and Estonia have belonged for centuries. The process marks a unique opportunity for the societies of the Baltic States to catch up with their neighbours, and to open up the gates for 50 years of accumulated European heritage. The ideas which Robert Schuman presented about a unified Europe can today be implemented at a totally new level of quality.

In 1995, Latvia, Lithuania and Estonia each concluded the so-called Europe Agreement with the EU, and this set out a foundation for further reforms and restructuring so that the three countries could draw closer to the EU. The Europe Agreement refers to trade liberalisation, lower customs barriers and increased market access. As a result of the agreement, Latvia is seeing increasing trade with the EU each year, and today the EU is the leading trade partner for all three Baltic countries. Russia's role in mutual trade, by contrast, is declining. This proves that European and Baltic companies are enjoying mutual advantage as the economy orients itself toward work in European markets.

When the Baltic States join the EU, they will become a frontier for the union – the eastern border of the Baltic States will be the eastern border of the EU, set against the economic space which Russia and its confederate countries are establishing. By forming the external boundary of the EU, the Baltic States, along with Poland and Hungary, will have a more important role to play in defending the European common market.

From the perspective of European security, too, the Baltic States will have a critical role to play in terms of hard and soft security. It is in the interests not only of Latvia, Lithuania and Estonia, but also of the EU, to ensure that the Baltic region is a safe environment for democratic processes. This reduces the possibility of military threats and international tensions. In terms of soft security, the achievements which the Baltic States have reached in reducing corruption and red tape have served to create a good groundwork for a secure investment environment – something that is a critical prerequisite for further integration between EU member states and the Baltic States. The enlargement of NATO and the EU's initiatives in setting up a European common defence policy are also placing increasing responsibility on the new member states when it comes to regional security. That is why the process of improving defence and security systems in the Baltic States in line with the EU's *acquis communautaire* is very important in terms of preparing for the duties of an EU member state.

The experience of the Baltic States in dealing with nationality issues – unique experience for all of Europe

The Soviet occupation not only kept the Baltic States from developing along with other European countries under conditions of democracy, it also left the three countries with a very serious ethnic situation. Russification and industrialisation of the Baltic region led to vast immigration of other nationalities into the Baltic republics from Russia and other parts of the Soviet Union. In the early 1990s, for example, ethnic Latvians made up only 52% of the country's population. Despite the fact that the Baltic States enjoy Nordic calm, and their societies are generally tolerant toward other ethnic groups, a very critical boundary was approaching in terms of maintaining ethnic identity. This could have created the threat of explosive situations among various ethnic groups at the time when the Baltic States were casting off the influence of the Soviet Union, when the Soviet armed forces were withdrawn, and later. Despite the complex situation, however, the Baltic States have managed to balance the interests of various ethnic groups peacefully and in the spirit of mutual understanding. Policies regarding language and the integration of society drew counter-reactions initially, but in the end they served as a basis for consolidation in the Baltic societies. Today nationality issues are no longer on the political agenda of the Baltic States. A legal foundation and public understanding have emerged when it comes to the need to establish consolidated societies. In the context of the new Europe, the Baltic States have set an example in the peaceful coexistence of various ethnic groups, and this experience can be useful in dealing with nationality issues in such European hot spots as the former Yugoslavia and its constituent parts.

The role of the Baltic region and its opportunities in the EU

The Baltic States are located in a region that is both politically and economically active. They are at a crossroads between Northern and Central Europe, as well as between the easternmost parts of Russia and the westernmost parts of Europe. The geographic placement of the three countries, as well as the fact that they have seaports that are ice-free all year round, are the things which really dictate the region's role as a bridge between Russia and the rest of Europe. The Baltic States are something of a "mouth", through which sea transport, transit pipelines, railroads and roads pass, connecting Russia with the rest of the world. This makes the region very important in the export of Russian oil products, as well as in the sale of potassium, wood and chemicals. The food industry is also important, as its share in the regional economy will only increase as Russia's economy expands and the purchasing power of Russia's residents strengthens. The Baltic States, indeed, can become a centre for logistics and distribution in the whole region.

Although Russia and the other countries of the CIS have started down the path of reform, they all face unpredictable political situations, economic crises, frequent changes in law and an unusual business mentality which serve to create an insecure business environment that scares off entrepreneurs from the European Union when it comes to doing business in Russia and the CIS. Businesspeople in the Baltic States, however, have extensive experience and know-how in Russia, and they can maintain economic contacts even in the wake of that country's massive economic crisis. Traditional contacts make it easier for EU businesses, too, to access the Russian market.

Scandinavian companies took note of the advantages of the Baltic States relatively more quickly than most EU member states did. Scandinavian capital is taking over an increasing share of the Baltic market in such areas as banking and finances, manufacturing and retail sales. Integration between the economies of the Scandinavian countries and the Baltic States allow us to predict that the Northern European region – including those countries which surround the Baltic Sea – will eventually become the most rapidly growing region in Europe, as well as a region which undergoes rapid development at the global level.

Cooperation among the Baltic states and Latvia as an advocate of Baltic unity

There are relatively few residents in Estonia, Latvia and Lithuania, and this serves to limit economic development in purely domestic terms.

With the aim of expanding market opportunities, the Baltic States in 1993 concluded a free trade agreement which led to a dismantling of customs barriers and the creation of a unified economic space. This was a political step of great importance, because the integration of the three Baltic economies moved forward very significantly. Manufacturers gained easier access to neighbouring markets, and conditions were set up for free capital flow across boundaries. This approach made the joint Baltic economy most powerful and competitive.

Latvia has always been an advocate of unity among the Baltic States, because the economic role of the three countries increases, and they become more attractive for investments, when common economic opportunities and market integration expand. Latvia, therefore, is continuing to pursue policies which seek to eliminate the various factors which can hinder the business environment in the three countries. The three Baltic parliaments have set up the Baltic Assembly – the highest political forum in which politicians from Estonia, Lithuania and Latvia take part. This mechanism makes it possible to harmonise national policies and to work on joint infrastructure projects. This, in turn, stimulates the Baltic economies and improves the business environment.

When it comes to integration into the European Union, Latvia has also favoured the simultaneous admission of all three Baltic States to the EU. The EU's decision to eliminate the process in which candidate countries were divided up into groups certainly increases the possibility that this will happen. The pace of integration of the various candidate countries depends on political will and a readiness to undertake reforms. The process of reform has differed in the Baltic States – Estonia has implemented faster economic restructuring and privatisation policies, Latvia has moved ahead more quickly on human rights and language issues, and Lithuania has worked very hard on bringing its defence system in line with NATO requirements. Overall, however, the pace and nature of reform have been very similar in the three countries, as have economic development processes. If the three Baltic States were admitted to the European Union at different times, this would unquestionably lead to complications and greater costs in mutual trade among the three countries. The Baltic States must seek to catch up with one another in various aspects of the reform process in order to avoid this and join the EU together.

All three Baltic States must deal with the same challenges in preparing for EU membership – harmonisation of laws with EU laws, modernisation of public administration systems, and increased economic competitiveness.

Latvia's experience shows that institutional reform of public administration is a critically important factor in EU integration, the aim being to set up a civil service and related institutions which can implement and supervise the *acquis communautaire* and also implement EU laws in a way which is understandable to members of the public. Restructuring, which Latvia has done in its central administrative system and in the various ministries, has led to significantly increased capacity and quality, but the changes which have been made in order to strengthen the central administrative apparatus have not been far-reaching enough. If the country is to undergo harmonic development and make full use of its comparative advantages and the opportunities which globalisation affords, the country must set up powerful and modern administrative structures in local governments and in the country's regions. This is a process of reform which is still largely in the future for Latvia and the other Baltic States.

A knowledge-based society

The Baltic market is comparatively small, there are limited numbers of workers, and the three countries are not rich in natural resources. This means that the traditional pattern of economic development – one which is based on the production of low added-value and the rational use of natural resources – is not applicable if the Baltic States are to develop quickly.

Latvia believes that the establishment of an educated society and a competitive labour force are the main factors in ensuring competitiveness in economic development. Latvia has long-standing traditions in education and science which have served as a foundation for high educational standards in the country. Latvia is among the world's leaders in terms of the share of the national population with a completed higher education. The new economy in Latvia will be based on the intensive use of knowledge and advanced technologies, emphasising a knowledge-based economy in place of a labour-intensive economy.

Computerisation and the rapid development of information technologies have allowed professionals from Latvia, Estonia and Lithuania to find their niche in the world. The political ambitions of the Baltic States to draw closer to the developmental level of the EU's member states have stimulated the process of adapting more quickly to the opportunities which the e-world and related IT development afford. In the next five years the Baltic States can become a true frontier for the e-economy in Europe. Estonia already has among the highest per capita computerisation indicators in all Europe. Latvia's experience in linking various national information systems and registers in a unified megasystem is unique on the continent. Since Soviet times the Baltic States have been developing traditions in IT education and science, which means that our societies have many IT specialists who can serve as a cornerstone for e-economy development in the Baltic region. Laws in the e-sector are being drafted to adopt the latest norms of the world's developed countries, and the telecommunications infrastructure is being rebuilt, making use of the most modern available technologies in this process. All of this is leading to the emergence of a modern and dynamic environment which serves as a basis for the successful development of other economic sectors. It may seem a paradox, but it is a fact of life that small economies have distinct advantages in various e-projects. Small countries have an easier time in reaching agreement among various government and private interests in this process. All of this means that the Baltic States have every opportunity to become a breeding ground for new and non-traditional economic opportunities.

Baltic integration into the EU – of interest to all of Europe

This is unquestionably a period of historical opportunity for the Baltic States, along with other countries in Eastern and Central Europe. The design, construction and reconstruction of these countries are all occurring at the same time. This is an era in which the development of countries and regions is no longer a closed and narrow process – today they are occurring in a transnational and global context.

This is a period of challenges, but it is also a period of opportunities. Making use of these opportunities is of interest to all of Europe, so that we can ensure the long-term security and stability of the region, and so that we change Europe, making it more powerful and open in international trade and enriching it in terms of cultural variety.

It is entirely in our power to make full use of these opportunities.

2
COMPETITIVENESS

EPP-ED

2.1 The new economy

2.1.1 Training and new forms of work: prerequisites for a dynamic labour market

Guido PODESTÀ
Vice-President of the European Parliament

Introduction

The crisis in traditional employment based on Taylorist principles of production began in the 1970s. In the last few years, the organisation of work has undergone an even more fundamental transformation, with the advent of 'lean' (or 'flat') organisational configurations that change constantly in response to the product/market. This new approach involves a process of continuous change known as the 'flexible enterprise'.

This change has been brought about by the interaction of three key factors in the ever-changing environment: human resources, markets and technology. However, the vast majority of companies still operate according to the traditional mode of organising work, on the basis of low-skilled jobs that are completely inadequate to face the challenge of the new economy.

This situation places a particular strain on the most vulnerable sectors of society, particularly the elderly and the young. For these groups, integration into the active and productive world becomes a formidable challenge, which can only be overcome by promoting digital literacy and exploiting untapped resources of 'tacit knowledge'.

The challenges of the new economy for employment

A number of the socio-economic challenges involved can be summed up in the following question: how can worker security be reconciled with firms' need for flexibility in the global market? This raises, inter alia, the following questions for public institutions and social and industrial partners:

- How should work be organised, in which organisational structures?
- Which new technological instruments will be required for the new jobs in the new organisations?
- How can these instruments be made user-friendly and what training is required?
- How should retraining be organised so that the current industrial work-force can satisfy increasing demand in terms of skills and competences?
- How will the new organisation conform to and fulfil ergonomic and environmental safety requirements in the work place?
- How are rules on working hours to be adapted to the new, flexible system?
- How can adequate support be given, particularly to SMEs that want to change but lack the resources or skills to do so?

For almost a century, work has been based on the same fundamental principle: a rigid hierarchical organisation with a high level of specialisation in specific, simple and often repetitive tasks. Every separate stage of the production process took place within the firm. Fordism, a modern interpretation of Taylorism, introduced synchronised and sequential production processes to optimise quality subject to technical constraints.

One main problem associated with the traditional production system is the fragmentation of work into short and repetitive tasks. Work methods are laid down in detail. The system does not allow sufficient room for creativeness, which would lead to improvements and innovations in the routine. To achieve constant improvement, it is important that workers participate actively; if they are to do so, they must have opportunities to develop their knowledge in relation to their work, through interaction with colleagues and continuous training. The rigidity of the traditional system forms an obstacle to the development of workers' professional skills and competences.

Some labour market trends

Quality of work and workers' motivation are the critical factors affecting the firm's competitiveness. The capacity to motivate is more important than methods of organising work and is best achieved when conditions in the work place match requirements in terms of quality, safety and flexibility. There is a need to strike a balance amongst three key elements that generate change: human resources, markets and technology.

Optimising human resources: In classical economics, labour is a factor of production on a par with land and capital – a cost to be reduced. However, in a knowledge-based economy, people represent a key resource. Organisations are valued not only on the basis of their products and their machines but principally on the creativity applied by labour to the machine, on 'tacit knowledge'. The integration of this ability and the productive capacity of the machine leads to the generation of Integrated Product Unity (IPU) in which the economic value of the worker becomes complementary to that of the machine.

The pace of innovation and technological change is so fast that the competitive advantage of firms and national systems will depend on innovation and the capacity to apply knowledge. Recent data show that approximately 70% of this workforce have above-average secondary education qualifications and approximately 20% have a university degree.

Research that generates technological innovation has a multiplier effect on success. Today, for both financial and organisational reasons, SMEs are structurally incapable of and show little interest in investing in research in new technologies. The potential of SMEs to adapt to the rapidly changing markets is beyond doubt due primarily to their flexibility and entrepreneurial capacity. However, SMEs are not used to cooperating with large research organisations on new technologies, given their very limited or non-existent connections to universities and access to applied research.

Markets: Consumers are more demanding and discerning than ever and do not accept simple standardised products. They seek innovative goods and services; they want variety, novelty and high quality. Market forces generate competition between firms to organise production in such a way that consumer preferences can be satisfied. This creates the need for close links between the market and the firm, which call for the capacity to manage innovation and highly flexible work. Competitiveness and success will increasingly be based on the skills and adaptability of organisations and less on the traditional concept of producing more at a lower price.

Technology: Over the last 20 to 30 years, a new technological revolution has started, based on the introduction of information and communication technology (ICT). One of the principal effects of the 'Information Society' on productive activities has been the reduction of data transmission time to zero and the extension of the market to infinity. Production takes place in the most remote area of the world as if it were just around the corner. This development has dramatically reduced the cost and the time associated with the storage, processing and transmission of information. These changes have a profound effect on the way in which wealth is produced and employment is generated. The main lesson to be drawn is the need for an integrated method combining the introduction of ICT with continuous training.

Which new skills and competences?

A model that is emerging increasingly via the use of new ICT technologies is the decentralised organisation where workers become responsible for a range of tasks, rather than the execution of a single task in a linear sequence. Workers perform a service within the firm by applying their knowledge to the chain of production to ensure the quality of the production process, thus functioning as 'knowledge workers'

The 'knowledge worker' has good cognitive, reading and writing skills as well as the capacity to interact with the new technology and the specific demands of the work place, where there is a need not only for highly specialised skills but also for broader competences. This is why continuous learning, the up-dating and development of skills and capacities, as well as investment in the quality of human capital, are of crucial importance for improving the competitiveness and productivity of the European economy.

The main challenge for workers, social partners, the business community and political leaders is to find a balance between flexibility and security. The reorganisation of work often causes uncertainty. Workers must above all be reassured that after the changes have been implemented they will still have a job and that this job will last a reasonable amount of time. At the same time, once the changes are implemented, the new organisation of work can provide increased security for workers through greater participation in their work, greater professional satisfaction and opportunities to develop employment-related skills and potential in the long term.

The changing job profiles: the Italian case

Historically, the rate of digital literacy in Italy has been low, due to the strong presence of 'low-tech' traditional industry. Yet, during the course of the nineties, the relative size of the different professional categories in Italy has changed and is presumably set to change further, towards a progressive increase of employment for people who can offer high-level competences on the labour market.

The ISTAT breakdown of professional categories and data on the share of each category in total employment indicate that, between 1993 and the second quarter of 1999, the percentage of members of legislative bodies at various levels, entrepreneurs and senior executives in the public and private sectors increased from 2.8 to 3.3%. A similar trend emerges in the intellectual, scientific and highly specialised professions, whose share increased from 6.5 to 8%, and intermediate professions, including technicians, whose share increased from 17.4 to 19.7%. Together, these categories accounted for 26.7% of employed people in Italy in 1993, compared to 31% in 1999. The executive professions also show some growth relative to administration and management in the public and private sectors whose share of employment increased from 11 to 11.7%.

In short, these statistics confirm the parabolic trend currently affecting employment in technologically advanced societies, where the reorganisation of sectors and firms, the automation of production processes and computerisation caused a contraction of demand for less skilled professional categories (ISTAT statistics 2000).

Lifelong learning for a skilled worker becomes an asset for the production process, regardless of the type of product or service the firm produces. A highly skilled 'knowledge worker' hence becomes independent from any specific type of production or product. Moreover, since technologies are increasingly becoming user-friendly, a skilled worker can rapidly change and adapt existing skills to alternative types of industrial production and industrial sectors.

In addition, as workers develop a wide range of skills they become more versatile and independent, thus allowing the new organisation of work to further facilitate geographic mobility. This mobility, in turn will enable workers to exploit their production value more fully and exercise their right to choose better working environments. An increasingly important criterion affecting this choice will be the safety of the work environment as well as the 'atmosphere' in the workplace. These features will play an increasingly important role in attracting and keeping skilled knowledge workers. In the future, the attractiveness of a firm will shift from the issue of salary to the quality of work and the opportunities for the development of skills and competences. The firm that is able to attract the best knowledge workers will have the greatest productive and competitive potential.

Combating the exclusion of the weakest groups: the digital divide

In the context of the gradual extension of the 'new economy' into all areas of the economy and society, the sections of the population that are most at risk are senior citizens and youth. The former have the knowledge but not the skills of digital technology, the latter have, at best, the skill but not the experience and the economic means. Both suffer from the digital divide syndrome, or exclusion from the digital revolution.

Literacy re-training for senior citizens (60-75 years) as well as tailored targeted training are the prerequisites for accessibility to the new job profiles. The opportunities of the digital economy will lead to a revalorization of the experience of older people, in particular through the use of tele-services and tele-work. Literacy re-training is the prerequisite for accessing the new economy, which is a valuable opportunity to transcend age, space and time.

The inclusion of senior citizens in the knowledge society opens the way for a new system of learning technology which takes the specific needs of the elderly into account with particular reference to activities aimed at maintaining and/or restoring high levels of health and fitness by learning appropriate techniques ranging from physical and mental exercise to measures to improve one's memory.

On the contrary, and in addition to literacy and knowledge, young people must be able to learn fast and constantly develop their own knowledge, through continuous learning in relation to the development of new technologies, in order to face the challenges of new forms of work. Work is being digitalised and becoming more abstract. Obtaining and keeping a job will depend both on mastery of one's own field and on the creative and educational content of the training received.

It is therefore important to teach young people to learn continuously throughout their lives, so that they can better adapt to a rapidly changing socio-economic context. Both the form and content of work in the knowledge society is dynamic: knowing how to re-orient oneself towards new knowledge and professions will be the knowledge worker's 'master-key'.

Concluding remarks

The new way of organising work will challenge industrial relations. The old method is characterised by the specialisation of tasks and abilities and by the separation of RTD and the production phase. Under the rules of the new economy, industrial relations will have to be developed on the basis of co-operation and common interest ('co-petition'). New forms of labour relations (union and non-union) will have to be developed on the basis of greater participation of workers in all areas, including management, since efficient and optimal production requires a greater degree of both trust and responsibility within the firm.

Knowledge creates value and will be the key to employment in the new economy. With higher levels of competence, workers with 'knowledge' skills will have the privilege of choosing their work and, therefore, enjoy greater security in terms of employability. In this scenario, flexibility will necessarily go hand in hand with security as one will be the prerequisite for the other. Striking this balance between flexibility and security lies at the heart of these new forms of work.

2.1.2 The new agricultural policy: combining farmers' and consumers' concerns

Franz FISCHLER
European Commissioner responsible for
agriculture and fisheries

'We cannot stand still while the world around us is moving'. This statement, made by Jean Monnet around fifty years ago, stressing Europe's need to make dynamic progress, is more valid than ever before, in particular with respect to the Common Agricultural Policy (CAP). When the EU was being established, the main agricultural priority was ensuring supplies. Accordingly, Article 39 (now 33) of the EEC Treaty stated that the aim was 'to increase agricultural productivity' and 'to assure the availability of supplies'.

Now, entering the third millennium, these goals only sound quaint: Europe had assured its self-sufficiency in food supplies even by the end of the Sixties and we have been plagued with surplus problems since the Seventies.

The new CAP

Society no longer expects agricultural policy to explain 'how much is being produced' but rather 'what is being produced and how'. Disasters such as the dioxin-contaminated chicken meat in Belgium, the BSE crisis or the antibiotic scandal in pig breeding have shown what can happen if we pursue increased productivity and maximised profit without sufficient controls. Feasibility cannot be the key criterion for agriculture; that has been brought home to us over the past few months. We must work with nature, not against it. Surely that is the most important lesson to be drawn from the BSE crisis.

It would be mistaken, however, to assume that this comes as news to me. Nor is it necessary to clamour for changes to the agricultural policy, as these have already been ushered in by the European Commission. The EU created a new model of agriculture with the 1992 and 1999 CAP reforms and the emphasis is no longer on maximising output, but on developing sustainability.

Sustainability has three well-established dimensions: not only an ecological one but also a social and an economic aspect. Agricultural holdings that are not economically healthy are also unable to operate in a sustainable manner, therefore our farming businesses must be competitive. Fair income opportunities must be provided. Finally – and this is the social component – we must make structural change bearable.

Highly promising interim results

So far, the results of the CAP reforms prove that we are heading in the right direction. As regards economic sustainability, the farmers are clearly responding more to market signals. In going for artificially high prices, the EU used to spend a major part of its agricultural budget on its cereal, meat and butter mountains or getting rid of part of its produce on the world market at dumping prices. About 90% of our 1991 agricultural budget was spent on export refunds and interventions. Only 20% of the farming budget is being used for market support now that we have opted out of the production race.

The positive effects of this new approach are clearly visible: by curbing the artificial drive towards production, market balance has been restored for most agricultural products. This has drained the milk lakes and levelled the mountains of meat and cereals. As fate would have it, exactly two weeks after selling the most recent intervention purchases of beef in attempts to contain BSE, there was a new BSE outbreak that completely upset the market balance once more.

However, the cereal mountains have also dwindled, because normal market prices and reduced output have refuelled the demand for European cereals in Europe. Pig and poultry feeding has become more natural. While during the 80s feed grain consumption in the EU fell by 1 to 2 million tonnes per year and cereals were increasingly replaced by industrial waste and substitutes from overseas, today, following the reform, about 25 million tonnes more cereals per year are being used than in 1992.

The example of feed grain shows that economic and ecological sustainability do not have to be mutually exclusive, but may complement each other. It makes ecological sense to adopt a more sound, efficient way of using our resources. Thus the new CAP has also seen a sharp drop in the use of artificial fertilisers and pesticides.

Agriculture and environmental protection

These are not the only ecological aspects of the agricultural reform. Agenda 2000 prescribes several measures specifically targeted at developing greener agriculture.

Firstly, every national programme for rural development must include agri-environmental measures. This means encouraging organic production as well as landscape and wildlife protection. Secondly, Agenda 2000 authorises Member States to cut or block direct payments should farmers not comply with the binding environmental commitments (the so-called Cross-compliance measure). And thirdly, Agenda 2000 allows Member States to exercise a degree of flexibility. It enables the Member States to cut direct payments to large low labour-intensive farms by up to 20% and to spend the money saved on further agricultural and environmental measures.

Clearly, Agenda 2000 contained some measures that fostered greater sustainability in the ecological context. However, it cannot be denied that the Commission would have preferred to go still further in its proposals but Member States were unwilling to follow suit at the Berlin summit.

Divergent national and Union interests cannot and must not stand in the way of future additional reform. Agricultural policy – like any policy – must reflect society's interests and these interests have changed radically over the past 50 years. It is not enough to concern ourselves only with assuring food supplies, as we became more than self-sufficient over 30 years ago. It is no longer acceptable to focus only on ensuring farmers' incomes without considering the ecological consequences. Modern agricultural policy must adopt a holistic approach. We must consider the entire agricultural system, not only the farmers, who, after all, only represent a small percentage of the working population. That includes:

• an economically sound rural community

• producing products that consumers have full confidence in

• environmentally-sound production which respects animal welfare

• developing every aspect of economic and social activity in rural areas

• and improving the quality and range of infrastructure to provide more opportunities.

Rural development – the comprehensive approach

Agenda 2000 has established rural development policy as the 'second pillar' of the CAP. Rural development policy is concerned both with promoting full-scale agricultural sustainability and with implementing structural transformation in the rural areas by widening the spectrum of alternative employment possibilities outside farming.

Yet agricultural policy cannot forcibly drive sustainable agricultural development. Agriculture is unlike other industries, as it provides services that are needed by all of society and which are not provided by the free market. Conversely, this also means that society must support the farmers providing these services. Naturally, farmers must earn consumers' trust by providing uncontaminated goods. Yet at the same time consumers should also be willing to pay a fair price for product quality. Therefore trade must stop treating food products – especially perishables – as bargain items. And other policy areas such as the environmental, energy and transport policies must help provide the rural areas with opportunities outside farming. Farming is a key economic sector and can only be sustained economically, ecologically and socially through a comprehensive approach.

The mid-term review of Agenda 2000 – A chance to make further adjustments

The European Commission is ready to continue the process launched with Agenda 2000. Reforming agricultural policy is a process that must be completed one step at a time. We must not rush things, just because the BSE crisis has led the public to crave speedy action. In any case, the Berlin decisions oblige us to carry out a mid-term review, to monitor the effects of Agenda 2000 and to propose necessary changes. The mid-term review gives us the opportunity to find answers to urgent questions, such as:

- Why does the CAP focus on products and not on product quality?
- Why are only 10% of funds channelled into rural development although almost half the farmers in the EU are already only part-time farmers and it is becoming increasingly important for their families to find suitable alternative work in the countryside?
- And what are the factual reasons for spending about 45% of the EU- agricultural policy funds only on crop farming, although four times as many people are employed in the dairy and meat production industry or, for example, in the fruit and vegetable sector?

These are the sort of questions we need to address now. This year, the European Commission will closely analyse the developments so far; the final outcome of the mid-term review will be presented next year. However, the mid-term review is not only the Commission's concern; the Member States' governments, the lobbying groups and the general public are called upon to ponder the future of agriculture and the rural environment. It would be counterproductive to wait to hear what Brussels has to say and then, as is so often the case, subject it to heavy criticism.

The international dimension

One thing should not be overlooked in our reform fervour: we are not on an island where we can carry out agricultural policy experiments at will. As the second largest exporter of agricultural products, the European Union profits from global trade and therefore it is in our own interests to include the current negotiations within the WTO in our considerations. During the Uruguay round of the GATT negotiations, Europe was forced onto the defensive due to its obsolete subsidy policy and had to give in on many issues. However, we are on the right track with our new model of agriculture and we are also ready to defend this approach in the WTO.

This time, we are better prepared and our negotiation paper is a constructive and balanced proposal. On the one hand, we are willing to keep whittling down trade-distorting domestic support and export subsidies. At the same time, we are also resolved to safeguard the full scope of agricultural issues: i.e. environmental protection, food safety, animal welfare and conservation of the landscape etc. These are issues that involve European society and therefore we demand the right to remunerate these services accordingly. Nor are we alone in doing so. The citizens of other WTO Member States also expect these services from farmers and so I am confident that we will be able to reach an agreement on these aspects in the long term.

There is no reason for European agriculture to be typecast as the villain in the international agricultural debate. Agenda 2000 has introduced a transparent, stable subsidy scheme. While our support is limited by a fixed upper ceiling, agricultural expenditure in the USA has rocketed. In the past year American farms received almost three times as much in direct subsidies as their European counterparts. The writing is on the wall; we are on the right track with the new CAP. We will still have to smooth the path as we proceed and we are prepared to do so, but the goal is clear: ecologically, economically and socially sustainable agriculture in dynamic rural areas.

2.1.3 Can the welfare state survive?

Bendt BENDTSEN
Chairman of the Danish Conservative People's Party

The State must loosen its grip in order to safeguard the welfare state

The future of the welfare state depends to a great extent on whether we in the highly developed western democracies are able to adapt to developments. The striking social developments which we have witnessed throughout recent decades confront us with new challenges and tasks.

Many societies – very much including Denmark – have over a number of years experienced increasing public sector domination in an increasing number of sectors of society. It has almost by definition become a task of the public sector to manage the problems with which the individual perhaps has difficulty in coping himself. In step with the growth of the welfare state an increasing number of us have become accustomed to the State, region or local government intervening when a problem or an undesirable trend needs tackling.

We wish to preserve, safeguard and consolidate the welfare state but do not want to see ourselves as citizens in a 'social democratic welfare state guaranteed for the future' where everything from 'cradle to grave' is arranged by the social democratic concern with all its ramifications – ranging from children's and sporting organisations and cooperative housing associations – in order to end up ultimately as a customer of the movement's firm of funeral directors.

The private sector must be encouraged in order to secure a sustainable future both for the private and public sector. No-one can dispense with the State. It is the national framework for the community of which a society consists. Yet the State (or the public sector) must be there for the individual – and not vice versa. As individuals we are citizens who must enjoy maximum scope for individual development – not at the expense of others but for the benefit of all.

The public sector must therefore be adapted to future developments. The time is past when every social task must as a matter of course necessarily be performed by society. We have made such progress in ensuring that basic rights are guaranteed that the individual will in future be assuming greater responsibility for himself and those closest to him within the community.

The challenge of the future is not therefore to safeguard the role of the State but to guarantee that more space and greater room for manoeuvre are created for the individual. When we (and the electorate) have allowed matters to get to the point where the public sector in a country like Denmark confiscates over half of disposable income (on average), then we have gone too far. Enterprise and endeavour are trampled under foot for the sake of a passive existence when all significant actions become a public responsibility. We must and shall change this.

Technological and economic developments create greater opportunities for the individual if we allow them to happen. It is therefore crucial for the future of the welfare state that we change the allocation of roles in that society that is the framework for everyone – and hence for the individual.

If we are to succeed in maintaining the level of welfare which no one either can or should go without, we must create the right framework for ensuring that there are adequate resources available. What is assistance for everyone is in reality assistance for no-one – since State generosity does not come out of the blue. Ultimately it is the taxpayers that are footing the bill. It is that simple and that is of course how it should be to a certain extent but we must therefore ensure that the bill is written out in such a way that people are both eager and willing to pay it.

Welfare is the sum of the achievements which the individual is capable of producing. Welfare is not something which the State has devised on its own but something for which it can help ensure a common basis.

The achievements of industry and the private sector are what we all have to live off and at a time when the average age is steadily rising there will, all things being equal, be fewer people to foot the bill. It is the section of the population that is of working age that must provide the basis from which we all must live. For this reason as well we are forced to channel more resources into the private manufacturing and services sector in the form of an extra intake of labour. In other words, we must ensure that there are enough busy hands available.

The public sector in many of our countries must be adapted to the new reality. Denmark has far too many people on the public payroll regardless of whether they are employed in central, regional or local government or whether they are in receipt of transfer payments in the form of early retirement pensions, bridging and leave-of-absence benefits or unemployment benefit, etc. There are too many people parked in the public sector's welfare budgets as passive recipients of automatic benefits. To this should be added the natural obligations which a modern society has for pensions, etc. for our older fellow citizens who must also be provided with the necessary resources in the health and care sector. This, too, is a joint obligation.

It is absolutely essential that we focus more sharply on the imbalances in society – not for the sake of blind controversy but so that we can face up to reality. The time has come for a positive showdown with the handout mentality underlying the conventional protection of the role of the State.

We must redefine our role as individuals in a dynamic society. The individual citizen must as far as possible be able to run and plan his life himself.

Yet we must also be ready to engage in the political struggle since a restructuring process of this nature requires a showdown with many prejudices and unreconstructed thinking on the part of many people. The traditional social democratic approach to society does not contain the answer to the challenges of the future. We can to some extent in certain areas agree with our political opponents on the objectives which we wish to set ourselves but the means often divide us. Any talk of a reform of the structure on which society is based encounters deep-seated reluctance on the part of many. We believe in free enterprise and private entrepreneurship. We trust the individual; we do not mistrust his or her motives.

'The world is no larger than can be encompassed by thought', were the wise words of a leading Danish businessman at the beginning of the last century. Today these words are truer than ever before and they are increasingly often seen to be confirmed by the globalisation that has become a part of everyday life. We have already been living for a long time in the global village. We are now moving into the next phase – the global conurbation where we are all affected by a crisis on Asian stock markets, by turmoil in a particular part of the world or by a change in energy production in another part. We are all dependent on one another in a completely different way than before. We must therefore adapt.

The structures to which we have been accustomed for decades – and many have perhaps been comfortable with – cannot in the long run deliver what we need. A rigid and inflexible labour market can be a needless obstacle to sensible growth whilst unreconstructed thinking locks us into an outdated model. A conformist primary school that does not allow the individual's talent to develop can be another such obstacle. A health sector that sets limits where no limits are needed is also outdated. A tax system that thwarts the individual's desire to make an extra effort hampers growth and employment and must be replaced by a reform that eases the tax on work.

A research policy that does not match existing requirements must be designed so that we can secure the necessary investment in the future. An industrial policy that puts the business world into a straitjacket at a time when it needs a new and broader framework within which to develop along with society must receive the same priority.

If we are to save our welfare state we must create the right framework. There is a need for a new balance between the public and private sectors – between the State and the individual. The allocation of roles must be altered before the welfare state suffocates in new taxes and charges and in new conformist structures, the aim of which is to preserve the existing division of power.

In other words: we must let our citizens keep a far larger share of what they earn. Society and the community must have their share but it can never be a goal in itself for the public sector to discharge the maximum possible number of tasks for the individual.

The citizen must have his freedom back.

2.1.4   *Environmental protection or economic competition?*

Avril DOYLE
Member of the EPP-ED Group in the
European Parliament

There is no basis for commonly-expressed dichotomies such as "Environment or Employment". On the contrary we assert that the quality and protection of the environment are directly dependent upon the strength and health of the local economy.

Furthermore I believe that unchallenged environmental protectionism can be harmful to the very assets that it purports to nurture, whenever it distorts the long established symbiosis that exists between human beings and their habitats.

History has shown how competition – political, economic and intellectual – promotes stability and progress. However in mature societies competition is always managed, primarily to avoid monopolies of power, privilege or values.

Unchallenged environmental protectionism has the potential to become a distorting and unsustainable value monopoly, whenever it seeks to avoid the needs of an economically successful and competitive Europe.

The European People's Party and European Democrats Group believes that the environment should always be considered within the wider social economic context – without compromising its inherent natural limitations and vulnerabilities. From this argument a distinctively European vision emerges where environmental protection is made more challenging by the need to accommodate and sustain the economies of those people on whose prosperity the future of Europe's environment depends.

The false paradigm

It is not true to say that society must choose between *"Employment or the Environment"*. Wealth, growth, enterprise and development need not and do not "consume the environments" of mature societies. On the contrary it may be observed that there is a clear relationship between the quality of the environment and the wealth of the nation. Throughout Europe and North America recent years have seen dramatic reversals in the pollution of air and water due to technological improvements driven by legislation and societal expectations. In the same period there have been profound increases in the extent and quantity of habitats and natural resources that are formally recognised and protected. The infrastructure, organisation and technology that are needed for a cleaner environment are all achievable because of the wealth and surpluses of the local economies. Significant environmental pollution of air and water and the unsustainable exploitation of natural resources have become characteristic of the early stages of developing industrial economies – as they were over a century ago in Europe and North America. Environmental protection requires surpluses, education and vision together with institutional maturity and stability.

Wealth sustains the environment

I believe that the promotion and protection of European competitiveness is inextricably linked to the protection of the environment. Wealth in mature economies is sustained by competitiveness as well as innovation and productivity.

Environmental protection can either be integrated into the maintenance of European competitiveness or it can become a liability whenever it is pursued as a narrowly-focused restriction on development.

Well-managed environments are themselves a source of wealth creation – through agriculture, tourism and the maintenance of assimilative capacity. A high-quality environment is also one of the principal determinants for "Quality of Life" indicators which are becoming such a vital resource in sustaining the well-educated workforces who are the intellectual capital of the emerging knowledge-based economy. Environmental protection is therefore a matter of enlightened self-interest for the future economic well-being and competitiveness of Europe.

Seen in this light environmental protection becomes part of a 'Virtuous Circle' whereby a high-quality environment is sustained by wealth which in turn is sustained by competition which in its turn requires a high-quality environment.

Environmental threats to competitiveness

These assertions must not, however, be allowed to be used to promote the idea that environmental protection can have priority over all other considerations. Environmental protection which is not proportionate, integrated, accommodating and flexible can quickly become a distorting effect within an economy.

I recognise and embrace the need for constant vigilance in matters of environmental protection. Environmental protection must however be placed within the context of the criteria that apply to other concerns of society.

Environmental orthodoxies must be constantly scrutinised and re-evaluated to ensure that the protection required is proportionate and effective. Environmental scaremongering hampers open debate by inflating statable risks (for example the presence of a toxin) so that it becomes an inaccurately perceived threat (i.e. by failing to acknowledge that the quantity of toxin falls significantly below any threatening dose).

"The right to free speech doesn't confer the right to shout "FIRE!" in a crowded theatre" is an old expression that has contemporary relevance for environmental debates.

The overstatement or exaggeration of environmental risks; the overzealous or disproportionate pursuit of absolutes in matters of conservation and pro-tection; the excessive and paralysing invocation of the precautionary principle are all examples of how the pursuit of environmental protection can become a threat to economic competitiveness.

Restoring the balance – the key challenges

A strong lobby in favour of environmental protection is a good and necessary part of any mature democratic society. We are committed to ensuring that the widest range of opinions and values are nurtured, expressed and considered because debate can only increase knowledge and improve the quality of decisions.

Environmental issues should be resolved by debate that is subject to the same norms that are used for any other issue in society, namely that the consideration should be ethical, inclusive and non-discriminatory.

Social and economic audits of environmentalism

The Environmental Impact Assessment of projects, plans and policies is an established and successful method for ensuring that developments do not lead to unintended adverse impacts on the environment. Similarly there is now a need to ensure that the pursuit of environmental objectives is subjected to a balancing audit. This would seek to ensure that the consequences of policy for social equity and economic competitiveness are clearly and fully articulated as part of any decision-making process.

Environmental discrimination

I believe that great sensitivity, tolerance and compassion must be employed whenever it is proposed to apply the environmental standards of a developed economy to the economies and environments of emerging economies.

Europe's history has shown that localised overloading of environmental carrying capacity can be a temporary phase of an emerging economy. We need to acknowledge the resilience of natural systems and their ability to subsequently recover once a plateau of economic stability has been achieved. This has been the pattern over most of the developed world. We must avoid discrimination, on environmental grounds, against economies that are at that stage of the development cycle.

Urban and rural values

The majority of Europe's population is urbanised, leaving a small and shrinking minority who own and manage the countrysides of Europe.

We must be vigilant against a presumption that the values and needs of the urban majority will coincide with those of the rural minority. We must ensure that these urban-generated value systems and needs are not translated into inappropriate, unsustainable or unworkable restrictions and regulations on rural life. Environmental protection is too often proposed without due consideration for its effects on the lives and economies of the countryside that contains these natural resources.

A European environment

The countryside of Europe is like a book that records the pages of change and it is changing again during our lifetime. Agriculture will be restructured. We will protect our natural and cultural heritage. Our populations will further urbanise. All of these forces will change the face of Europe and its environment. In my vision the emerging environment of Europe will be the result of a balanced consideration of the need to prosper as well as to preserve. In our vision the characteristics of a successful European environment in the year 2020 will be:

Distinctive

Europe's greatest source of wealth – cultural, intellectual as well as economic – has been how its extraordinary environmental diversity occurs in such a spatially-condensed area. This diversity lies at the root of Europe's distinctiveness. The structures and functions of the European Union must constantly strive to sustain and enhance this distinctiveness. Policies and practices must not contribute to making landscapes, land-uses or habitats the same throughout Europe. The key to sustaining distinctiveness is to accept that human land-uses – modifying and wisely managing the land for economic gain – have been, and must remain, an integral part of Europe's environment.

Productive

The European territories are endowed with agricultural and natural resources of global significance on account of such factors as the extent of its productive soils, its oceanic fisheries, and its climate as well as deeply-rooted agricultural practices dating back six millennia.

In a world of growing population Europe has a responsibility to utilise these natural resources to their greatest potential consistent with wise and sustainable land management.

Productivity and profitability are important pre-requisites for environmental protection and enhancement, particularly on a regional and local basis.

Competitive

More rational use of interventions and incentives can facilitate world-market pricing for environmentally-based economic activity, such as agriculture, tourism, mineral extraction, fishing and water management.

Such open market practices and pricing will increase long-term stability, productivity and profitability in these sectors. The pursuit of such competitiveness will require constant and balanced analysis to ensure that short-term efficiency gains are not sacrificed against long-term equity rights and responsibilities.

Robust

The diversity, productivity and competitiveness of Europe's environment should, whenever possible and reasonable, be based upon the inherent competitive advantages offered by the local and regional environment. The policies and practices of the Union must be constantly scrutinised to ensure that they do not promote or sustain interventions which diminish competitiveness – particularly that which arises from natural factors – such as soil, climate or cultural practices. Inappropriate and unresponsively uniform intervention can create economically, socially and environmentally unsustainable land-uses that are prone to abrupt changes when policies change.

This uncertainty promotes vulnerability and is a disincentive to investment, planning and social commitment. Stability, continuity and certainty are important characteristics of a healthy robust environment.

Conclusion

The EPP-ED Group has a clear vision of the future of Europe's environment. We see it being shaped by a confident and knowledgeable use of Europe's diverse and deeply-rooted natural endowments.

This knowledgeable use includes a balance between the need to prosper and protect. We recognise the need for sustained economic competitiveness to provide the resources required for a high quality of environment. We believe that environmental protection is achieved by economic competitiveness. There does not need to be any contradiction between these two objectives.

2.2 The euro between the dollar and the yen

2.2.1 Competition in a social market economy

Mario MONTI
European Commissioner responsible for competition

More than ever, the European Union is today confronted with the challenging task of upholding economic expansion in a context of less favourable
global conditions. Despite the somewhat slow down of the economy in some
other parts of the world, growth prospects remain encouraging in Europe,
given its sound fundamentals. Recently it has been questioned whether the
euro-zone could not do more to help the rest of the world, playing a role of
"locomotive" in the world economy. Although I am not convinced that there
is a serious risk of recession, there is nevertheless scope to seriously and effectively address the problem of how to improve the economic performance of
the European economy and its long-term growth potential, which would
increase confidence in the euro.

The recently adopted 2001 Broad Economic Policy Guidelines have recommended a policy strategy which, in the framework of a monetary policy
oriented towards price stability, would press ahead with the process of
rejuvenation of the EU economy. The Guidelines stress that, not only do we
need to improve the quality and sustainability of public finances, but in
order to be able to contribute substantially to reverse the current global
growth slow-down, European governments are required to forge ahead with
structural economic reforms to ensure efficient product markets.

While significant progress has been made in recent years in the functioning
of EU product markets, a number of areas remain where further efforts are
needed. The good shape of the EU economy – 2000 was one of the best years
of the last decade – was undoubtedly the result of sound macro-economic
policies coupled with improved competitiveness. Average growth in the EU
in 2001 has been revised downwards to 2.8% as exports are expected to be
less dynamic following the expected decrease of world GDP to 3.3% in 2001,

compared to 4.8% last year. Average inflation in the euro area was slightly above 2% in 2000 and is expected to remain so this year. However, improving the growth potential of the EU economy will need to emerge above all from strengthening production efficiency, quality and innovation.

What can competition, and competition policy, contribute to the development of the EU economy? Are the instruments at our disposal sufficient to address the new challenges? I am convinced that competition plays a key role in encouraging the optimal allocation of resources and that the Commission has started a review process of existing tools to ensure a more rigorous enforcement of competition rules.

The Union, and in particular the Commission, has been assigned broad powers in the competition field in order to ensure the application of the principle, enshrined in the Treaty, of *"an open market economy with free competition"*. Since its adoption more than 40 years ago, the Treaty acknowledges the fundamental role of the market and of competition in guaranteeing consumer welfare and in granting to economic agents the appropriate incentives to pursue productive efficiency, quality, and innovation. Competition policy was a fundamental feature of the "Social Market Economy".

An open market economy can only be effectively maintained by preventing collusive agreements between firms or abuses of a dominant position, by ensuring competitive market structures through merger control, and by abolishing those unjustified State subsidies that distort competition by artificially keeping non-viable firms in business.

I consider all these legal instruments as tools to achieve a single aim: to maintain a vibrant and competitive economy in Europe. In short: competition is the key to a viable and sustainable development of our economy, fit to meet the challenges that lie ahead.

Is this model in need of fundemental change?

I think it is worthwhile to reflect whether the Social Market Economy can still be considered a model for the European economy. Everybody recognises that this model is one of the greatest success-stories in modern history.

It combines the efficiency and dynamism of the market economy with a policy of social balance, leading to more productivity and competitiveness while ensuring social and economic cohesion, which is essential for a high degree of social consensus.

It implies the development of a legal framework for the economy with a clear set of regulations. Ludwig Erhard's ideas were always regarded as a particular form of economic order of "rules" to be enforced by competent and sufficiently independent authorities. It is therefore not surprising that one thing is inseparably bound up with Erhard's economic miracle and the Social Market Economy: it is the system of competition rules, which became one of the pillars of German economic policy at the end of the 1950s.

The fact that competition rules were at the same time made a cornerstone of the EEC Treaty from the very beginning was due not least to the influence of Germany. Since then, German politicians and competition specialists have taken a leading role in the shaping and practical development of European competition rules.

This illustrates perfectly that competition policy is a constitutent element of the Social Market Economy. It ensures that the economy remains open to reform and is in a position to be flexible enough to face up to the challenges of a changing world.

Nevertheless, we have to increase our efforts to make clear to the European citizen the underlying positive social effects of liberalisation and competition. It is one of my objectives, as Commissioner in charge of competition, to underline the citizens' role as guardians of competition policy. I realise that many citizens only see the down side: restructuring, job losses and fears about the preservation of the European social model including services of general economic interest. I must acknowledge that sometimes competition decisions, as in the field of state aid, can have negative short-term effects on employment. These effects probably cannot be avoided but they can be attenuated through specific conversion programmes and training. On the other hand, improved competitiveness of European companies will lead to the creation of sustainable jobs.

It is my firm conviction that the Social Market Economy still is the best model for Europe. Its basic principles are still appropriate and desirable in modern economies.

Competition and globalisation

This certainly does not mean that we should move on without actively addressing new challenges. The economic, legal and institutional environment has fundamentally changed.

Let me turn in more detail to a market development that requires our particular attention: the increasing internationalisation of our economies. Globalisation leads to increased competition for the companies active in Europe. This competition comes not only from inside the Union, but also from Third Countries like the USA or Japan. It takes place in a context where markets tend to become wider and where the critical mass that is necessary to be an active player tends to increase.

Consequently, competition law enforcement is taking on an increasingly international dimension: antitrust agencies the world over are finding that the consumers whom they are mandated to protect are being adversely affected by anticompetitive behaviour taking place outside their jurisdiction.

In response to these challenges, the Commission has adopted a dual approach. First and foremost, we are developing our bilateral relations with the competition authorities of the EU's major trading partners.

Secondly, we have always believed that multilateral efforts are necessary to ensure convergence and co-ordination between the vast number of competition enforcement systems around the world. The Commission has been very active to achieve cooperation among antitrust enforcement authorities. We have pioneered the idea of a Multilateral Framework Agreement on Competition Policy in the WTO. Such a framework would include core principles of competition law and would serve to underpin the impressive progress which has been made in trade liberalisation over the past few decades, by ensuring that governmental barriers to trade are not replaced by private ones which have the same effect. We have also contributed to the debate by offering some ideas on what could be an international forum for competition among authorities from all over the world. The "Global Competition Forum" has been gathering momentum over the recent months. It should not be a new institution, but is intended to draw together all interested parties – both public and private – to discuss subjects ranging from substantive competition law and policy issues to enforcement-related and systemic matters.

The introduction of the euro

No other change could thrust us towards a single market in such a dynamic way as the introduction of the euro. The financial services sector facilitates trade and consumption and can be used to hedge all kinds of risks. Its performance is essential to improve competitiveness in the economy as a whole by assisting optimum allocation of investment capital. These are the reasons which led us to set a priority in ensuring that competition rules are fully applied in the financial services sector. This requires, at Community level, a strong impulsion to remove the remaining barriers to cross-border provision of financial services.

If strong domestic institutions are further strengthened by government intervention, there is a risk that existing competitors will be weakened and potential market entrants will be discouraged. Such a situation could foster market segmentation and present an obstacle to the opening up of financial markets.

Let me, in this context, turn to State aid policy in the banking sector. The Commission's activity in this field has increased dramatically in the last few years. It did not only focus on Germany. The usual State aid rules have to be applied in this sector without exception. Otherwise distortions would occur to the detriment of competitors, undermining the trust in the viability of the whole banking sector, with consequences for the European currency system.

The financial services sector is the foundation of an open market economy and has a fundamental impact on all other sectors, without exception. For this reason, the Commission is committed to making the application of the competition rules to the financial services sector one of its top priorities.

The modernisation of the competition rules

Our competition procedures have to adapt to new challenges. Competition authorities need effective tools. We are committed to an ambitious modernisation programme with the aim of ensuring that our competition rules, whilst building on the past, represent an evolving dynamic: the main purpose of the Commission's reforms and reform proposals is to render our competition law enforcement regime more efficient, and better suited to economic and political realities in the European Union of today and tomorrow, while maintaining the Commission's central role.

A proposal for a regulation designed to modernise the procedural rules implementing the antitrust provisions of the Treaty is currently being discussed. It will allow the Commission to focus on the most serious infringements and, by creating a network amongst national antitrust authorities, it will greatly facilitate the strengthening of a common competition culture in the EU.

Antitrust is not the only area where we need to adapt our instruments. Merger controls also need to be kept up-to-date in order to cope with the ever-increasing number and complexity of cases. It is for this reason that we are undertaking an in-depth review.

These processes of modernising our legislative and interpretative rules aim to keep up with the pace of economic and technological development in the 21st century. The basis principles, however, will not change.

With the experience of forging and applying competition rules in a set of integrating economies, within the framework of a Social Market Economy, Europe will be able to meet – and to anticipate – the challenges ahead for all of us. Thus, European economic prospects will in this way improve, whilst still remaining based on a foundation of social and economic cohesion.

2.2.2   Who needs Economic and Monetary Union?

Alain MADELIN
Member of the EPP-ED Group in the
European Parliament

Since its launch, the euro has lost roughly a quarter of its initial value against the dollar. At 1 January 1999 the rate of exchange was € 1 to US$ 1.17. At the time of writing (27 March 2001) it is worth only US$ 0.90.

The scale of this – totally unexpected – depreciation continues to give European leaders cause for concern. Many see it as an undeserved punishment, an unjust sanction by the markets, the reasons for which they do not understand.

Their perplexity is compounded by the fact that the recovery that occurred at the end of 2000, when the euro climbed to US$ 0.95, was followed by a further slide. For economists, factors such as the harsh slowdown of the American economy since autumn, the fall of the stock markets, fears of a severe recession and the Fed's lowering of interest rates ought normally to have led to a reversal in the relative fortunes of both currencies. Supported by a European economy in better health than America's, favoured by a smaller difference in rates, the euro should, in theory, have recovered against the dollar. But this is not what has happened. Once more the economists – not to mention the politicians – have got it wrong.

And this is undoubtedly because economic explanations do not tell the whole story. Something else, something more fundamental, is at stake. But what, exactly?

* * *

During the summer of 2000, debate raged as to the causes of the euro's fall. With hindsight, we now understand better what happened. At the time, the euro was paying the price for a temporary crisis of international liquidity caused by the unfortunate conjunction of the sudden rise in world petrol prices with the American monetary clampdown that had occurred in spring to correct the excesses seen at the end of 1999 as a result of fears about the famous 'Millennium bug'.

Since its launch, there have been three successive phases in the euro's fall:

- The first phase – until June 1999 – reflected the economic growth differential between the USA and euroland – about 2% for European GNP and almost 4% for America. This growth differential – now much smaller – caused a significant exodus of capital from Europe to the United States. Investors and firms threw themselves upon the American market and on assets denominated in dollars.
- The second phase – from November 1999 until May 2000 – was essentially linked to interest rate differentials. Following the Fed's decision to raise rates, bonds fell in relation to shares, and it became more beneficial for American firms to borrow on the new European market, in euro, rather than in dollars in the United States, even taking into account the additional cost of the exchange risk. The flow of sums borrowed in this way into the United States caused the dollar to rise.
- The third phase – from July to the end of November 2001 – was caused by the oil effect. When oil prices rise (as a result of the very strong growth and increasing dependence of the United States on imports), the liquidity goes out of the American monetary system and the dollar becomes a rare currency. In the past, the victim tended to be the yen (Japan having the second most important banking system in the world). This time it was the euro's turn to be affected.

The exceptional factors that were present in the summer of 2000 have now disappeared. The price per barrel has fallen back to under US$ 25. The deposits of foreign central banks with the Federal Reserve in New York are on the increase again. The American economic boom has slowed down, while the money supply is growing rapidly again. All these elements ought now to operate in the euro's favour. However, although it gained almost 10% during December alone, at the first quarter of 2001 the euro has fallen to levels not far from its previous record lows.

* * *

The economy has a large influence on how currencies behave, but it is not the only determining factor. Another key element is the movement of relative prices between monetary zones.

In order to gauge the influence this has, economists use *purchasing power parity*, i.e. the exchange rate that serves to keep at a consistent level in local currencies the cost of a specific basket of goods and services. The PPP determines long-term currency movements in relation to each other, while the economy and interest rates are responsible for variations in the effective parity around this trend.

For several months it has been as though, in its efforts to bounce back, and taking into account the differentials in the economic situation, the euro has been colliding with a kind of ceiling that has prevented it from reaching its appropriate exchange rate.

One possible explanation is that, since the euro's launch two years ago, the level of its *purchasing power parity* against the dollar has changed to its disadvantage. This is the hypothesis put forward by the London-based Lombard Street Research Institute in a paper published in January.[1]

In the past, the accepted wisdom was that with regard to foreign exchange, the most important factor was the trade balance. That was what brought about the financial movements necessary to ensure the accounting adjustment, the movement of currencies serving to compensate for that which could not be financed.

Since the 1980s, with the progress of globalisation, the generalised liberalisation of trade and the ever-increasing freedom in capital movements, everything has changed. The sequence of adjustments has been reversed: the financial flows now come first, the balance being re-established by an adjustment of the trade balances driven by the movement of exchange rates. The change from one system to another has resulted in a real revolution.

According to Lombard, for several years now a new change of the highest order has been taking place, linked to the dynamics of the American 'new economy'.

While, up until now, direct investment abroad (investment by firms, for example) accounted for most of the financial flows, today portfolio investments (purchase of shares, pension fund placement) are growing much more quickly.

The proportion of stock market investments made abroad, which accounted for 2% to 3% of the GDP of G7 member states between 1990 and 1997, increased to more than 8%, while direct investments remained stable at around 12% to 14% of total GDP.

For the euroland countries, the movement was even more spectacular – the volume of portfolio investments increased by six or seven times, to reach 15%.

The current stock market crisis may change the outlook again. Nonetheless, this change in the structure of international monetary flows has a significant consequence: it means that the list of activities in which the market is now a global one, and which are the principal determinants of a country's competitivity – and thus also the relative evolution of the value of its currency – has been extended to encompass a whole range of new sectors of

---

1. Lombard Street Research, Monthly International Review 102, 15 January 2001: 'How far might the euro rebound?'

services, far beyond just the manufacturing sectors for which the evolution of costs, prices and productivity tend to be the only ones taken into account by economists calculating the PPP of the two currencies.

This has led some to revise the calculations to include services, where it is well-known – especially since the new revolutions of the virtual economy – that relative trends are less favourable to Europe because of the regulatory framework that exists there and the fact that the level of obstacles to competition remains significantly higher than in the United States.

Gabriel Stein and Charles Dumas, the authors of the study, discovered that, if PPP is calculated only on the basis of the evolution of unit costs in manufacturing sectors, the 'correct' value of the euro against the dollar would have increased from an average of 90 cents for the period 1985-95 to approximately 110-115 cents today.

But if we take as the starting point the figures on the whole economy, which include services, we obtain a result of about 94-95 cents, a figure which corresponds, more or less, to the 'ceiling' observed at the end of last year.

In other words, if we accept their hypothesis that, as a result of globalisation and the new technological revolution, the international competitivity of an economy is now dependent upon a much wider range of activities, which is not confined to industrial activities alone, the euro's apparent weakness is simply the result of a fall in the competitive capacity of the European economy linked to the growing globalisation of markets and the existence of an institutional environment in which it is less easy for services to exploit new technological opportunities than it is in the United Sates. The 'euro mystery' is no more.

* * *

The French see monetary policy essentially as a power factor. The currency is a political tool to serve the ends of a legitimate authority.

In such a scenario, the single currency is both the lever and the symbol of the emancipation of Europe in the face of Anglo-Saxon economic and financial power. In this vision of things, the State is the 'founder' of the Nation: Europe will be built as France was, by observing imposed rules (such as the single currency), the practice of which will gradually cause to emerge among the different peoples feelings of belonging and loyalty, and thus union with a shared institution.

Last year, powerless to explain the reasons for the euro's fall, those who subscribed to this way of thinking naturally started to blame the weakness of European political power. The euro was weak because Europe was still a 'political dwarf'; because the euro did not yet have the State it needed to back it up.

The solutions proposed involved stepping up 'political' management of the currency. By improving the procedures for economic cooperation between governments. By reconsidering the excessive degree of independence accorded to the central bank. If necessary, by appointing a 'Mr euro', or a 'triumvirate', who would finally be capable of talking on equal terms with such powerful men as the chairman of the Federal Reserve or America's Secretary to the Treasury. In other words, the message of the euro's weakness was that Europe needed a greater degree of supranationality, more centralised power.

Such a way of seeing things is based on an unrealistic and archaic view of political power, informed by the mercantilist ideologies of the 20th century, and totally out of step with the new realities of the open universe of the 21st.

In the single financial area in which we now operate, currencies are little more than barometers that tell us how economic agents the world over rate the relative capacity of the economic, social and political institutions of a certain country or area to deliver a higher or lower growth rate, and thus higher or lower profits.

In this context, the euro's continuing weakness should be seen, essentially, as the expression of a message that reflects the market's conviction that, whatever uncertainties and concerns may exist with regard to the coming months, it is still America that offers the best hopes for economic growth.

The relative movement of currencies sends a political signal, but one that differs greatly from that seen and believed by those who remain convinced that the only solution is to create a central superstate with superpowers.

In the case of the euro, the message is this: that while it is true that European nations have made considerable progress in liberalising their economic structures, these efforts – which must not be underestimated – are still not enough to close rapidly and in any significant way the growth gap of 1.5 points that has separated the European economy from the American one for several years.

Taxation policy, the intervention of States in the economy, the mushrooming of rules, insufficient competition and the weight of redistributions are so many relative obstacles that weaken the prospects of increasing the returns on capital invested and thus prevent the potential of the new technological revolution from being exploited to the full.

To put it simply, the behaviour of the euro in relation to the dollar is expressing this truth, a truth that too many people are refusing to acknowledge.

So those unwilling to face the truth seek scapegoats, such us the 'untimely' interventions of Wim Duisenberg, or the excuse of insufficient political centralisation.

* * *

One question that is really worthy of an answer is to what extent the creation of the euro is itself partly responsible for this situation. Can monetary union contribute to the reduction of this growth gap, or, rather, does it hamper convergence?

The Brussels rhetoric sees only advantages to the single currency. It systematically ignores the costs involved. But they do exist. It is possible that what the euro's persistent weakness is telling us is that the costs, in reality, are far from being as negligible as is generally supposed.

* * *

One of the main positive consequences of the creation of the euro has been the emergence of a truly European financial market which, today, means European firms can benefit from sources of investment and financing that are infinitely more liquid, and more closely resemble the conditions found on the other side of the Atlantic, which has not been the case in the past.

The Wall Street Journal has published excellent articles on this aspect (on 6 November 2000 and 8 January 2001 in particular). It quotes several industry experts and bankers who confirm how, thanks to the euro, the famous 'financial revolution', which was the main reason behind the past performance of the new economy, is spreading to euroland:

1) The creation of a single currency in eleven countries has improved the liquidity of European stocks, shares and bonds, including the emergence of a market in high yield securities (junk bonds), which opens access to the financial market to numerous firms hitherto excluded from it.

2) The deepening of this capital market reduces the average cost of financing in Europe, reduces the traditional dependence of borrowers on the banks, and makes it much easier to finance mergers and acquisitions. The overall value of such transactions in Europe today is approximately twice the 1998 figure. Such rapid growth has never been seen in the United States.

3) Operating in a larger market reduces transaction costs for large borrowers, allowing them to make even more ambitious investment plans. As for investors, the growth of the average size of issues allows them to enjoy greater liquidity of investments and more attractive investment prospects.

4) Overall, a good many European firms today are certainly enjoying interest rates that are significantly lower than those which, all other things being equal, they would otherwise have paid.

But there is a conflicting aspect of monetary union that is systematically swept under the carpet, since it is seen as 'politically incorrect' to mention it. That aspect is the harmful effects of what is known as 'fiscal federalism'.

* * *

One problem that has occupied economists – and politicians – for a long time is that of the inequalities in development and growth between regions in the same trading area.

The accepted wisdom is that if the market is left to itself, the normal inter-play of competition with the laws of supply and demand will lead to a growing momentum whereby inequalities increase, with the richest regions becoming richer still, while the poorest become increasingly worse off.

The idea was thus born that an economic and federal union can only work if significant provision is made for assistance and transfers in order to support and increase the competitivity of the least-favoured regions, such as aid to promote employment, industrial reconversion programmes and finance for infrastructure.

In fact, today, there is a wealth of empirical evidence to show that within a unified trading area (without barriers to trade), the logic of growth is not one of a cumulative worsening of inequality, but, on the contrary, of a conver-gence in living standards.[1]

In their 1995 study for the World Bank, Robert Barro and Xavier Sala-i-Martin referred to an average rate of convergence of 2% to 3% per year[2]. It is slow: it would take between 25 and 35 years to make up half of the relative gap between rich and poor regions. But the effect exists, nonetheless, and it occurs independently of all other variables except initial standard of living and level of relative income.

It is a classic mechanism, based on the dynamic of the capital/labour relationship and relative productivity. A large supply of less costly labour attracts investment, which benefits from higher returns since capital is harder to come by. The levels of training and human resources improve, which leads to a gradual increase in real salaries and, thus, in the standard of living.

This is the way things work, for example, in the single American market.

Despite its internal disparities, the American market is relatively homo-geneous. The same language is spoken. Culture, tastes, customs and social institutions are much more homogeneous than in Europe. As a result, the Europeans concluded that they could not expect the spontaneous processes of convergence to occur to the same extent, and that it was necessary to compensate for the specific handicaps linked to the greater disparity of situa-tions in Europe by means of a voluntarist policy of transfers, which was all

---

1. See Fred McMahon, 'The Road to Growth: how lagging economies become prosperous', Atlantic Institute for Market Studies, Halifax, Novia Scotia, Canada, 2000. www.aims.ca
2. Robert Barro and Xavier Sala-i-Martin, 'Economic Growth', New York, McGraw-Hill, 1995

the more necessary given that regulatory harmonisation acted as an additional disincentive to mobility.

But the result of this redistribution, as pointed out by the economist Jean-Luc Migué[1], is that instead of moving, firms and the inhabitants of regions subsidised in this manner are encouraged to remain where they are and to continue in the least productive activities. The lack of connection between the level of prices observed in each country or region and its local costs serves to recreate the equivalent of a form of commercial customs barrier.

Conversely, it is now in the interests of those who control capital and resources in the most prosperous and productive regions to move elsewhere, in view of the relatively higher weight of tax deductions, since it is they who bear the cost of these transfers. By means of taxation, the cost of economic and monetary adjustments is borne by the most economically dynamic regions (since they operate the most liberal policies).

This kind of strategy thus penalises growth factors, and in particular those regions that are the driving force of growth within a particular area.

From this perspective, the behaviour of the markets *vis-à-vis* the euro is far from irrational. Perhaps they are just expressing their extreme scepticism with regard to the beneficial effects of the euro on growth.

* * *

Overall, there is no shortage of reasons to explain the euro's disconcerting behaviour on the exchange markets.

It is true that for many Europeans, life will be much more pleasant when they can move across the whole Union without having to pay any exchange costs. The same will be true for company leaders who will no longer have to juggle with different currencies. But just because such a situation is desirable does not mean that we should rush headlong towards it. Everything depends on the costs – especially the transition costs – that are involved. As Bastiat explained, there are both hidden and visible costs. The former is the tangible expenditure incurred by governments and firms to bring their accounting and management procedures into line. The latter are a result of the growth deficit to which the change in the system of monetary regulation will lead.

The trials of the euro seem to be showing us that by deciding to go all out for the single currency, the Europeans have certainly underestimated the scale of these economic costs. In doing so, they have sacrificed an alternative (a common, rather than a single currency) which, with a little patience, could

---

1. Jean-Luc Migué, 'Monnaie et politique: le débat oublié', on the Institut Euro 92 website, address www.euro92.org/edi/bull/archives/arch23migue.htm

have led to the same result, but without the same costs being incurred.[1]

The euro exists. There is no going back. We must do everything in our power, in the institutional framework that is now ours, to ensure that it is a success. But that should not prevent us from acknowledging that a mistake has been made, and that that is no doubt what the markets are penalising.[2]

---

1. Some further clarification is necessary.
   Basically, the issue here is that it is certainly not by replacing political and collective disciplines with a way of thinking whereby responsible markets make adjustments that the relative economic performance of a region will be improved. In fact, the reverse is true. While it is true that the slightest mobility of resources between the regions of Europe hampers the spontaneous process of economic convergence, compared with what happens in a country like America, economic logic would dictate that the European Union ought to confine itself to the introduction of a common currency, without abolishing the national currencies, rather than to take shortcuts to arrive so quickly at the single currency. By leaving firms and individuals free to hold their assets in the currency of their choice, such a system of a single market with competing currencies would have had the advantage of making the cost to all of the most irresponsible policies clearly apparent.
   True, the freedom to devalue the currency is an easy way out for governments guilty of this. But it is a politically costly one. Those who tend to devalue in order to encourage exports, or which levy the highest taxes in order to subsidise subsidies for declining industries quickly find that resources flow from their territory. They may react, or continue as though nothing was wrong. But in any event it is they – since their citizens then have the opportunity of expressing their opinion through the ballot box – who will assume the financial and human consequences of their own decisions. When exchange rates are irrevocably fixed, this mechanism becomes unavailable. It is as though the thermometer were frozen.
   The constraints on politicians are becoming increasingly virtual (let us take the example of the Stability Pact, where no-one can be sure that it has the slightest chance of ever being enforced, other than in the case of a small Member State), rather than real. They cease to be automatic, since they depend only on processes of negotiation and compromise that are subject to political intricacies and the arbiter of the competition for advantage and financial gain. Thus compensatory transfers are nothing more than bargaining chips that those who have been the least economically responsible in the past extort from the richest and most dynamic as the price for their cooperation. They neutralise the processes of adjustment through the migration of people and resources that begins automatically when regional imbalances appear in the relationship between prices and local costs. The result is that the area's potential economic dynamism is reduced in relation to what would have happened if a strategy of more gradual economic and monetary *rapprochement* had been chosen.

2. Cf. conclusion by Professor Jean-Luc Migué, which states that competition for advantage and financial gain must be considered an intrinsic part of the political decision-making process. While no other constitutional constraint places an explicit limit on the discretionary nature of the management powers of the central authority, redistributory measures between the State and regions making up a geographical whole and collectively managed by multi-state institutions must be considered primarily as activities governed by the logic of political decision. Once this is taken into account, the result is that even by assuming that governments are only subject to light constitutional constraints, it is preferable that economic and monetary decision-making remain the preserve of individual States in so far as that implies that governments remain subject to the disciplines of competition eliminated by the move to union. Paradoxically, it is by retaining monetary sovereignty at the level of national governments that there is relatively less risk of them adopting harmful redistribution policies. In a democracy, it is better for decisions on economic regulation to be decentralised at national level because it is at this level that the institutional context that determines political decision-making processes is, relatively, the least unfavourable to monetary governance close to what may be considered optimal.www.euro92.org/edi/bull/archives/arch23migue.htm.

2.2.3 The readiness of Europe for a common monetary policy

Sauli NIINISTÖ
Deputy Prime Minister of Finland and
Minister of Finance

"A currency without a state"

The creation of the Economic and Monetary Union (EMU) was undoubtedly a remarkable achievement. Reflecting the ideas presented by Jean Monnet in the 1950s, deepening economic integration between European nations gained a pivotal role in the European integration process, even though the process itself has been based on political goals. The introduction of the single currency, the euro, is therefore to be seen as a product of a long-lasting and persistent co-operation.

The monetary union was a logical complement to the single market enabling full exploitation of the potential benefits of economic integration. The achievements of more sustainability in public finances and a high degree of nominal economic convergence alongside the creation of a new institutional setting made it possible to introduce the euro under favourable circumstances.

The European Union now has its own currency, central bank and common monetary policy. The euro is sometimes referred to as being "a currency without a state". As far as the uniqueness of the policy framework of the EMU is concerned, this is indeed a proper expression: monetary policy is executed by the independent European Central Bank (ECB), while the rest of the macroeconomic policies remain in the hands of the individual Member States. This framework is very different from the "usual" setting, in which a currency and a sovereign state are closely interrelated. In the context of the EMU, a clear division of policy responsibilities between different authorities ensures a credible foundation for the single currency.

New challenges for economic policies ...

As we know, nations, and especially their economies, are becoming increasingly interdependent. This is even more profoundly true for the countries of the euro area, where the effects of economic policy actions taken in one Member State are easily transmitted to the rest of the euro area via close economic linkages. The credibility of national economic policies in individual Member States is a precondition for sustainable economic development in the euro area as a whole. The need for co-ordination of fiscal and structural policies stems directly from this interaction. And although it is country-specific needs and conditions that determine the direction of national economic policies, it is essential for the Member States, in particular the larger ones, to take into account the euro area perspective when formulating their policies. Co-ordination is needed to ensure that economic policy measures do not adversely affect the other countries.

A number of different procedures have been designed to facilitate economic policy co-ordination, and consequently to ensure the smooth functioning of the EMU. This co-ordination is most explicit in budgetary policies, where the Member States have agreed to submit themselves to budgetary surveillance as defined by the provisions in the Treaty and in the Stability and Growth Pact. These procedures even enable the Council of Economic and Finance Ministers (ECOFIN) to impose sanctions on a country which fails to comply with the requirements.

Also, the importance of the Broad Economic Policy Guidelines (BEPGs) as an overall device for policy co-ordination is rapidly increasing. This is prompted by the need to clarify the policy strategy for Europe. More attention will undoubtedly be paid in the future to the formulation of the BEPGs now that Ireland is the first country to be blamed for not having its economic strategy in line with the BEPGs.

The BEPGs provide an instrument for formalising the co-ordination related to the enhancing of growth potential and employment in the EU. Structural issues in the labour markets, for example, differ considerably from one Member State to another and can thus be dealt with most efficiently by each of the Member States themselves. Co-ordination is needed to enable the Member States to compare experiences and to apply best practices so as to find ways to tackle existing problems and sometimes also to set common goals.

These processes concern all Member States of the European Union – irrespective of whether a country has adopted the euro or not. Nevertheless, the euro area countries clearly have a special obligation concerning the relationship between national economic policies and the common monetary policy. This was the main motivation behind the creation of the Eurogroup in which the euro area Finance Ministers, together with the President of the ECB and the Commissioner responsible for economic policy questions, meet regularly to discuss and exchange views on issues that stem from a common interest in the euro.

Informal economic policy co-ordination in the context of the Eurogroup consists essentially of assessing the economic situation and policy needs, comparing experiences and best practices as well as applying peer pressure in order to find ways to improve the functioning of the economies within the euro area. Furthermore, the Eurogroup has provided an important opportunity for a deepening of the dialogue between the Finance Ministers and the ECB.

... and for external relations

It is clear that the implications of this new European currency go far beyond the borders of the euro area. This imposes demands also on the external representation of the euro area.

Prior to the introduction of the euro, the Deutsche Mark held the position of the second most important international currency. Because of this, and because of the sheer size of the euro area economy, the euro area immediately gained an important role in the global monetary system. The obvious conclusion was that it is essential to ensure that the euro area is represented at the highest possible level in the global fora and that the euro area speaks with one voice.

These principles are now reflected in the format in which the meetings of G-7 finance ministers and central bank governors take place. The meetings are divided into two parts. The first part covers the world economy and exchange rate matters and this is the part that the President of the Eurogroup and the President of the ECB attend. Then the national central banks of the G-7 countries take part in the second leg of the meeting which deals with other issues concerning the international financial system. Similar arrangements are also implemented to ensure proper euro area representation in the International Monetary Fund, where the representative of the Eurogroup Presidency acts on behalf of the euro area.

... as well as for the rest of the economy

The single currency has indeed profoundly changed the economic policy framework in Europe. Shortcomings in national policies do not necessarily cause immediate market reactions, such as a rise in national interest rates or pressure on the exchange rate, as was often the case when having a national monetary policy.

But economic policies are not the only area where the situation has thoroughly changed. Enterprises also face a completely new situation. Indeed, the most profound economic effects emanate from the impact on small and medium-sized companies (SMEs). On the one hand, the creation of the euro area expanded the "home markets" considerably. This is particularly important to SMEs in small countries. On the other hand, competition became tougher calling for more rapid adjustment and also offering benefits to consumers.

From the point of view of firms, increased competition requires that production structures are able to adequately adjust to the demands of the new operating environment. This, in turn, encourages specialisation and production efficiency. The challenge is even greater in countries where, in the past decades, accommodation through exchange rate devaluations eased pressures on structural change and contributed to the preservation of existing industrial structures.

The euro poses equal challenges to the labour markets. Price stability cannot be maintained in any economic system without significant costs in terms of lost output and employment if wages do not adequately reflect productivity and cost developments. In this new environment, labour markets and wage setting need to respond flexibly to changing business circumstances; excessive wage rises are transferred into lower employment faster than before because there are no national correction mechanisms. This puts the traditional solidaristic wage policy into a new light: it is increasingly important to price labour in relation to competitors, not in relation to neighbours. Depending on the circumstances in individual countries, this may require enhanced wage flexibility both at the individual and company level.

First experiences are encouraging ...

An early assessment of the effect of the euro is not an easy task. This follows from the fact that it is impossible to isolate the specific impact of the euro from more general trends, such as rapid technological advances and globalisation.

Furthermore, it should be remembered that these are still early days for the euro. Naturally, the full effects of a major regime shift, such as the introduction of the single currency, can only be seen with time. Therefore, it is too early to assess, for example, the extent to which enterprises have been able to benefit from the considerable expansion of the "home markets". Similarly, it is not yet evident to what extent the labour markets have adapted to the new rules of the game.

Bearing these reservations in mind, it is nonetheless possible to draw some conclusions.

The functioning of the economic policy framework itself has been subject to intense debate. The present framework was built on the idea that the best contribution monetary policy can make to an economy is to provide stable price developments and expectations, while fiscal and structural policies are doing their part in promoting sustainable non-inflationary growth.

Overall, the experiences are positive. The ECB has so far succeeded well. Member States of the euro area have agreed on, and implemented, a number of important initiatives aimed at raising the growth potential in the euro area. Economic developments have been favourable. Budgetary positions have improved considerably, price stability has been maintained and employment is rising. Also, the single currency has shielded the euro countries from the effects of international disturbances.

The experiences from the arrangements made to ensure proper external representation for the euro area are also encouraging. The euro area is now being represented in the international fora in a way that guarantees its role as an equal partner with other major global actors.

It is, therefore, justified to say that the euro is making an important contribution to economic and financial stability both within the euro area and at the global level. Better allocation of financial resources and enhanced overall efficiency in the financial markets promote better risk diversification and reduce the likelihood of abrupt price adjustments. On the other hand, deeper integration increases the possibility of shocks being transmitted more rapidly across the system. This imposes important demands both on market participants and on financial market supervision.

The euro is, indeed, acting as a catalyst for the rapid integration process in the financial markets. As a result, the depth and liquidity of European financial markets have been greatly enhanced. Cross-border borrowing and investing are now possible, which has considerably expanded financing opportunities for growing companies. Furthermore, financial market integration has promoted a consolidation process in many business sectors as mergers and acquisitions are easier to finance.

It is perhaps worth stressing again that the benefits that the euro can and will offer, and to some extent has already offered, are first and foremost of a long-term and structural nature. For this reason the attempts to measure the success of the Economic and Monetary Union by the euro's external value are misplaced. In the end, short-term exchange rate fluctuations have very little to do with these structural developments.

... but more is needed

Based on the experiences so far, it can be stated with some confidence that the euro area is heading in the right direction.

While the European economy has made considerable progress, it must be admitted that further challenges still remain. These need to be tackled decisively. Our economies are still suffering from a lack of dynamism that has affected economic performance and job creation in a situation where structural adaptation is increasingly important.

In connection with the Lisbon Summit held in the spring of 2000, the EU adopted a new strategic goal according to which the European economy should, in the next ten years, become the most competitive and dynamic knowledge-based economy in the world.

This strategy should now be implemented. However, the current EU agenda is, unfortunately, still too dispersed and vague. A strengthened and a more visible line of action is needed to boost market integration both at the national level and at the EU level.

Also, the close-to-balance target in public finances is not enough in the present circumstances and level of ambition should be raised. This means reaching fiscal surpluses in the following years. Efforts to reduce the tax burden are not sustainable, if the tax reforms endanger the fiscal balance in the longer term. In this connection, we should also pay increasing attention to the social protection systems and to sustainability in pension financing. Active measures and stronger commitment to these aims would enhance the credibility of the long-term strategy.

In the product markets we need both a parallel reform process throughout the EU and cross-border market integration in order to prevent distortions in competition. Telecommunications and energy are priority sectors, but there are also other major areas in network industries in which further liberalisation and enhanced market integration could stimulate economic activity at the European level and also play an active role in developing new technologies. In the financial markets, too, the creation of integrated markets for financial services should be accelerated. At the same time increasing co-operation between EU financial market regulators and supervisors needs to be ensured.

Despite the favourable economic developments, high unemployment continues to be the most acute problem in European economies, suggesting the existence of prevailing structural problems. The benefits of the single market and single currency depend critically on the adaptability of our labour markets. Furthermore, to alleviate unemployment and social exclusion, labour skills and the functioning of the labour market need to adjust to the rapidly evolving economic environment. The European social model ought to be modernised to ensure that work always pays, to enhance the responsibilities of workers in the search and acceptance of new jobs and to stimulate regional and EU-wide labour mobility.

Finally, proper functioning of the single market presupposes some minimum level of co-ordination in taxation. This does not, however, have to mean pursuing general tax harmonisation in the EU. Nevertheless, it is clear that without tax neutrality, resources, such as capital, are not efficiently allocated and benefits of the single market will not be realised to the full.

In sum, to achieve a more dynamic economy in the EU and in the euro area, we need deeper market integration. In spite of the single currency and related progress achieved, the euro area still too strongly functions as 12 individual and separate economies. Markets are fragmented and strategies in many respects national.

This challenge is faced by authorities, enterprises and other market participants alike. The challenge is made greater by the fact that the euro area consists of many nations with different cultures and traditions. Special attention needs to be paid to the fact that institutions, circumstances and details still differ between different countries. It is therefore hardly a surprise that gaining a true euro area perspective is a time-consuming process.

This creates also further challenges for economic policy co-ordination in Europe. As discussed above, the single currency and the single market substantially increase interdependency between the Member States. One by-product of this process is that it should become easier to find a "common interest" among the Member States. This is indeed a crucial question. If national and common interests diverge it is not realistic to expect that significant steps forward can be taken. The challenge will be even greater in the future when the EU, and eventually the EMU, enlarge.

It should be kept in mind that the aim of policy co-ordination is to ensure proper functioning of the EMU and to boost market liberalisation and competition. Therefore, strengthened co-ordination is a call for common rules and a framework under which economies can function efficiently. However, attention should be paid to ensure that the objective to tackle the existing problems by increasing co-ordination does not paradoxically result in excessive regulations. In other words, already existing procedures should be employed more efficiently and not create more overlapping elements.

The European economy has already experienced a massive change in the past ten years. With the euro acting as a catalyst, the euro area is set to evolve even further in the future to reach its full potential. The signs are already there. We all should, however, be well aware that there is no room for complacency. Further work is needed in order to be able reap the full benefits of the single currency.

2.3 New technology

2.3.1 The e-revolution and economic development

Malcolm HARBOUR
Member of the EPP-ED Group in the
European Parliament

A maturing 'e-revolution'

Recent, much publicised, failures of 'dot.com' businesses, and the fall in shares of 'high tech.' companies have caused a welcome re-appraisal of the 'Internet revolution'. In the initial stages of the e-commerce boom, it seemed that every type of business would be revolutionised, or even made obsolete, by the power of this new communications revolution. Business pages were full of new entrepreneurs with new ideas, and investors were eager to back them. A number of lessons are now clear from the first stage of the 'Internet revolution' – firstly, that any new venture needs a sound business plan, backed by proper market research, if it is going to be successful. Companies using Internet web sites to attract customers are no exception. Secondly, e-commerce business models must have an efficient and responsive organisation to deal with customer expectations of fast and reliable service. A-well designed and attractive web site is only a small part of a successful e-business model – investors should look at the 'guts', not the glamour.

But the present, more realistic view of e-commerce activities should not mask the underlying revolution that will have profound effects on global economic development, and present new challenges for policy-makers and legislators. While the high-profile failures may have made the headlines, out of the limelight companies have been getting on with the steady progress of incorporating e-commerce into their business models. A recent European business survey[1], carried out in the aftermath of the sectors' recent troubles,

---

1. E-Europe – Connecting the Dots, published by Andersen Consulting (now Accenture) 2000

showed that 97% of companies are using forms of e-commerce, and that 80% have plans for its further exploitation.

This article examines the impact that this maturing revolution will have on economic development, and the appropriate responses for Centre-Right policies. The focus will be on the European Union, particularly on the evolution of the internal market, and the strategies to be adopted by the applicant countries. The global dimension of e-commerce and the resulting intensification of competition will also be considered. Issues for policy-makers will be examined, as it is apparent that traditional measures to stimulate economic growth or regulate business conduct will need rethinking. Questions for the political process itself, and the need to adopt new formats that address the speed, responsiveness and all-embracing coverage of electronic communication methods, will also be addressed.

Leaping across market barriers

It is already clear that e-commerce offers a huge opportunity to accelerate the completion of the European internal market. E-commerce offers big opportunities to accelerate cross-border trading, reinforcing the impact of the euro in making pricing more transparent to consumers and businesses. Increased trading activity will, in turn, level trading barriers, expose high-tax, high-cost economies and nullify protectionist practices (such as unnecessary advertising restrictions).

EU business is taking up the opportunity in a big way. In the survey already cited, 72% of firms are now using e-commerce for sales and marketing. They are expanding their message to a wider audience, and developing new forms of interaction with the customer. Not all the first attempts have been successful, and there is now much more realism about the real customer benefits of Internet shopping methods. In some sectors – apparel for example – actual sales on-line have been much less than expected. In many cases, customers prefer to try goods before they purchase. However, the Internet is offering new opportunities for product and price comparison, and allowing well-informed consumers to do a lot of research before they buy. In the UK, consumers have been quick to use on-line brokers to source cheaper cars from other EU countries, for example.

Some fears have been expressed that e-commerce will reinforce the use of English and lead to an increased uniformity in marketing and advertising. These fears do not appear to be borne out in practice. It is quite clear that multi-lingual sites will be an essential requirement for local market success, and that a local sales presence will still be needed if companies want to stay close to their customers. Indeed, it is likely that the Internet will stimulate the use of minority languages, since astute companies will be able to offer a regional language option on their web-sites. Product offers and promotions are also likely to become more diverse. E-commerce is already driving reforms in those countries with restrictive laws on advertising or customer offers. Consumers can easily see the benefits available in other countries, and want equal treatment.

Alongside local marketing offers, e-commerce gives companies much more freedom to organise their operational activities – such as ordering, ware-housing and distribution – based on considerations of costs and logistics. Orders can be processed centrally, and payments accepted, anywhere in the EU. Studies have shown that the costs of making sales over the Internet – handling the order, collecting and processing payments – are much lower than 'face to face' methods. In setting up pan-EU or regional sales centres, companies will consider the cost and availability of the required skills, establishment costs and taxes, and communications infrastructure, in making their decisions. E-commerce will reinforce the trend towards outsourcing product supply activities to specialist companies, which will help the competitiveness of smaller firms who will not have to bear the costs of establishing new pan-EU operations.

Overall, it is clear that, in sales activities, e-commerce will have a powerful effect in enhancing consumer choice, lowering prices, accelerating pan-EU competition and reducing marketing costs. But it is not just the customer-facing activities that are benefiting – e-commerce is also making a big difference to the 'upstream' side of business operations.

E-commerce within the business

The tools of e-commerce – instant, easy to use, communication and the ability to widely share information – are reconfiguring the internal operations of large and small companies. Using private Internet connections – or 'Intranets' – many organisations are streamlining all their internal processes, improving the way they track data and follow customer needs. Better information systems can reduce product development times, improve quality and help manage complex projects. In turn, better team working is encouraged and organisations are becoming less hierarchical, more structured around processes or customer accounts. In the business survey previously cited[1], 50% of companies reported that e-commerce had helped team working between departments. New markets can also be researched and developed more effectively – no less than 86% of companies consider that e-commerce will help in new country access.

---

1. See p. 143

Procurement of components, goods and services is becoming one of the key areas for e-commerce activity. Purchasing is being opened up to a much wider range of companies and traditional 'buyers' are expanding their international horizons. Specification, quality and cost data can be made very accessible, enabling prospective buyers to compare products and prices very easily.

The interactive nature of e-commerce also opens up new possibilities for shared purchasing networks. Many sectors are now pooling common needs and setting up tendering systems or on-line 'auctions'. These systems will drive down prices and encourage consolidation in previously fragmented sectors. They will put pressure on the competitiveness of small and medium-sized enterprises, but also provide new opportunities for the successful SMEs to get access to big orders.

Not surprisingly, the combined impact of e-commerce on business competitiveness, dynamism and costs is substantial. Studies indicate that e-commerce between businesses (business to business) will continue to be much higher than business to consumer for the next 5 years. Companies are already reporting substantial cost savings and efficiency improvements. Even basic, long-established businesses cite 10% savings, while for newer sectors as much as 40% is claimed[1]. It is, therefore, not surprising that the recent growth record of the US economy is attributed to the dynamic effect of e-commerce. There are, however, other factors that need to be considered in the successful development of the e-economy.

Unleashing the e-entrepreneurs

Despite the well publicised problems of a number of e-commerce start-ups, it is clear that the new tools now on offer in the e-economy are an irresistible magnet to new entrepreneurs. The emerging technologies – such as mobile e-commerce, or m-commerce – will also open up huge opportunities for new products and services. Many studies confirm that the tax and business climate in the US has actively encouraged new, internet-based businesses that are exploiting the new technologies. Not surprisingly, many US firms have become dominant in the key areas of computer hardware and software that are powering the Internet revolution. The European Union must provide the same sort of opportunities if it is to take real advantage of the economic development potential of the new economy and to generate new product and service concepts that will become globally successful.

A very welcome impact of e-commerce is that it is forcing Governments to address these problems, and to press for political action to overcome them.

1. Source Goldman Sachs, as quoted in Business Week (January 2000)

The 2000 Lisbon summit identified the following concerns:

– High social costs of employment
– Inflexibility imposed by excessive employment regulation
– High cost of company start-ups and high penalties for failure
– Excessive taxes on capital gains, particularly stock options, discouraging new entrepreneurs from taking risks

Despite the identification of the problems, progress has been slow – the forthcoming Stockholm Summit will provide a progress report and identify gaps in performance. In the meantime, prospective e-businesses will register their companies, and take on employees, in any EU country that offers the most advantageous conditions. A true market-driven approach would soon have governments competing with each other in encouraging e-business. This could be stimulated by a start-up scoreboard giving fledgling entrepreneurs all the facts needed to make their decision.

The new companies will need access to capital. The development of the Single European Market for financial services will bring about more dynamism and competition in the capital market. In the meantime, new EU-based venture capital funds are growing rapidly with a strong focus on high technology investments. European stock exchanges are responding to the need for market making in Internet and hi-tech companies, and to provide ways of encouraging the flotation of successful start-ups. As part of the e-Europe initiative, the European Investment Bank is providing capital for venturing operations as well as supporting other infrastructure projects.

Given Europe's relative weakness in new business start-ups, it is particularly important for larger organisations to develop entrepreneurial skills within their own companies. Large companies should be encouraged to develop, and then spin off, e-commerce start-ups using their existing human and financial resources. There are many middle managers who would leap at the chance of developing a new business idea, and becoming their own boss. Spin-off companies, with the risks being underwritten by the strength of their parent, would have the chance to grow quickly. They would also encourage the development of entrepreneurial skills and practical knowledge within their feeder company and help its competitiveness in the new information-driven economy. A number of large European companies – including well-known names like Shell, Nokia and Vivendi – are already pioneering 'incubator' or 'corporate venturing' operations.

Although open markets will be the prime enabler of e-commerce, the existing European grant instruments – regional and social funds – can be targeted to help e-commerce ventures. In both rural and urban communities, e-commerce will provide powerful tools to tackle unemployment – by encouraging new business ideas, by giving fast and cheap access to market information, by developing networks of entrepreneurs and job-seekers. In many cases, e-commerce will help to reinvent old business models and transform traditional, slow-moving industries. People with existing skills can be encouraged to develop niche products for targeted customers and market them globally.

The other key element to address is infrastructure. Low-cost, widely available, broad-band electronic communications will be an essential foundation for a powerful e-economy. The European Commission has proposed a de-regulation package that encourages a single, open, electronic communications market, integrating fixed-line services, cable, digital television, and mobile. This should complete its legislative process by early 2001, when it will offer service providers open licensing and market entry opportunities across the EU. A key aspect of the proposals, already implemented in record time, with the support of the European Parliament, is access to the local telephone connection (local loop) in every market, opening competition for services to every household.

Digital television will also bring about a sharp rise in households with Internet connections. Electronic services will be available for selection alongside television channels. More TV offerings will have interactive connections offering alternative views, languages or information.

The EU is already significantly ahead of the US in mobile telephones. Third generation mobile technology will bring internet access to consumers at a much lower capital cost than a fixed computer, or TV-based system. The speedy growth of internet mobiles will also encourage new providers of simple, fast, useful data for phone users – based on travel, news, business and general information services, integrated with other services such as geographical data. These are areas where new European companies can gain a global lead.

Alongside the basic infrastructure, other elements such as data security for payment applications and common standards for electronic signatures will be important facilitators of e-commerce. The evolution of electronic money standards will open up new payment methods for consumers who do not have access, or do not wish to hold, a credit card. These changes bring with them the need for effective pan-EU measures to tackle 'cyber-crime'

But the achievement of the structural changes necessary to promote the e-revolution will only deliver part of the economic benefits. If the EU is to be the leading exponent of the 'New Economy', all citizens need to be involved, as consumers, users or employees. To sustain the growth of e-commerce, more and more people with skills in the technology, and entrepreneurial flair, will be needed.

Involving citizens in the e-revolution

Education must increasingly equip young people to be active on-line consumers and to develop the skills to work in the new information companies. EU Member States that have had particular success in developing a strong e-economy have made IT training in schools and universities their top priority (Ireland is a good example). Growth forecasts suggest that shortage of skilled people will be a constraint on e-business growth under present trends. Public and private sector organisations will need ambitious retraining and reskilling programmes. Alongside core skills in using information technology, developing entrepreneurial and creative skills must also be developed, in schools and universities. Incubator schemes for new businesses, based in universities, are already showing their value in taking young entrepreneurs through the first critical stage of a business start-up.

The information society has the potential to offer big benefits for the less fortunate and the less mobile – disabled people, and the elderly, for example. But there are significant concerns that the benefits of the Information Society will not be shared equally, and that a 'digital divide' will result. Many potential users cannot afford the equipment to access electronic communications and do not have the necessary skills. All Member States are making public investments in programmes that provide community facilities and training for accessing electronic services. Industry partners – particularly service suppliers – are keen to support these programmes, since it is clearly in their interests to foster the widespread use of the new information tools. The availability of information society services through television and mobile networks will also spread access through all levels of the community. Once the infrastructure and skills are in place, issues such as service cost and transparent pricing will become more important in securing universal access.

But e-commerce will never achieve its full potential unless consumers are confident and secure in using it. The openness and pervasiveness of the Internet provide many opportunities for criminal activities and unscrupulous trading. The ability to set up and dismantle web sites very quickly, and to move them from country to country, make redress very difficult. Consumers are concerned about providing private data and payment details over the Internet, and want better guarantees of security.

The development of on-line security and trust must be a shared responsibility between Governments and industry. The development of 'Trust-Marks', giving on-line consumers the reassurance of fair dealing and ability to obtain redress, should be supported by all reputable e-commerce players. Electronic signature certification and standards for 'Smart' cards are already operational. Proposals for dispute resolution systems, operating at a pan-EU level, are under development. Governments have a key role in providing the legal framework within which self-regulation will operate and ensuring that standards are maintained. They must also develop an international judicial framework within which consumers can obtain redress if voluntary mechanisms fail. In setting up these new security and trust measures, the needs of the smaller company must be paramount. It is the small companies, not the big brand names, that will gain the most benefit from growing consumer confidence and security for 'web trading'.

Towards e-government

In their internal organisations, and in their contacts with citizens, government (at all levels) can make enormous gains by embracing the information society. Most EU administrations have already made commitments to move all their major interactions with citizens 'on-line' within the next decade. The cost saving and efficiency benefits are very attractive as pressure continues on public expenditure. Governments also need to address their internal structures and to re-examine their traditional 'vertical chimneys' based around departmental boundaries. These may become an increasing barrier to policy development and operational efficiency. As the European Parliament's recent opinion[1] pointed out, the European Commission must address this issue as well.

Governments also have a key role in market development as purchasers of e-commerce services. They should be encouraging 'best practice' and ensuring that their procurement systems are open to smaller, innovative companies. E-procurement systems have enormous potential for public purchasing, and can provide the means within which the EU Treaty provisions for open public procurement could finally be delivered.

At a local level, through town and district administrations, health and community services, the potential for better and more responsive delivery is clear. Governments should encourage the development of local solutions and resist imposing large-scale, centralised plans. The information revolution is moving so quickly that central plans become out of date as quickly as they are approved. Devolving local responsibility, while sharing information on performance and best practice, is likely to be the best way of disseminating the benefits of the new tools available.

---

1. Report on the White Paper on Reforming the Commission (aspects concerning the Committee on Legal Affairs and the Internal Market), rapporteur Malcolm Harbour, Ref:94905PA

Light but strong legislation

Companies operating in e-commerce would like the security of a legal frame-work within which their activities can develop, but they are very much against over-regulation. Securing the right balance will be critical. Politicians should accept that their success will be judged on how little they do, not on how much! Legislation must be 'technology neutral' – thus being flexible enough to encompass future developments in a fast-moving market place. In the EU, the Commission has followed the right approach. Since 1997, it has been moving ahead with framework directives in crucial areas such as electronic signatures, market access and copyright.. The e-commerce Directive, approved by the European Parliament in mid 2000, ensures market openness by preventing Member States from blocking cross-border transactions.

Laws will need to be regularly reviewed, updated, or removed once their objectives have been achieved. Speed will become a more important factor. It may be better to get a legal framework operational in a new and uncertain world, than to spend a further 6 to 12 months on detailed refinement, with no guarantees that the end result will be much improved. Networks must be established to share experiences of the operation of new e-commerce laws, identifying where they are working well or where complaints have remained unresolved.

Enlargement and the e-revolution

It is clear that the information society 'toolbox' offers large benefits to the candidate countries. It must be a major EU policy objective to help the candidate countries take maximum advantage of the 'e-revolution' in their plans for developing both economies and civil societies. Policy-makers should be imaginative in their thinking and be prepared to help business and government move directly to new models, unconstrained by past thinking. There a real chance for the accession countries to gain a competitive advantage by jumping a whole evolutionary cycle.

Education must reflect these priorities, and equip young people to work in the new electronically-enabled organisations. A new generation of entrepreneurs must be trained in e-commerce business models. In view of the relatively low penetration of internet with private consumers, the initial focus should be on the use of e-commerce for business to business transactions, and as an enabler of efficient supply chains. Venture capital will be essential, and existing funds should be encouraged to move into these new markets. E-government will be a priority – and countries should be encouraged to move straight to new, open technologies in key areas such as land

and property registries.

The EU legal framework for a single, open, electronic communications market will be adopted by candidate countries as part of the 'acquis'. It is clear, from the reviews already carried out by the Commission[1], that there are wide variations in the readiness of accession governments to press ahead with de-regulation. This needs to be a negotiating priority, so that the capital and expertise necessary to achieve fast upgrading can flow quickly. Mobile network development should be a priority for the accession countries, since universal service infrastructure could be achieved with a lower capital cost than fixed wire systems. In 3rd Generation mobile, the accession countries should be encouraged to play a role from the beginning.

The EPP-ED – at the heart of the e-revolution

The EPP-ED Group is actively shaping the political response to the e-revolution, both in the European Parliament and in national and regional government. This approach is underpinned by a deep understanding of the economic and social changes being brought about by information technology. Based on these insights, the Group wishes to see a political framework that maximises the beneficial power of the e-revolution, while ensuring that consumers, and society, are fully safeguarded. This will be a delicate balance, which could be de-stabilised by heavy-handed regulation. So far, the Group's approach has sustained that balance, and set a positive lead for others to follow. It intends to stay at the heart of a fast-evolving world.

---

1. See EP Enlargement Briefing 46 – Telecommunications and Information Technology

2.3.2 The usefulness of Research and Development Programmes

Marjo MATIKAINEN-KALLSTRÖM
Member of the EPP-ED Group in the
European Parliament

Introduction

Research and Development is one of the most exciting and active policy fields in the European Union. Fuelled by the framework programmes – we are currently in the fifth with the sixth programme under construction – and a European Research Area on the horizon, European R&D has a strong forward momentum. Although the road ahead has its share of ups and downs, a political consensus exists in Europe which agrees that R&D is an area which deserves all our efforts.

Research and Development Programmes recently came under the spotlight of EU politics in a most unfavourable way. R&D programmes were associated with the corrupt practices of the previous Commission, mainly the financing of dubious programmes by the then Commissioner Edith Cresson. The negative connotation attributed to R&D is extremely regrettable as R&D represents one of the most important factors in the future of Europe and its economy. It has a tremendous impact on the lives of all Europeans. Without additional R&D we risk slowing economic growth, increased unemployment and loss of competitiveness.

The so-called information revolution is leading human endeavours to new and uncharted waters. Technological developments are moving at an unprecedented pace. The EU has shown that the United States alone does not dominate the information revolution. At the same time, whether we like it or not, the forces of globalization are shaping the world into a single entity, characterised by increasing interaction and interdependence, undoubtedly leading to increasing competition as well. The importance of R&D cannot be undermined in this "new" era. More than ever before the role of R&D is essential in remaining on top of the global economy. Only by sustaining adequate R&D can Europe rise to the challenges it faces in the short as well as the long term. These challenges include not only the need for innovative outcome but issues such as education and employment which must run alongside the technological evolution.

A substantial fault in European R&D is the lack of a coordinated approach. Although the EU's framework programmes play an important part in European R&D policies, they fall short of a much needed, all-inclusive vision of efficient R&D policies. The EU's R&D policies cannot remain separate from its Member States' R&D policies. This does not imply the need for an institutionalized European approach, but rather the need to find new efficient channels to distribute resources and efforts more evenly. Instead of having competition and overlapping among EU Member States, Europe should profit from the spillover effects and sharing of each other's strengths in competing as a single research entity at the global level. Europe needs further all-inclusive discussion on the organization, distribution and funding of research, as well as discussion on the interaction between research and education and the ethics of research.

European R&D policies

Overall there are good points and bad points to European R&D policies. The EU has already done a great deal to activate European research. However, it could do much more. Currently Europe is using nowhere near enough of its potential for R&D.

R&D in the European Union lies first and foremost within EU member states. It is crucial to realize that R&D is not and should not be exclusively a public affair. The role of the private sector, including corporations, research institutes, universities, etc., is at least as important to R&D as programmes that are financed with public money. It is, however, the responsibility of the public sector to ensure that the private sector has the tools and the framework it needs to conduct adequate policies, such as R&D.

The EU's overall research effort in relation to its gross domestic product has been in a constant decline since the late 1980s. Unfortunately, the gap is widening in relation to Europe's main competitors, the United States and Japan. If one compares the latest figures it is plausible to argue that as long as the European Union on average invests one per cent less of its GDP in R&D than the US and Japan this unfavourable trend is more than likely to continue. Even more alarming than the lack of revenue is the lack of innovative results being produced in Europe in comparison with the US and Japan. The EU produces considerably fewer patents than its main competitors. Equally the EU has fewer researchers per capita and fewer highly-educated people than the United States. However, overall one can argue that Europe has a better-educated workforce, which could potentially be a strong asset in the information society. This is a factor which must be better exploited in Europe. Nevertheless, whichever way one looks at the R&D statistics, Europe lies behind its major competitors and needs to increase its efforts.

Currently the contribution that comes directly from the EU's budget is only four per cent of the total public sector R&D funding in Europe. Therefore the main burden of R&D still lies within the competence of the member states. EU Member States' approach towards allocating money to R&D differs widely from state to state. While the lowest contributors, Greece and Portugal, only direct a marginal amount of funding towards R&D, at the same time Sweden and Finland, for example, are global leaders in R&D funding. In absolute terms of funds allocated to R&D, Germany and France are also at the top.

The Treaties provide the European Union with a legal framework for organizing and supporting cooperation within the EU in the field of Research and Development. The EU's R&D policies are set out in the framework programmes, the main tools of the EU in R&D. We are in the fifth programme which covers the years 1998-2002 and which will receive funding of € 15 billion over the four-year period. The sixth framework programme is currently being prepared and will set the tone of EU-led research for the years 2002-2006.

The framework programmes have done a great deal for European research and have taken us closer to where we want to be. However, although the programmes have created additional networks and research ties around Europe they have also demonstrated that there is a growing need for deeper and more exclusive cooperation in this field in Europe.

Climate for innovation

The first and foremost goal Europe should aim to achieve is to produce innovative results. Since the world is dominated by technological advances it is essential that Europe is able to produce applicable innovations. As I have stated above, in this field Europe is dragging dangerously behind its main global competitors.

The eEurope initiative sets goals for Europe to become the leading global area in the information society. It is needless to say that words alone will not do much to achieve this goal. To achieve this ambitious goal we cannot afford to neglect R&D. Up till now Europe has been lagging behind the US and Japan in creating the basic components which are shaping this new economy. While we all agree with the declared aims of eEurope, we must accept the fact that currently we are nowhere near being in the lead in this field. Our intention is to be able to create innovative solutions which drive this new economy and thereby find our way to the top. We cannot hope to compete efficiently unless we are able to be innovative and not just adapt to the innovations of others.

A crucial aspect in achieving these goals is the creation of an environment favourable to R&D in Europe. In Europe R&D is too often associated with unnecessary expenditure which is the first to be cut when difficult times arise. The image of the corrupt use of money in research projects is indeed regrettable. Elsewhere, such as in the US, research is associated with progress and man's continuing desire to know more, and in general R&D is seen in a progressive and positive light. In Europe, in addition to association with corruption, R&D is seen in a variety of ways, many of which are not always positive.

Currently the US offers a much more favourable environment for researchers than Europe. Not only does the US invest more money in R&D, but the US also encourages innovation and allows more leverage for researchers by promoting more high-risk funding for research among other things. This is one of the most obvious faults in the European R&D culture, or atmosphere. Research projects and programmes are made accountable for their results with too high expectations. This is especially true of EU-funded research. Researchers are under pressure to produce results and are too closely monitored by bureaucrats. This takes away the leverage needed to create new innovations. We must be ready in Europe, as they are in the US, to invest more in economically-risky and long-term research. R&D projects could then create spillover and permanent structures, not just projects which die after the initial funding has stopped. This is one of the greatest problems for the current fifth framework programme. The truly innovative and ambitious research projects lose out in funding to more "conservative" projects, whose outcome can be predicted. We should not conduct research to find out what we know but rather to investigate areas which we do not know.

It is difficult to predict the future, especially in the field of technology. Therefore we must not tie the hands of our researchers from exploring new possibilities by demanding immediate results. Although this kind of research is deemed politically and economically risky, one look across the Atlantic shows that very rarely is such expenditure wasted in the long run. Our most talented researchers are being tempted abroad partly in search of more freedom in which to conduct research. Indeed, contrary to public demand for more oversight on research projects, what Europe needs is less bureaucratic involvement in these projects. Authorities should encourage and support research, not tie it down with red tape and inflexible rules and procedures. Direct contact between research fellows and research institutes has been reinforced. Increased networking among European researchers is already a reality, but needs to be improved. We are on the right track.

The result has been that the most qualified and potential young researchers in Europe have been drawn across the Atlantic, leaving Europe lacking the vital know-how needed for its own research projects which cannot offer the same benefits or opportunities as our American competitors. The overwhelming majority of European post-graduate students studying in the US have remained there after completing their doctoral studies. The EU has been trying for years to keep its talented researchers from going to better jobs in the US.

There is no quick solution to stopping the "brain drain". It is a question of creating a whole new atmosphere for R&D including, but not restricted to, the financing of projects. Naturally this problem is not restricted to the use of public expenditure. The R&D environment requires a balance between public and private sector policies. However, it is the responsibility of the public sector to help create the foundations on which the private sector can build its R&D efforts. It has been said that had Bill Gates been a European the world would never have heard of Microsoft. This illustrates the difficulties of creating new technologies in Europe, and the barriers that exist for R&D.

This includes above all putting additional emphasis on education. It has been estimated that millions of jobs in Europe relating to new technologies will remain unfilled in the coming years. Naturally the lack of qualified personnel reflects strongly on R&D as well. At the same time unemployment remains a problem in Europe. This double-sided problem of employment might seem absurd but it is unfortunately a likely scenario. It is the responsibility of the public sector to provide the private sector with the human resources it needs, in this case properly qualified and educated people. We must begin making the transition to a knowledge-based society immediately, and education is at the heart of the matter.

Above all R&D needs to become the topic of wide-ranging social discussion. All sectors of society must be brought in to share their views on the future of R&D. An example could be taken from the Finnish Parliament which has set up a special "Future Committee" for such discussion. Its aim is not to predict the future, but rather to discuss issues that need to be addressed in the future. Such a body might be useful at a European level to deal with issues such as the future of R&D.

The European Research Area

The sixth framework programme currently being prepared will begin to tackle the difficult R&D issue. This programme must take additional steps in strengthening EU-funded research and allowing EU-level coordination of R&D. However, due to the restricted role of the EU in overall R&D these framework programmes, although extremely useful, can only go so far. Additional measures are needed and they are currently being envisaged and prepared.

In January 2000 the European Commission put forward a long awaited proposal for creating a single European Research Area. The Lisbon European Council in March 2000 approved the Commission's proposal. The European Parliament, which has for years been concerned with the topic, eagerly gave its support for the plan in May 2000.

By creating the European Research Area, we hope to tackle the problems mentioned above. By coordinating and cooperating in the field of R&D we can achieve the goals of efficient and innovative results. We must work more intelligently and not just harder. Currently the EU is the world's largest single market and the world's largest trader. We have the largest industrial potential in the world. However, in the field of R&D we are at best middle-weight. In the past we have failed to take advantage of our size and wealth in R&D. Notably the US invests an estimated € 70 billion more a year in R&D than Europe. We must make use of our enormous potential in this field. We need more spillover and national R&D policies need to open up.

Although we act united in most other fields, in R&D Member States are still competing amongst themselves. Member States conduct research which is overlapping amongst themselves. As the sharing of resources and informa-tion is at a poor level many states are "reinventing the wheel" because they are not able to profit from the research done by their European partners. This is the root of the problem in EU R&D policy. With the European Research Area we hope to make Europe a single R&D entity which in turn will be a force to be reckoned with on a global scale. Creating European R&D into a single entity is essential in order to correct the fragmented, isolated and overlapping characteristics of R&D in Europe today. The eventual enlargement of the EU will put additional pressure on coordinating efforts. Applicant states can be seen as potential assets to European R&D, bringing along new know-how to the EU. Europe has many cultural differences which can only be an asset. We must find a way to exploit these differences and find the best ways to gain from each other's strong points and become a single entity, so that instead of competing amongst ourselves we support one another.

The European Research Area, which is a long-term goal, will provide tools for communication and networking among European researchers. It will also provide a common approach to finding finance for large research facilities in Europe, establish a common system of scientific and technical reference, provide better use of instruments and resources to encourage investment, ease the mobility of European researchers within Europe, give more promi-nence to women in research, stimulate the interest of young people in research, bring together the public and private scientific communities of Europe, improve Europe's attraction to foreign researchers and promote social and ethical values in scientific and technological matters.

Interaction between policy makers and industry – the role of SMEs in R&D

In the long run the role of government in pursuing our objectives can only take us to a certain point. In order to achieve innovative results, and above all to benefit from them, private enterprises must take more and more responsibility for R&D. Arguably the large high-tech corporations in Europe such as Nokia, Siemens and Ericsson are leaders in their field due to their vast R&D programmes. The problem in Europe has been that private sector R&D lies almost solely in the hands of the large corporations. SMEs have a hard time keeping up with fast-moving technologies. It is the SMEs which we must strive to help keep abreast of developments in the field of R&D.

Governments can enhance corporate R&D not only by providing the environment and educated workforce needed but also by direct assistance. Cuts in taxation and tolerance towards R&D can also contribute to enhanced SME research. This centres around the concept of a university-industry-government troika. The enhancement of economic utilization of publicly-funded research is a key concern. One way of doing this is by creating so-called university spin-off companies, which utilize academic research in a commercial manner. This is a method that has long been used in the US and proven successful in building a bridge between public R&D and private enterprise. It allows SMEs to be innovative without having to bear the financial risks involved with long-term R&D projects. At the same time it allows universities and other publicly-funded projects the possibility of transferring their know-how to the business sector.

Conclusions

Our vision of Europe is one where we continue to develop our society to make the life of EU citizens as fruitful as possible. With research and development programmes we hope to be able to tackle the big problems that face us in the future, such as finding environmentally-friendly technologies, easing unemployment and facing the challenges of globalization.

The information age took the world by surprise. The sudden emphasis on new innovative technologies changed the nature of global competition. Today a good idea combined with technological know-how can create unprecedented opportunities in the global marketplace. Small start-up companies powered by a single innovation can now challenge the large established companies. Indeed innovation is the key to mastering business or trade, and as we know there can be no innovation without R&D.

By providing an increasingly favourable atmosphere for innovation, improving the financing of R&D and supporting the R&D efforts of SMEs, we can achieve a winning hand in this new era. The sixth framework programme will be the next step in this direction, followed by the European Research Area. We are definitely moving in the right direction; however, much more needs to be done and more money allocated.

2.3.3　Globalisation as the consequence of technical innovations

Wim VAN VELZEN
Vice-Chairman of the EPP-ED Group in the
European Parliament

What is globalisation and what is a global society?

Globalisation can be seen in several ways: as a process that is beneficial and also inevitable or as a process that increases inequality within and between nations, which threatens employment and living standards.

Globalisation is a historical process, because it is the result of human innovation and technological progress. In brief, globalisation is integration through trade and financial flows. People nowadays can have access to more capital flows, technology, cheaper imports and larger export markets. Globalisation is a complex concept.

The origin of globalisation

In the last century it turned out that the nation-state as a whole could not solve all the problems nor give an answer to all the needs of the population because of growing interdependence. With the industrial revolution countries opened up their borders bit by bit to other countries and social mobility for the population began to grow slowly.

The process of globalisation started to take off after the Second World War. Although at that time the term 'globalisation' did not really exist, looking back we can distinguish a process which later on we labelled globalisation. The term 'globalisation' has been used since the eighties.

The beginning of the process, after 1945, was known as and was *integration*, focused on cooperation amongst nation states within institutional frameworks. Europe with its specific historical background had another start to the integration process. Here it began with the integration of coal and steel, as an effective instrument against another world war, and later the main focus was on the internal market. Later on the deepening of integration with other policy objectives took place. The acceptance of one currency, a common security and foreign affairs policy, a rapid defence force and enlargement are examples of deepening and widening EU integration. In other continents *integration* started in trade and financial markets.

This deepening was due to the liberalisation of capital flows. Institutional arrangements followed like ASEAN and NAFTA, although the EU has its own sui generis character. Nowhere in history can we find a comparable development.

In the meantime a whole set of new international organizations (UN, WTO, OECD etc.) have been established in order to cope with increased interdependence, both politically, and more especially, in trade, financial markets and the economy.

Interdependence

Interdependence exists on two bases, on the multilateral base and on the regional base. The WTO is the best example of a multilateral organisation in a globalised world. It is based on a strong framework of rules, within which open markets are able to operate. Parties within the WTO are constantly discussing social, cultural, civic and environmental concerns and how to encourage economies to override them.

On a regional basis we can mention the EU, NAFTA, Mercosur and the ASEAN organizations, while other bodies like G-7 and G-8 are more loosely coupled organizations. Nevertheless the world now has many models available on how to cope with increased interdependence. China for instance is looking with great interest at how the EU is introducing one currency and is talking with its neighbours about developments in the EU. The purpose of globalisation is binding us together in mutual interdependence, that is to say open, regulated access to all the world's markets, free trade all over the world and the liberalisation of all businesses. The objective is to attract foreign investment at low costs. The consequence of globalisation in the trade market is a large number of mergers of companies in the same business; they become world-companies which are looking further than borders and cultures. As a consequence those companies are becoming more and more able to move freely from one place to another where market conditions are better. That development has created a bad image of globalisation because governments and local populations want enterprises that take their full responsibility in society.

Here is the conflict between the law of the international capital market, share values, the necessity to produce at the lowest cost, and the local responsibility of an enterprise. Moreover, as a consequence of increased interdependence and the "CNN culture" information and communication technology is able to bring into each living room the breaking news in the global world: the global village. There is widespread discussion about the impact not to say the dominance of Western culture and living style on other cultures as a consequence of globalisation and information and communication technological developments.

We can see every day on our television screens or through the Internet what the consequences are of a lack of access of products from developing countries to Western markets, what the impact is of climate change in several continents, or how degrading the traffic in illegal immigrants is.

Unilateralism or developments towards a "fortress" Europe or US are answers that ignore the consequences of globalisation and developments in information and communication technology.

In this respect we can see that one of the biggest tendencies in our current global world is the time lag that exists between developments in financial markets, trade, economy and information and communication technology on the one hand, and the political and institutional cooperation at the global level on the other hand. The UN is far from playing a key role in setting conditions for this process of global interdependence.

What is the impact of ICT on globalisation?

Information exchange is an integral aspect of globalisation. Information and communication technology is able to put people in contact with each other to a very wide extent all over the world. Nowadays it is easy to get the information you need from a professor in Denmark or one in South Africa. We are at the eve of a new and completely different form of globalisation. In the past globalisation had to do with trade, financial markets and CNN. In the future more products and services open to the public will be influenced by globalisation through information and communication technology. Citizens can check the effectiveness of their governments by comparing them with the activities of other governments (benchmarking). The same is true with hospitals, schools, universities etc. Information is available everywhere, so the controlling of information by governments as totalitarian regimes tried to do will become more and more difficult. People and companies will operate from different countries at the same time, or will work in a sequential way making the best use of the availability of the labour force because of the facilities of communication technology. ICT makes society a global society. Developments within the world of mobile communication and the Internet and the high-speed second generation of the Internet will enhance this process.

The ICT society can only exist in a global society. Putting it more strongly, we could say that the information society is, without any doubt, a global society. The world of ICT is infinite in two ways. ICT does not recognize borders: all forms of information and communication technology, which are being used in the ICT are literally going across borders and frontiers. ICT supports co-operating networks and ignores/does away with distances, two prerequisites for a global society. The problem however with doing away with distances is that it makes the application of national laws problematic. What about the consumer protection law, intellectual property? And which rules apply to "offshore banking" to avoid tax and social security responsibilities? What should be done with the different systems of added-value taxation? How can world-wide safe payments be guaranteed or contracts with "virtual" business partners? New crimes are emerging such as hacking, and "cybercops" need to work together at a global level. Again we can see a time lag between the speed of development in the information and communication technology sector and the public domain. The institutional framework is lagging behind. A global framework alongside multilateral agreements, such as already exists in the WTO, is therefore very much needed for an open market in ICT. And to complete the circle, ICT makes this possible.

In addition to bringing expansion of capital and so on, ICT also brings technical innovation. Knowledge about production methods and management techniques etc. represents a valuable resource for developing countries. And this development of new technology seems infinite also.

At a European level we are now working on the further liberalisation of the electronic communications market. We are trying to promote a 'level playing field' in that sector. In the European Union, in our opinion it will be necessary for the division of scarce means, like frequencies for mobile phones, digital television and the wireless local loop, to be harmonised. Harmonisation signifies creating a pan-European market within the fifteen Member States of the European Union, in which the first priority will be fair competition between Member States. And fair competition can only exist in a global market.

Until now liberalisation of the electronic communications market appears to be successful in the European Union. Prices have already dropped, the number of telecom operators has increased, and there is competition on the world market.

Responsibility in a global world

Besides the hardware and software technology we have to ask ourselves what kind of society the information society will be? And what the people who are living in it look like? In the information society a lot of possibilities are opened up for individuals and societies by ICT. The modes of communication are widely spread and have influence in every aspect of the individual life of the people. The members of the information society will have unprecedented access to information and to new modes of communication with each other.

Electronic commerce and financial services are probably the most discussed issues in the world of communication and services, because right now they are deeply integrated in our society in the same way that the integration of financial markets is being made possible by modern electronic communications.

Within the above framework of possibilities for individuals, responsibility is closely linked. In a global world, the responsibility of the individual goes beyond just his or her own life, neighbourhood or country. With all the implications of electronic communication for citizens we touch on fundamental matters such as the rights of citizens to have access to information that is vital for democratic choices, and for active participation in the economy. And here responsibility plays a big role.

With responsibility comes caring about situations in other parts of the world, situations which in the past were not our concern and did not affect us. We have to make sure that big differences between continents will not arise because of the information society. Without specific measures the Third World will be left behind, and here we see a task for Europe and the US to reduce the gap between those parts of the world. At a European level we have to develop programmes to make sure that these countries can take part in the ICT society and to promote digital inclusion. Now and in the future we will have to deal with all kinds of problems due to the opening up of the information society.

ICT and globalisation are asking for a growth in values, into which will fit democracy, respect for people and human rights, freedom of information and speech. Development in the global community has to ensure that everybody has decent living conditions, good health care, education etc. Only then will there be peace and prosperity in the global village. Everyone deserves to have a decent life.

A global world does not exist without technical innovations. Technology is the main stimulator of globalisation. The advances and the developments in the electronic communications sector offer enormous possibilities for individual people. They have the potential to facilitate improvements in the quality of life of everyone living in the information society. The unprecedented access to information makes the world smaller and therefore the responsibility of the individual person grows beyond his borders. 'Access' will be the code word for the future. The Internet has to become a fundamental right in order to make the whole world participate in the advantages of the ICT society.

3
VISIBILITY

EPP-ED

3.1 The European Union maintaining stability and peace in the world

3.1.1 From Balkans to broadband: the new European agenda

Carl BILDT
Special Envoy of the United Nations
Secretary-General to the Balkans and
former Prime Minister of Sweden

We have just entered the second decade of the second start of the process of building a new Europe.

The first start was intimately connected with the need to overcome the divisions that led to major continental and global wars during the first part of the last century. It was to pave the way for the economic and social reconstruction of Europe after the devastating wars.

Then, economic integration in the West and military deterrence towards the East were the formulae that for four decades gave Europe both political stability and the possibility of economic revival.

But the second start is connected with the need to overcome all the divisions that were created by the half-century Cold War and the domination of much of Europe by the Soviet empire. And this goes hand in hand with the need to transform the economic structures of Europe as the third industrial revolution gathers momentum.

We often forget how momentous the changes were during the last decade of the last century.

Little more than a decade ago, there was still a wall dividing Berlin, Germany and all of Europe. And there was certainly no world wide web. It was in late 1989 that the wall came down in Berlin, and it was approximately a year later that the world wide web was born at the European CERN laboratories in Geneva.

And since then we have been dealing with the consequences of the death of the wall and the birth of the web – with the gradual disappearance of what divides, and the gradual strengthening of what unites.

We see that the old Europe of the wall is gradually giving way to the new Europe of the web.

It was in Maastricht in late 1991 that the then leaders of the then European Community decided on the agenda for Europe during the 1990s by transforming their community into the European Union, opening it up for new member states willing to join, embarking on an effort to create a common foreign and security policy and aiming at creating a common European currency before the end of the decade.

Only weeks after that meeting in Maastricht, the red flag was lowered from the Kremlin, and the evil empire that had dominated half of Europe for a generation, and cast its shadow over all of it during most of the century, came to its end.

The 1990s was dominated by the Maastricht agenda laid down in 1991. By 1995, the Union went from twelve to fifteen members, as the former neutral countries of Austria, Finland and Sweden became new members. With the exception of Norway and Switzerland, the Union then embraced all of what could be defined as Western Europe.

And the common European currency was indeed created. It is fair to say that most observers for most of the 1990s doubted that this would in fact happen. It was seen as a political project beyond the capabilities of the political leaderships of Europe.

The starting point was indeed a difficult one.

The early 1990s saw the spectacular collapse of the Exchange Rate Mechanism – the then effort to achieve the desired monetary stability in Europe. Most of the public budgets were heavily in deficit, we were very far from currency stability, and signs of a true process of economic convergence between the key economies were in fact rather few.

But the train set in motion at Maastricht did reach its destination. Against the expectations of most, there is today a well-functioning common currency covering 12 nations from Portugal in the south to Finland in the north, now including even Greece.

And observers on the other side of the Atlantic often point to the successes of the euro in terms of facilitating an integration of European financial markets, thus contributing to a more competitive economy, as well as giving Europe more weight in the world of international finance. The aim was never to achieve a defined parity with the dollar or any other major currency, understanding that these will fluctuate over time, but to provide better conditions for non-inflationary growth of the Euroland economy itself.

The part of the Maastricht agenda which turned out to be far more problematic was the creation of a common foreign and security policy. There were many reasons for this, but the paramount reason was the fact that we were utterly unprepared for the challenges we were going to face in the Balkans.

There were, in the early 1990s, three very major tasks concerning the security structure of Europe that we were faced with. We mastered two of them far better than expected, and failed with the third of them in a most tragic way.

The reunification of Germany within the framework of both the EU and NATO, as well as the withdrawal of the massive Soviet forces stationed in Germany since 1945, was achieved. This was an achievement that bordered on the miraculous. And with this, the fate of Soviet power in Central Europe was sealed.

The second major task was the re-establishment of the independence of Estonia, Latvia and Lithuania, and the withdrawal of Russian forces from them.

This was even more challenging, since here we were dealing with areas that had been part of the Soviet Union proper, and where some Russians claimed rights going back to the days of Ivan the Terrible. And the military forces here were not primarily forces for offensive warfare, as those in Germany, but for the defence of the Russian heartland itself. Nevertheless, this was achieved as well.

The third challenge was the transition of the areas of Yugoslavia from one order that clearly did not work towards another order of self-sustaining stability. Here we failed, and failed massively. We failed to avert a war in Croatia in 1991, failed to avert the war that started in Bosnia in 1992 and failed to avert the war over Kosovo. We were clearly up against forces stronger than we had thought, and forces we only partly understood, but the failure was nevertheless ours.

Today we have approximately a quarter of a million young men and women in uniform committed to service in the Balkans, with key issues of some of the core political conflicts of the area still wide open, and being far away from that self-sustaining stability that we started to seek for this area a decade ago.

And the image of Europe as a power capable of conducting serious foreign and security policies suffered accordingly. Although facts were different, the impression was nevertheless created that only the Americans have the policies and the powers necessary to create peace in Europe.

Now, the Maastricht agenda has run its course. It was the agenda of the first decade of the new Europe. We have entered the phase that will be dominated by the twin agendas of Helsinki and Lisbon.

The Helsinki agenda is the one set by the last meeting of the European Council of the 1990s. And the Lisbon agenda is the one set by the first meeting of the European Council of the new century.

The Helsinki agenda is the agenda of peace, and the Lisbon agenda is the agenda of prosperity. The first deals with the challenges coming from the fall of the wall, and the second deals with the challenges coming from the rise of the web.

In Helsinki, the leaders of the European Union decided to embrace the most ambitious agenda possible in terms of the coming enlargement of the Union in the years ahead.

Once upon a time, the process of closer European integration was started as an instrument of peace, trying to bring the former enemies of France and Germany so close together as to make further wars between them not only impossible but also unthinkable.

Having achieved this, the peace-creating powers of the process of European integration will now be extended to all of Europe to the west and to the south of Russia and the Ukraine. It will one day encompass an area that stretches from the Arctic Ocean in the north to the outskirts of the plains of Mesopotamia in the south. It will bring in major areas of conflict and tensions of the past, trying to create a peace for the future.

This will, to put it mildly, not happen overnight. There are truly gigantic problems to be overcome. But as the experience of the Maastricht agenda and the emergence of the euro show, once a goal has been set, the European Union tends to move – step by step, crisis by crisis – towards achieving that aim.

Perhaps we can envisage the fulfilment of this part of the agenda in three phases during this and the coming decade, thus having the issue of enlargement and its consequences dominating this and the coming three periods of the European Parliament and the European Commission.

The first phase, bringing in the Baltic and the Central European nations, should be possible to complete within the period of this European Parliament and this European Commission. It should be completed so that the new member countries can take part in the next European elections in June 2004.

The second phase will in all probability coincide with more major steps in the institutional evolution of the Union, resulting in a treaty crisper and clearer than the present amalgamation of past treaties, now in the form of a constitution. It will extend the process of enlargement into south-eastern Europe, and it should be completed so that those countries from that region that are ready could take part in the 2009 elections to the European Parliament.

The third phase will in all probability focus on the highly important issue of Turkey as well as on those countries of south-eastern Europe that were not previously ready to join the Union. Although important progress has been made in Turkey, the size of the country as well as the magnitude of the task of bringing its society and economy up to the levels required for full membership make it likely that, even if membership negotiations are opened during the next few years, it will not be until June 2014 that the people of Turkey can also take part in the elections to the European Parliament.

By coincidence, 2014 will be just a century after those fateful events that, after a long period of relative stability and globalisation of the economies, initiated the period of wars and dictatorship in Europe in the 20th century.

With the Helsinki enlargement agenda then completed, we will be dealing with a very different European Union. Then, the largest city of the European Union will no longer be London with its links also across the Atlantic, but rather Istanbul, which literally straddles continents, cultures and traditions, thus reflecting the new realities that we already see emerging in the large cities throughout our continent.

After the age of deterrence during the Cold War, we are now trying to create peace through integration. But the Helsinki agenda is also about making Europe more credible as a power for peace by giving it the instruments to conduct a truly common foreign, security and defence policy.

This will be far from easy. With stagnating or declining defence budgets, it is most unlikely that the force and capability goals for military capabilities decided in Helsinki can be met without seriously fudging the figures. We see how already the present commitments in the Balkans, which are unlikely to be substantially reduced even in the medium term, are straining the military capabilities of Europe to the extreme. Any further commitments of an order even remotely approaching Balkan size will be extremely difficult.

But although these hardware issues are serious, I am even more concerned with what I would call the software deficiencies. In the aftermath of the Kosovo war, much has been written about how we are lacking in terms of smart bombs and other sophisticated technologies. While this is a problem, I am far more concerned by how the wars in the Balkans have demonstrated what we have been lacking in terms of smart policies.

Military force is no more than an instrument of policy, and the success or failure of any use of force will ultimately be decided less by the hardware employed but by the software of policy guiding that employment towards well-defined and realistic policy goals.

If we do not have the software capabilities in terms of smart policies to deal with complex issues like the ones we will be faced with in the different fracture zones around the periphery of Europe in the decades ahead, no amount of hardware capabilities will help. Smart bombs without smart policies are about as useful as capable PCs equipped with defunct software.

To develop common philosophies and strategies for the use of military force in the different possible contingencies along the periphery of the European Union, or world-wide as part of United Nations-mandated operations, will be a task as demanding as important for the success of any European foreign and security policy. It is a question of forging a strategic and cultural consensus on the use of military force between nations that have extremely different backgrounds and traditions in these respects.

Still, I believe it will happen. At every one of the crises we will face, we will have to stare the consequences of failure in the face, and thus be forced to succeed.

Because a Europe that does not integrate more might well be a Europe where the forces of disintegration get the upper hand, national rivalries once again come to the forefront, the prospects of peace diminish and the prospects of war increase.

To prevent this is the essence of the Helsinki agenda for peace.

The Lisbon agenda is, in contrast, about prosperity. By it, the leaders of the European Union have set ambitious goals for the future. They have committed themselves to policies to ensure that the European Union within a decade becomes "the most competitive and dynamic knowledge-based economy in the world".

We live in the midst of a revolutionary technological shift, the impact of which we are all feeling in our daily lives, and which we are certainly starting to see in our economies.

The relentless increase in microprocessor capability – Moore's law might continue for some time to come – in combination with the tremendous increase in telecommunication capabilities and the rapid rise of the use of the Internet is truly transforming the conditions for our economies, but at the end of the day for social and political life as well. That was the case with the previous great transformations, and there is no reason whatsoever to believe it will be different now.

But there is no doubt that we are lagging behind the United States in this development. Not necessarily because we are significantly less good in basic research and innovation – the web was, after all, invented on this side of the

Atlantic – but because we lack some of the flexibility and some of the entrepreneurial spirit that the Americans have in their society.

The web was invented in Europe in 1990, but it was commercialised in the United States three years later, and ever since the other side of the Atlantic has driven developments.

This cannot go on. During the past year we have seen the dollar and the euro drifting apart, to a very large extent due to the fact that funds have been flowing from Europe into the US economy in the belief that prospects for profits are better there than they are here. And with more funds being available, and with markets being more flexible, we will see a stronger development there than here.

Although the term "new economy" is hotly debated, there is no doubt that the advent of a series of profoundly new technologies introduces something fundamentally new in our economies, and that the success of any region, country or parts of the world in the years to come will be determined by its success in adapting to these changes and becoming truly competitive under new circumstances.

In Europe, there are areas where we are beginning to see something resembling a new economy. But if we look at the macroeconomic figures, it is not easy to see the impact as of yet. Investments in high technologies in European industry still run at levels half of those in the US, and recent studies claim that on average it takes twelve times as long to start up a new company in Europe as in the US.

The Lisbon agenda sets out to rectify this. It is about liberalizing markets, creating new rules for a new economy, encouraging entrepreneurship, restructuring old welfare state models and getting Europe as a whole to embrace the possibilities of the new technologies.

I believe this will be as challenging in the years ahead as will the Helsinki agenda. And here it will primarily be a case of challenging old political doctrines and the old structures that these old structures have created. There are certainly differences between the countries, but the need for reform is there in every single one of them.

We see some signs of change starting to happen. Germany is undertaking a tax reform that points in the right direction, although other steps taken in Germany rather complicate the picture. Sweden has pushed through a fundamental reform of its pension system that could well serve as a model for other countries. Finland has undertaken reforms that have made it one of the clear growth leaders in Europe. And the European Commission is moving aggressively forward with its e-Europe agenda for regulatory and other reforms in the years ahead.

But the challenge is substantial. The target we are aiming at is constantly moving. Technology is continuing to develop, and we might well be faced also with new competition from the economies of East Asia, as well as other places in the world, in the years ahead.

The one area where we are ahead is the emerging area of the mobile Internet. And here there is a distinct northern light over the emerging of the new economy in Europe, with Finland and Sweden emerging as the world leaders not only, and perhaps not even primarily, in the relevant technologies, but also in the wide-spread application of them throughout society.

The Helsinki agenda for peace and the Lisbon agenda for prosperity are united by the fact that they can only be achieved by common efforts and by taking our common endeavour in the European Union forward.

There is no way any nation state can master these agendas fully on its own. The fall of the wall and the rise of the web are forces that call for more integration between the countries of Europe. Only thus can we succeed.

But this in no way signifies the death of the nation state. I believe that cultural and national identities are important, and I even believe that they might become even more important in a period of dramatic and for some even traumatic change.

It is only when people feel secure in their national and cultural identity that they will be ready to fully endorse and take part in the common European efforts that will be so necessary. But it is also in a Europe where peace is more secure and where prosperity is stronger and more widespread that we can fully enjoy the richness that is there in the national and cultural diversity of Europe.

3.1.2 United States-European Union relations: a partnership for tomorrow's world

James ELLES
Vice-Chairman of the EPP-ED Group in the
European Parliament

The most important relationship

The bilateral relationship between the United States and the European Union is the most important bilateral relationship in the world. There are some who may think this an exaggeration. But it is not, such is the significance of US-EU relations for the global economy and global politics. America and the EU are bound together by a dense web of economic, political, security, cultural and social ties that make each the most important partner of the other. Together they account for half the global economy and set the political agenda in multilateral fora.

It is a relationship that is constantly under scrutiny, not only from professional journalists, analysts, academics and other commentators, but also from the politicians and officials upon whom its daily health depends. Quite properly, the relationship receives much attention from the European Parliament, whose formal links with the US Congress are established through the Transatlantic Legislators Dialogue, based on the formal delegations, while a more informal, future-oriented discussion and debate between politicians, business and academics is hosted by the Transatlantic Policy Network.

Since the end of the Cold War, a minor industry has grown up in both Europe and the US predicting the inevitable withering away of the Atlantic Alliance in the absence of the threat to its collective security from the Soviet Union. Labourers in this particular industry have emphasised the damage inflicted by trade disputes such as those over bananas, foreign sales corporations, hormones in meat and aircraft manufacturing subsidies. They have warned that we may soon be saying the last rites over an historic relationship built in 1949 on the Marshall Plan and the creation of NATO. Their pessimism was fed and their case apparently strengthened by initial transatlantic divisions over intervention in the Balkans. Another nail in the coffin, they say, may well be the arrival of President George W. Bush, perhaps much more interested than his predecessor in pursuing a unilateralist agenda.

The gloomiest of such views tend to base themselves on the latest headlines rather than on any broader perspective on where the relationship has come from and where it is heading. Instead, we have the myths of decline and fall; of the two continents drifting apart on tides of contrasting social and moral values, and two visions of global needs and development that are increasingly difficult to reconcile.

In my view, the reality is very different. There are tensions and difficulties in any relationship – what matters is whether the political will, the procedures and habits exist to enable their resolution. All three are very much part of the transatlantic relationship. The trade disputes of which the media make so much account for much less than two per cent of transatlantic trade and investment flows, totalling $36 billion a day. US investment in Europe is seven times greater than it was six years ago and US-owned companies employ 3 million Europeans. European companies are the top investors in 41 out of 50 US states and the 4,000 European-owned businesses employ one in 12 Americans.

The "values gap" between the European and American peoples is by no means as straightforward as some would have us believe. Attitudes to the death penalty, globalisation, the environment, social welfare, liberal markets and food safety are all said to be diverging and complicating the management of the transatlantic relationship. I doubt that the gap is that significant. In this age of the cybercommunities, I am much more optimistic about the prospects of converging values – European campaigning on genetically modified organisms, for example, has done much to arouse consumer feelings on this issue in the US.

Some commentators believe there are geopolitical changes that are pulling Europe and the US in opposite directions.[1] I take the view that their impact can be minimised and accommodated. The US is still the only global superpower – a role which is often uncomfortable and lonely. The only actual and potential partner it has is the European Union. Although today the EU is not a partner that can match the US in military and political power and certainly not in its capacity for decisive action, I believe the requirements for a successful global partnership with the US will drive the EU to seek more effective implementation of its Common Foreign and Security Policy.

---

1. "Trade disputes ... reflect more profound tensions between a dynamic and fast-moving process of market integration – driven by technology, capital mobility and communications – and divergent polities, institutional systems and cultural attitudes." Guy de Jonquieres, 'How can Transatlantic trade disputes be avoided?' www.ft.com, May 7, 2001

Unreliable partners?

Concern among many members of the European Parliament about the very slow development of CFSP partly reflects the pragmatic awareness within this and other EU institutions of the urgent need to equip the Union to meet the global challenges confronting it. A similar impatience can often be found among American politicians and policy-makers.

The European Union's slow crawl to enlargement is criticised in Washington because of its potential undermining of the political and economic stability of many of the candidate countries and for its spill-over impacts on the NATO enlargement process. As the Union tries to prepare for the monumental internal transformation that enlargement will impose, it seems to some Americans exaggeratedly obsessed with reforming its institutions and processes to the exclusion of almost everything else. There is additional concern when the political motive for future EU development is seen to be specifically intended to distance Europe from the US[1].

Where once there was fear of US isolationism in many European capitals, now they worry about US unilateralism – Washington's tendency to take initiatives and pass laws with little regard for their impact on its friends around the world and on international multilateral agreements. This is not so much American exclusion from the world as the world's exclusion from America.

New times, new ties

Thankfully, the partnership's resistance to the periodic strains inflicted by the unpredictable behaviour of both sides has been strengthened by very important new ties that were put in place in the 1990s. These do not receive the attention and the credit they deserve from the prophets of doom.

After the fall of the Berlin Wall in 1989, far-sighted people on both sides of the Atlantic quickly realised that relations between the US and Europe were going to need "widening and deepening" if they were not to unravel in the absence of the security threat.[2] The Atlantic Alliance had, after all, triumphed after a long global confrontation. It had achieved and fulfilled the purpose for which NATO was created in 1949 and under the protective arm of American military power, western Europe had been able to build such a

---

1. Mr Jospin "consistently illustrated his notion of Europe's potential success with the negative example of what he suggested was the United States' unilateralism, brutal capitalist instincts and failures in human rights." John Vinocur, 'French Leader's Blueprint Sets Out a Socialist Europe', International Herald Tribune, May 29, 2001.
2. In November 1989, then Secretary of State James Baker called for "a significantly strengthened set of institutional and consultative links" between the US and Europe.

prosperous and attractive democratic Community that it became a magnet
for the peoples of eastern Europe, if not for their Communist governments.
But there was also a widespread feeling in European capitals that NATO
should not be discarded and that the world would be a safer place if the US
maintained its involvement in European security.

The then 12 Member States of the European Community were able to agree
on the need to keep the US involved in NATO, but they were far less united
in how to do so. In 1990, France, Germany and Italy saw perfect sense in
discussing the transformation of the Western European Union into the
defence arm of the EU while Britain and the Netherlands trembled at what
they saw as a divisive threat to America's commitment to the military
alliance. They warned that signs that the Europeans wanted to take care of
their own defence provided isolationists in the US Congress with all the
arguments they needed to order US troops in Europe back to their American
bases. Within a decade, both countries were to change their view.

At the same time things were moving ahead on other fronts. After four years
of negotiations, the US and the EU were working hard to bring the Uruguay
Round of multilateral trade talks to a conclusion and they eventually made
final agreement possible by bringing their views into line. Meanwhile, new
international challenges were emerging that neither side could effectively
address on its own. The Lockerbie bombing in December 1988 highlighted
both the ruthless danger of international terrorism and the need for some
common responses, while the Gulf War of 1990 showed that Europe and the
US were still able to make a joint response to a severe threat to international
peace and stability.

They also needed, however, a common work programme for the last decade
of the millennium. The first chapters were set down in the December 1990
"Declaration on US-EC Relations" whose purpose was "to endow the
relationship with long-term perspectives" based on obligations to consult
one another on important political and economic matters "with a view to
bringing their positions as close as possible." Bi-annual meetings between
the President of the United States and the Presidents of Council and the
Commission were established and beneath them bi-annual consultations at
foreign minister level and between the Commission and the US cabinet.

The Declaration could not prevent serious and open transatlantic divisions
on how to deal with the break-up of the Yugoslav federation. These in turn
prompted calls from European leaders in 1994 and 1995 for a new transatlantic "contract"[1] or "charter"[2]. The outcome was the New Transatlantic
Agenda (NTA), adopted, together with an Action Plan, at the EU-US
summit in Madrid in December 1995 after important preparatory work by

---

1. Volker Ruhe, then Germany's Minister of Defence
2. Alain Juppé, then French prime minister

the Transatlantic Policy Network. The NTA's four-part work programme[1] was broad enough to cover the entire gamut of political and economic challenges confronting the globe, and specific enough to generate a work programme by means of an Action Plan. Implementation of the NTA has been overseen by a group of senior level representatives who prepare a work report for the bi-annual summits.

The trade relationship, though bedevilled by regular disputes, had achieved pretty much all that it could – outside the agriculture and textile sectors – on the basis of tariff reduction. The concept of the "New Transatlantic Marketplace" was endorsed by both sides as an encouragement to face up to difficulties created by non-tariff barriers, above all different regulatory systems setting norms and standards. The Transatlantic Business Dialogue, launched in November 1995, was the first systematic and high-profile attempt to bring businesses on both sides of the Atlantic into an agenda-setting process for removing regulatory obstacles.

A great deal of the TABD's efforts have been directed at promoting agreement between the two administrations on Mutual Recognition Agreements (MRA) which allow each side to carry out tests on the other's behalf to make sure a product meets regulatory requirements. However, an MRA is a means of accommodating regulatory diversity, not of achieving the objective greatly desired by companies and administrators on both sides – regulatory convergence. In November 1998, the US and the Union launched the Transatlantic Economic Partnership with the aim of requiring regulators to aim for mutual recognition of technical regulations and professional qualifications. At the same time, the Partnership's broader goal was to achieve a close understanding on the key issues to be tackled in a new round of multilateral trade negotiations.

Sharing the security burden

These enormous strides were made in the 1990s despite the evident difficulties that each side has had in coming to terms with changes in political priorities and perceptions of the other. Periodic failures on the trade front have imposed wear and tear on the partnership and limited its horizons. More broadly, European political leaders, proud of the Union they are building, want a tone of voice from the US which is less commanding and more ready to deal with its European partner on an equal basis. US leaders, in politics and business, complain of a lack of consistency in European behaviour – particularly in handling trade problems – that sometimes calls into question

1. Promoting peace, development and democracy; responding to global challenges like international crime, the environment and diseases; contributing to the expansion of world trade; and closer economic relations and building bridges across the Atlantic.

Europe's integrity as a reliable partner. More recently, American critics see the same contradictions in the security area where the credibility of a real manifestation of burden-sharing – the European Rapid Reaction Force (RRF) – is undermined by falling European defence budgets.

But the charge of inconsistency is also levelled from the European side. Many European governments know that they must respond better than in the past to US pressure for burden-sharing, but they also insist that the US must be prepared to accept a more equal dialogue in return. Europeans and Americans must not waste time arguing which comes first. But it is clear that Europeans must shed their reputation as "free riders" exploiting US military resources while also insisting on their right to decide unilaterally on when and how these resources should be applied.

This is certainly how many Americans have seen the RRF concept and appears to be part of the reason why Washington just does not seem able to make up its mind about whether it thinks RRF is a good thing or not.[1] From the European Union's perspective this 60,000-strong force (from 2003) is an essential step towards sharing responsibility with the United States for the stability and security of the European mainland and the protection of its interests further afield. But negotiations within NATO on the details of RRF's access to the Alliance's military assets and planning resources have been dogged by confusion on all sides over the force's autonomy of NATO decision-making, particularly its planning and deployment, and by the role of non-EU NATO members.

Nevertheless, there will be agreement on the RRF which should, once in operation, relieve the Alliance of future strains rather than create new ones. It will, after all, reduce European expectations of US military support for peacekeeping or peacemaking in areas of only marginal concern to Washington.

We already have a partnership of far greater breadth and depth than is commonly realised. Writing in early 1999, two US Undersecretaries of State gave a vivid impression of its dimensions:

"Together we are knocking down global economic barriers and advancing peace in the western Balkans, the Korean peninsula and the Middle East. Together we are promoting nuclear safety in Ukraine and Russia, responding to hurricane devastation in Central America, stopping prostitution rings from entrapping women in eastern Europe and defending human rights in

---

1. "Each forward step towards European defence and foreign policy autonomy has met an American warning: recall Secretary of State Madeleine Albright's 1998 warning against the Franco-British defence initiative and Secretary of Defence William Cohen's speech to the NATO defence ministers meeting in October 2000, admonishing that the alliance was not to become a 'relic'." William Wallace, 'Europe the Necessary Partner', Foreign Affairs, May/June 2001.

Cuba, Burma and the Balkans. Together we are alleviating poverty in Africa, halting child pornography on the Internet, developing a global early warning network against commercial diseases and meeting humanitarian needs worldwide. And together, we are preventing nuclear proliferation and fighting criminals, terrorists and drug traffickers wherever they may be."[1]

This description would have been impossible 15 years ago, before the EU's own expansion in political and economic development. Clearly, the Union is an increasingly interesting and useful partner for the US:

"At President Clinton's first transatlantic summit in 1993, Americans and Europeans used the forum solely as a technocratic trade dialogue. By Clinton's fifteenth such summit last year, the agenda had expanded to encompass a broad range of security, transnational and economic issues."[2]

Towards a partnership treaty framework

The United States and the European Union have undoubtedly been much more successful in creating new foundations for their future relations than is commonly realised. To most Americans, NATO is the transatlantic relationship and very little else is. The European public has a slightly broader appreciation, but not much broader. Certainly political leaderships on both sides need to work harder to communicate a more three-dimensional sense of the Atlantic Partnership.

But the relationship needs a great deal more vision if it is to weather the challenges of the next 20 years. On the European side, it needs a stronger capability to speak and act together, for example through more effective implementation of its foreign and security policies. Defence spending will no doubt have to rise to equip military forces for tasks which will be quite different from those envisaged for a hot war confrontation with the Soviet Union. In addition, Europeans will have to demonstrate their ability to manage the consequences of a single currency, in particular with regard to labour mobility and the related issue of immigration: will this be possible with one interest rate for most EU Member States?

On the US side, it will need a genuine readiness to adjust policy objectives to accommodate European concerns. In future, Washington must avoid the apparent disregard for the policies of partners demonstrated by the abrupt announcement that the US would not be applying the terms of the Kyoto Protocol on global warming. Although it is too soon to be sure because of the

---

1. Thomas Pickering, then Undersecretary of State for Political Affairs and Stuart Eizenstat, then Undersecretary of State for Economics, Business and Agricultural Affairs. Article distributed by US Mission to the European Union, 1999.
2. Anthony Blinken, 'The False Crisis over the Atlantic', Foreign Affairs, May/June 2001.

doubts about its technical feasibility, President Bush's plans for national missile defence are another area where the US must show ready to base its policies on partnership rather than hegemony. The US should not be surprised by European reluctance to tear up the 1972 Comprehensive Test Ban Treaty. Rather, it should realise that Europeans need to feel that their security will be enhanced rather than diminished by the abandonment of that treaty in the cause of national missile defence. The US may need to win Russian support for its initiative to make that possible.

Transatlantic dialogue will be equally vital for establishing a common approach to the next round of multilateral trade negotiations. The excellent personal relationship between Robert Zoellick, the US Special Trade Representative and Pascal Lamy, the European Commissioner for Trade, is a genuine cause for optimism. But trade negotiators can achieve nothing if their mandates have been exclusively shaped by the interests of key domestic constituencies. Both sides need "an unusually self-critical approach and the courage to drive through often controversial changes in the face of uncomprehending, sceptical or resistant domestic constituencies."[1]

Perhaps the most important fact for all to grasp is the increasingly close relationship between politics, economics and security policies in the emerging new Transatlantic Partnership. This means that an overall view of its health and likely progress is only possible if all aspects are considered. Some experts, for example, in the security field are prone to commenting that there is no glue to keep the Transatlantic relationship together now that the Cold War is over and Russia is becoming more cooperative. And yet, a glance at the growing agenda between the EU and the US is sufficient to show that both partners have enormous responsibilities to ensure that a global system functions effectively.

Thus the transatlantic relationship continues to be characterised by both cooperation and competition. Both aspects have to be managed skilfully and with sensitivity. I believe that the future growth and development of the transatlantic partnership require us to build on the achievements of the 1990s. We need to evolve a more defined political framework for the future and to do so in such a way that holds public attention and wins public commitment, involving actively legislators on both sides in its activities.

The best way forward is by means of a partnership treaty framework which commits both sides to objectives, identifies mechanisms and includes the fora for regular and public debate between elected representatives from Europe and the US. This will be the millennium of decisive progress towards workable and acceptable world governance. The European Union and the United States should begin to blaze a trail.

---

1. Guy de Jonquieres, op. cit., p. 178

3.1.3 The European Union's responsibility for lasting peace in South-east Europe

Doris PACK
Chairman of the Delegation for relations with
South-east Europe
Member of the EPP-ED Group in the
European Parliament

The 'western Balkans' – part of Europe

The past ten years, and the war in the countries of the former Yugoslavia, have shown the European Union just how closely the region is tied to the EU at its south-east frontier. The region's destabilisation, culminating in military conflict, has had a direct impact on the Union. It has become very clear that developments here affect the whole of Europe. It is also clear that the European Union must bear a special responsibility – partly in its own interest – for peace and stability in the region, and that its credibility as a stabilising influence in Europe is at issue. What are known as the 'western Balkans' are part of Europe. To make the connection clearer, we will here use the term 'South-east Europe' for the countries of the former Yugoslavia including Albania.

Since 1989 the European Union has rather helplessly tolerated the criminal policy of Milosevic in Kosovo, Croatia, Bosnia and Herzegovina. In the acute phase of the conflict it was primarily NATO, under American leadership, and not the European Union that – albeit belatedly and after long hesitation – largely helped put an end to Milosevic's cynical policy, to the murders, ethnic cleansing and rapes. It was thus largely the United States that determined the 1996 Dayton peace agreement.

The major weaknesses in the agreement have all too soon become apparent. For one thing, it did not bring about a solution to the Kosovo problem, nor did it force Milosevic to change his policy in Kosovo. And in the Kosovo conflict it was again the Americans and NATO who took prime responsibility for the intervention. It was only in the phase after the war itself, in the second half of the 1990s, and 2000 in the case of Kosovo, that the European Union took over the leadership and main responsibility for reconstruction and peace-keeping, and formulated a long-term political strategy for the region. For another, the de facto division of Bosnia as a result of the Dayton agreement has until today been an almost insuperable obstacle to the functioning of the state as a whole and of its institutions.

European policy is at the end of an almost ten-year learning process for the Union. It has gradually realised that after the collapse of Communism in central Europe it must take on increasing responsibility for peace and stability throughout Europe, even outside its own frontiers. The conflict in South-east Europe, which has directly affected the Union's security interests, has made this problem very clear and prompted major progress in the Common Foreign and Security Policy.

Peace and stability in South-east Europe – only with the EU

The creation of an area of peace, prosperity and stability in South-east Europe is a strategic priority for the European Union[1]. The European Council defines its overall aim as the comprehensive integration of the countries of the region into the political and economic system in Europe, centred on the stabilisation and association process. The immediate short-term aim is assistance with reconstruction and the removal of war damage. In the medium term the aim is to set up lasting structures to promote democracy, the market economy and stability; the long-term aim is integration into the European structures.

To achieve this aim the EU has entered into a major commitment. It is by far the largest financial donor for the reconstruction of South-east Europe. From 1991 to 1999 the EU provided some € 4.5 billion for the five countries of South-east Europe; € 520 million for the assistance programmes in 2000; and an emergency aid programme for Serbia, agreed by the European Council in Biarritz after the fall of Milosevic in October, amounting to € 200 million. The CARDS Programme has replaced its forerunners, PHARE and Obnova, since the end of last year and is providing the five countries in the region with further funds. The Lisbon European Council recognised the Union's special responsibility in the region and made plain that it was deter-mined to safeguard the success of international efforts in Kosovo. With its 30 000 soldiers in KFOR, 800 policemen in the non-military area and € 505 million, the EU has already taken on the main role for the reconstruction of Kosovo[2]. In 1999 the Western Balkans became the first action area of the Common Foreign and Security Policy; at the same time, the European Agency for Reconstruction was set up under the Commission's leadership and the Stability Pact was founded under European leadership. The Commission has drawn up a new association strategy in the form of the

1. Conclusions of the Lisbon European Council of 23 and 24 March 2000.
2. ibid.

Stabilisation and Association Programme and has offered the countries of South-east Europe full integration into the EU in the long term within this framework.

There are three dimensions to reconstruction and the process of democratisation and stabilisation. The Sarajevo Summit defined them as key areas for the work of the Stability Pact. The political dimension covers the question of human rights, democracy, freedom of opinion and the rule of law. The creation of stable institutions and structures to promote the rule of law is a key issue for any further development of the region. Nor will economic reconstruction take off without legal security. Domestic and foreign investors will hold back while crime and corruption are not being dealt with effectively. Progress in the economic dimension, through economic reform, regional cooperation, the free movement of goods and capital and privatisation will therefore not bear fruit until they are closely accompanied by political reform. Finally, arms controls and confidence-building measures must also strengthen the region's security dimension.

The process of democratisation must begin in the field of elections, government and administration and civil society. Unfortunately, the Bosnian example shows that in spite of enormous international aid for reconstruction it remains limited in effect unless the reconstruction of institutions is equally successful at the same time. Reconstruction aid alone will not lead to economic growth or democratic development. If the EU wants to fulfil its aim of creating an area of security and stability in South-east Europe, it faces the challenge of achieving progress in the field of politics, the economy and security at the same time.

The EU's policy concept for South-east Europe

The European Union is the only actor on the international scene to have developed a clear policy concept for the development of peace and stability in the region following the military conflict. So among the large number of international operators the European Union has taken on a leading role in the reconstruction of South-east Europe, particularly in the form of the Stability Pact. This pact, signed on 10 June 1999 in Cologne on the initiative of the EU, is a central task of EU foreign policy in which the Union's political credibility must show its worth[1]. The Council, as well as the Commission, must engage in this task and coordination between the EU Commissioner responsible and the High Representative for Foreign and Security Policy is of

---

1. On the problems of implementing the Stability Pact, see also Doris Pack, 'The Stability Pact for South-east Europe – initial experience of implementation', in *CFSP Forum, Institute for European Policy (IEP)* 4/99, p. 3-5.

vital importance. The structure of the pact would be simpler and more efficient if its personnel were also located within the EU's structure, instead of setting up another 'special coordinator' who will have difficulty finding room alongside the Commission's External Relations Commissioner and the High Representative for Foreign and Security Policy. Besides, the proposals which are to be discussed in the so-called 'Round Tables' of the Stability Pact are by no means new, but have long been familiar to the Commission and to those who have for years been working locally in the field. Hence in the interest of consistency and efficiency it would have been better to give the Commission itself responsibility for running the Stability Pact.

The Stabilisation and Association Process (SAP)

The European Union began developing its relations with the countries of South-east Europe on the basis of a regional approach as long ago as 1997. The approach sets political and economic conditions as the basis for developing bilateral trade relations with the European Union. In view of the challenges of the Kosovo crisis and the changing situation in the region, and also the foundation of the Stability Pact, the Commission extended the regional approach into a long-term stabilisation and association process (SAP), with the prospect of full integration into the European structures. In the SAP the EU has formulated a clear policy concept and a new, extended approach to the countries of South-east Europe, which is at the same time a significant EU contribution to implementing the Stability Pact. But the EU must obviously ensure that the SAP becomes a load-bearing pillar of the Stability Pact and is also implemented in that area.

The Stability Pact rests on two operational elements[1]: closer association with the EU, including the prospect of accession for all the countries of South-east Europe as soon as they meet the criteria, and regional cooperation, to which the countries have committed themselves in order to overcome the obstacles to integration into the European structures at regional level.

The core of the association process is the SAP for the region's five countries (Albania, Bosnia and Herzegovina, Croatia, the Federal Republic of Yugoslavia and Macedonia) under the Commission's leadership. The clear prospect of accession places relations with these countries on an entirely new footing. While it is a real incentive for the region's countries to carry out essential but often painful reforms, it also implies the need to comply with tougher conditions for political and economic development and regional cooperation. The crucial point is that each country must be assessed

---

1. On the following comments see also 'Democracy, Stability and the Role of the Stability Pact in South-Eastern Europe', Belgrade discussion paper, EWI in collaboration with ESI, January 2001.

individually in the light of the progress it has made. Thus negotiations have already begun on a stabilisation and association agreement with Macedonia and Croatia. Negotiations for these agreements will only take place if the countries fulfil certain criteria such as the rule of law, democracy, media freedom, human rights and the rights of minorities; free and fair elections, completion of the first steps towards economic reform (privatisation), a readiness to cultivate good neighbourly relations and compliance with the Dayton agreement (cooperation with the Hague Court, the return of refugees, etc.).

To support the countries of South-east Europe with the necessary comprehensive institutional reform and bring them closer to the European community of values and creation of the market economy, from 2001 the EU is providing the five countries with further funds under the CARDS Programme[1], in place of the Obnova and PHARE Programmes. Aid from this programme is similarly tied to the fulfilment of clear conditions: respect for democratic principles, the rule of law, human and minority rights, basic freedoms and the principles of international law.

The conditional nature of European Union support is a fundamental aspect of the strategy for Europeanisation. It is a major opportunity for the European Union to exert an influence, and it needs taking up.

Regional cooperation

The EU's bilateral support of individual countries is not on its own a satisfactory way to create security and stability in the region, particularly where there are cross-frontier problems. Hence the concept of regional cooperation is the second main pillar of the Stability Pact. In the basic text for the pact of 10 June 1999 the participating states commit themselves to 'bilateral and regional cooperation amongst themselves to advance their integration, on an individual basis, into Euro-Atlantic structures'. This was reconfirmed at the Stability Pact summit in Sarajevo in July 1999. It defined regional cooperation as a catalyser for integration into larger structures. The commitment which the countries thus made to cooperation is significant, as regional cooperation is not an obvious political step for the countries of South-east Europe. For one thing, there is still a dormant fear of one country's domination of the others (a new form of 'regional integration'); for another, the countries fear ending up in the same basket. As President Mesic of Croatia put it, the move towards the EU cannot take the form of a caravan but must be a regatta; in other words, countries that make fast progress must be able to join the EU sooner. So it is an important task for the Stability Pact

---

1. Council Regulation 2666/2000 of 5 December 2000, OJ L 306, 7.12.2000.

to make it plain that regional cooperation is not an alternative but an essential complement to moving closer to the European Union. Since the association strategy is part of the Commission's responsibility the various 'tables' of the Stability Pact should concentrate on questions of regional and over-arching cooperation.

There are two aspects to regional cooperation. It can help to solve problems that confront all of the countries in equal measure, such as democratisation, legal and economic reform, institutional reform and so on. Here the main aim must be to exchange experience and know-how. But it is still more important for the countries to address regional problems that can better be solved by common action. They include, for instance, politically complicated questions such as the status of Kosovo, the peace process in Bosnia and ethnic relations in the region. Other issues of a more operational nature include the return of refugees, combating organised crime and creating a regional infrastructure. It should be a priority for the Stability Pact to draw attention to areas where regional strategies can be developed and apply the necessary mechanisms to make them happen.

The Stability Pact should concentrate its work on projects that deliver added value compared with other international activities.[1] This is particularly feasible with initiatives that go beyond the individual 'tables' of the Pact. The Belgrade discussion paper on the Stability Pact mentions two practical examples of such projects: the free movement of persons and visa regulations, and building an energy network. A project of this kind would serve the aim of moving closer to the EU, as well as of regional cooperation. It would also make it possible to tackle one of the key problems of the region, organised crime and the trafficking in humans, including trafficking in women, children and body parts. The Stability Pact could build up expertise in the field of frontier systems and migration, thus contributing to the exchange of technical experience, greater police cooperation and the introduction of institutional reform. The Pact could make a considerable impact in terms of synergy in this way.

A second project for the Pact could be the creation of an energy network in South-east Europe. A network of this kind necessarily has a cross-frontier dimension and can be set up much more efficiently as a joint measure, especially as in the energy sector recourse can be made to the common structures that used to exist. In this way regional cooperation could help to solve one of the region's major problems and create not only more security of energy supply but also greater internal stability. Cooperation in a strategically important area can help to build confidence between regional

---

1. See also 'Democracy, Stability and the Role of the Stability Pact in South-Eastern Europe', Belgrade discussion paper, EWI in collaboration with ESI, January 2001.

entities, as happened with the European Coal and Steel Community between France and Germany after the war.

So the Special Coordinator's priorities should concentrate on the area of regional cooperation and should make specific recommendations for priority areas, suggest the methods and identify the partners in the region. In this way the Stability Pact could make the two pillars of European strategy for South-east Europe, closer association with the EU and regional cooperation, work together in a complementary and efficient way.

South-east Europe – overcoming conflict by political means

The end of the Milosevic regime in Belgrade has given the whole region new hope and a new sense of purpose. While Milosevic – the main cause of the conflict in South-east Europe – was still in power, none of the neighbouring countries had the confidence to embark on the necessary reforms. Now even Yugoslavia is making progress, even if it still has major problems to contend with. The European Union has clearly recognised that the key to peaceful development in South-east Europe was deposing Milosevic. So with its emergency aid of € 200 million, which was agreed immediately after Milosevic had gone, and reached its destination with unusual speed, the EU was supporting the local people on the road to democracy, particularly in order to remove evidence of the consequences of EU sanctions against Yugoslavia under Milosevic. This was emergency aid and intended to help people quickly, without red tape or special conditions. But any further EU funds will now be tied to the same conditions and reforms as in the other countries of South-east Europe. In this respect there cannot and will not be any exceptions for Yugoslavia. The new leadership that has finally been established in Serbia since the elections has rapidly made clear its readiness for reform.

The EU's political strategy for South-east Europe after the end of the war centres on the region's close involvement, leading ultimately to inclusion, in the Union. The strategy has done much to enhance the EU's credibility in South-east Europe. For the EU itself the strategy reflects a determination to extend its peace system to the periphery and by effective integration of a crisis region create a security belt for itself. This makes the EU's peace initiative in South-east Europe an outstanding illustration of the way in which the EU is actively intervening in political development outside its frontiers in order to fulfil one of the priorities of its Common Foreign and Security Policy. What is unusual in the European Union strategy is that – unlike the foreign and security policy of the United States and NATO – its instrument is not the containment of conflict by military means, but overcoming conflict by political means. In the past ten years the two strategies have been applied effectively together, in cooperation between the Europeans and their trans-atlantic partners. Without NATO's military intervention the conflict might have lasted very much longer and done very much greater human, political and economic damage. The strategy for rebuilding the region cannot be confined to reconstruction aid, but must draw greater attention to and provide assistance for education in these countries, with the aim of preparing their young people for a better future and the necessary ability to co-exist with people irrespective of their ethnic origin. Without such a strategy the region would have no chance of a future in peace and freedom, and the European Union would face a constant source of unrest among its closest neighbours.

3.1.4   A leading role in the establishment of democratic institutions all over the world

José Maria GIL-ROBLES GIL-DELGADO
Member of the EPP-ED Group in the
European Parliament
Former President of the European Parliament

The European Union has played a crucial role in influencing global democracy, peace and prosperity. It is now that this fact becomes evident. But it was not so clear 50 years ago, when Schuman, Adenauer, De Gasperi, and other prominent members of our Christian Democrat family launched the ECSC (European Coal and Steel Community), the first step in what was seen as a very long and difficult road to travel.

Now fifteen countries share this project and twelve other countries are intensively negotiating to become members of the club as soon as possible.

Such a great success has been possible because the Community, and then the Union, was never conceived as a "closed shop" to build as a close space, but as a tool to expand democracy, peace and prosperity inside and outside Europe, all over the world.

***

Inside Europe, thirty years ago Greece, Portugal and Spain were under authoritarian regimes, trying to isolate these countries from the European democratic pattern. Our political family never accepted this situation, and fought inside and outside these countries for a change towards democracy. European institutions were highly useful instruments working on this project of extending the democratic Community to these countries. May I recall the Birkelbach report (1962), in which the European Parliament established for the first time democracy as a precondition for becoming a member of the Community?

The result of that engagement was so successful that today not only are Greece, Portugal and Spain full and active members of the Union, but democracy and European integration appear to their peoples as the two faces of the same coin.

Central and eastern European countries are still on their way towards membership of the European Union. Unfortunately, the lack of appropriate institutions and instruments in our Union has prevented us from intervening or stopping quickly enough heavy bloodshed in former Yugoslavia.

It was only very recently at the European Council in Nice in December 2000 that the Union took the decisive step of endowing itself with an armed intervention force that will in the future be capable of helping to build up and guarantee stability and democracy within the Union's limited remit.

The EPP is strongly committed to the goal of extending the Union throughout the whole of Europe, supporting the establishment and the consolidation of social and territorial cohesion. We are confident that in the first quarter of the 21st century this goal can be achieved if all Europeans, inside and outside the Union, make the necessary efforts.

**

Peace, stability and prosperity in Russia and all the CIS countries (Commonwealth of Independent States) are essential for Europe's and the world's security. They can be obtained only by the establishment, development and consolidation of democratic institutions. Relations with the European Union must be established on a partnership basis, and this partnership is not easy to build. The Communist past is still alive as often perceived in political and military behaviour, and transition to a market economy has been rather chaotic.

Time and a strong political will are necessary on both sides. The financial support which the Union is providing through TACIS and similar programmes is not enough. The EPP is working for the establishment of political, academic and social links between the European Union and the CIS countries, using all the possibilities the Union can provide to this purpose. We are very active in the participation of Russia and other CIS countries in the Council of Europe.

The European Union is seen by CIS countries as an interesting way of overcoming their historical conflict and, for some of them, as a club to reach which they wish to adhere to in the medium term. We have, therefore, the possibility of exercising some influence in order to speed up the evolution towards fully democratic systems, provided we respect the sovereignty and national identity of those countries.

**

Central America has been a remarkable example of how European Union institutions can play a leading role in building democracy in other parts of the world. Through intensive political and financial cooperation situations of war and dictatorship have been washed away, and the roots for the necessary regional cooperation on economic and democratic grounds have been established. The San José Conferences, as they are established now, are one of the best examples of inter-regional partnership for peace and democracy. Our political family has been in the first line of this process. The future of democracy in Latin America is closely linked with economic and social democracy. The EPP and our partners in the IDC are deeply involved in building up a transnational integration model like the Mercosur, and the third generation of association agreements (with Mexico, Mercosur and Chile) are necessary elements for the partnership between Latin America and the Union.

**

Africa is going through a painful post-colonial process, lasting much longer and with more bloodshed than expected. The European Union tried to be helpful via commercial and financial facilities, as established in the successive Lomé Conventions – the idea of our former colleague Bersani – which have survived as useful and peaceful devices in a panorama of everlasting conflicts.

There cannot be development without peace in the same way that peace is not possible without a sustainable development based on democracy, the rule of law and respect of human rights. That is why the strengthening of democratic institutions is one of the key elements of the development policy of the Union.

The Fourth Lomé Convention, signed in December 1989, was the first international treaty in which the Community and its Member States declared their commitment to the respect and promotion of democracy and human rights. This commitment has been developed and incorporated into other international instruments as a substantive element of the external relations of the Union.

**

The Barcelona Process is an attempt to improve democracy and stability in the Mediterranean Area.

The building up of democratic institutions, of economic and social stability, of establishing the rule of law and enhancing good governance in the Mediterranean region is the objective of the so-called Barcelona Process.

This political initiative was taken in parallel to the European Union's Nordic extension when our Scandinavian members joined the Union. Though a very slow and tiresome undertaking, almost put to a complete stop by the Near East conflict, the Barcelona Process meanwhile is making its way with some of our neighbours in the South Mediterranean area. But the initiatives and help we provide via this process are of enormous value to those States that develop towards democratic systems and rule of law, as we can now see happening for example in Morocco, Jordan and elsewhere.

The European Parliament has played, and continues to play, a role of capital importance in all these processes. With debates and resolutions, with questions and conferences, Parliament has influenced the path that the other institutions were about to take, strengthening the commitment of the Union in favour of democracy everywhere in the world. The EPP-ED Group has played a leading part in Parliament's action.

3.2 Supporting the development and addressing the needs of the regions

3.2.1 Present and future European Union regional policies

Kostantinos HATZIDAKIS
Chairman of the Committee on Regional Policy,
Transport and Tourism in the European Parliament
Member of the EPP-ED Group
in the European Parliament

Back in the mid-1950s, when the European Community emerged, it would have been hard to guess to what an extent the founding and subsequent member states would get engaged in an assortment of common policies. The Common Agricultural Policy (CAP) was the first to be adopted, but later on it was followed by others, which have given a substantial boost to the process of European integration. It would not be an exaggeration to say that EU regional policies are quintessential to this process, for reasons both economic and *par excellence* political.

Regional policies so far

In 1988 and then again in 1992, the EU decided to strengthen its support to regions with structural difficulties by recognising that a closer market-driven economic integration alone is not sufficient to reduce regional disparities. The degrees of socio-economic development of EU Member States and regions were much too varied – and still are – to let the Common Market accommodate all the disparities between them. A need for structural intervention was clearly identified and "translated" into what emerged as a set of EU regional policies.

The same holds true of economic integration of future Member States. Trade flows between the Union and the candidate countries have increased markedly during the 1990s, reflecting the progressive move towards a free trade area. Currently, the EU accounts for 60% of total exports of the candidate countries, whereas only 10% of the Union's exports are directed towards them. Yet, trade alone is not enough. Structural intervention will definitely be needed in the new Member States, even though that will not be an easy task.

The finance made available through the Structural Funds rose from an initial 0.27% of EU GDP in 1989 to 0.46% in 1999, with the increase being more pronounced in the so-called "cohesion" countries (Ireland, Spain, Portugal and Greece). For instance, the amount transferred varied from 1.5% of GDP in Spain to 3.5% in Greece. It is widely acknowledged that without these transfers, investment and growth rates in the "cohesion" countries as well as other beneficiaries would have been significantly lower. Although the size of Structural Funds agreed in Berlin in 1999 for the 2000-2006 period fell back to the 1992 level of 0.31% of EU GDP, the concentration of finance in Objective 1 regions will be maintained in terms of the average amount of aid per head. From now on, some 60% of total Structural Funds transfers are allocated to regions which, together, account for no more than 20% of EU GDP.

However, in assessing the EU regional policies in a nutshell, it should be said that, despite the considerable achievements in the direction of cohesion, EU regional policies have not eliminated the distinction between developed and developing regions. One might even add that, while less developed regions, notably in South Europe, are definitely pushing "forward", certain regions in the Union have been moving at a "fast forward" pace, thus further increasing their lead. A question then is to be posed as to what kind of regional policies we need from now on in the EU, particularly in view of the next enlargement. First, the needs posed by the accession of the candidate states will be *enormous* in quantitative terms and, second, to a large extent they will be qualitatively *new*. Regional and cohesion policies, as conceived and imple-mented so far, clearly will have to be overhauled and re-designed. This will not be a self-fulfilling exercise, but the only meaningful response to regional disparities in the EU.

Growing disparities ahead?

Much as it might be upsetting, one must face the facts of life, as illustrated by some telling examples. It is true that the scale of regional disparities has been reduced over the 1988-1998 span. Thus, the ratio of GDP per head in the richest regions to the poorest ones declined from 2.9 in 1988 to 2.6 in 1998. At least one of the (until recently) poor countries, Ireland, has managed to crawl out of the so-called "cohesion" group, as its per capita income is now above the EU average; as a result, the "cohesion" group now comprises

Greece, Spain and Portugal. Yet, the gap between the wealthiest and poorest Member States in terms of income per capita is still evident.

Moreover, with the accession of new Member States, the economic landscape of the EU will change drastically, as disparities will double in scale. For instance, the ratio of GDP per head in the richest regions to the poorest will nearly double from 5.5 to 10. The average GDP per head in the richest 10% of the EU27 regions will be almost 6 times as high as in the poorest 10%. This widening gap will be difficult to tackle and it is estimated that the convergence of regions in the enlarged Union will take at least two generations.

Perhaps a starting point for any discussion should be the rate of regional concentration of economic activities in the EU, for this would at once reveal an obvious discrepancy: the fact that the central areas of the EU, which account for only one-seventh of the Union's land mass and one-third of the population, produce nearly half (47%) of the total GDP. This is undoubtedly a negative development, not only for the peripheral regions – all the more so for the new peripheral regions after enlargement – but also for the central regions themselves, as they suffer from a high degree of transport congestion and pressure on the environment.

As regards sectoral analysis, one of the areas to look at is agriculture and its share in the structure of the future EU27 economy. Currently, agriculture in the candidate countries accounts for 22% of total employment against less than 5% in the current Member States, which are rapidly turning to service-based economies. Clearly then there is a huge gap to be filled in this particular sector, in spite of the noteworthy rise of EU citizens moving back to rural areas over the last several years!

Another serious cause for concern in view of the accession is the expected increase in disparities as regards poverty levels. Although reliable data is not always available for the candidate countries, there is general consensus that a relatively high proportion of the population has a per capita income which is much lower than respective levels in the current EU Member States.

It goes without saying that poverty – or wealth respectively – is intertwined with the dynamism of the labour market. The current level of unemployment in the candidate countries, averaging 10.2% in 1999, is fairly close to the EU rate of 9.3%, but this figure does not necessarily reflect the economic restructuring that lies ahead. More importantly than employment levels, productivity rates in the candidate countries are still well below those in the Union and that fact should no doubt be taken into account

Curiously enough, over the years to come, employment will pose a new problem, one that Europe has not faced so far: a bizarre combination of high unemployment rates and a labour shortage at the same time! While millions of Europeans will be out of work, a number of jobs – particularly IT-related – are expected to remain vacant. Currently, there are no less than half a million job vacancies across the EU and, what is more, their number is expected to rise even higher! A possible solution would be for the EU to attract qualified workers at a time of labour shortages, particularly from younger age groups. It is of interest to know that the proportion of young people (between 10 and 25) in the candidate countries is relatively large at present.

One should also note the need for Union support for investment and development. "*What kind of investment*" is the question. Not just investment in fixed capital, but in know-how and labour-force skills. Because what is even more important than age is *education* and *professional training*, parameters that can only be utilised in the context of Research and Development (R&D). In this area, too, regional discrepancies are looming large. The top 10 regions account for nearly a third of the total R&D expenditure in the Union for a similar share of patents and, as is only to be expected, these regions display the largest numbers of people employed in high-tech sectors.

All these examples illustrate the "horizontal" or "sectoral" approach. However, in a number of cases geography matters as well. Certain specific regions, such as mountainous, coastal and maritime regions as well as islands and archipelagos, have to be treated on a different level. The fact that all these areas have similar physical and geo-morphological features – e.g. fragile environment, a low degree of accessibility, etc. – has to be taken into consideration. Quite naturally, 95% of mountain areas and islands are currently eligible under Objectives 1 and 2 of the Structural Funds.

The Structural Funds in a broader context

Being fully aware of the fact that a lot of these figures may sound tiresome or even "Greek" to the readers, let me now dwell for a moment on the very concept of cohesion and the wider goals of the Structural Funds. A couple of political remarks to begin with. This unique structure, initially called the European Community and then turning into a Union, has been based on the fundamental notions of cohesion and solidarity. This principle should be observed even more piously in view of the next enlargement, the biggest and most challenging enlargement in the entire history of the EU.

Secondly, a year or so after a Europe-wide debate on the federal prospects of the EU started, the notions of cohesion and solidarity are more appropriate than ever. No discussion on the federal concept would make much sense without incorporating cohesion – and, therefore, regional policies – in the political agenda. All the rest is technicalities, to put it bluntly.

On the other hand, once the political will is there, technicalities matter as well. Well-structured, widely accepted and easily implementable regulations are instrumental to the efficient and transparent use of EU funding. I know quite well that European citizens may sometimes think we

"Eurocrats" are much too obsessed with figures, charts and PowerPoint presentations. I firmly believe, however, that sound management is the only way to cement European citizens' trust in good governance provided by EU institutions.

Regional policies in an enlarged EU

Let me finish this, hardly exhaustive, presentation of EU regional policies by putting forward some suggestions as to how we should go about regional development in the years to come.

- First of all, no policy whatsoever makes much sense without the necessary resources. If the EU is to live up to the challenges of regional development, it will inescapably face the need to increase the Union's "own resources" above the meagre 1.27% of EU GDP. The current level of "own resources" is clearly incompatible with the prospect of growing disparities after the next enlargement. It is evident that the demand created by the accession of much poorer new Member States cannot be met with the current financial tools the Union has at its disposal. Unless the EU keeps its commitment to cohesion by sufficiently raising its "own resources", regional disparities within Europe will inevitably destabilise weaker Member States, will further fuel the wave of euroscepticism, and will thus expose the entire EU vision as a poorly structured project.

- Funding for regional policies will never be enough, which is precisely why it should be spent wisely. This is why "value-for-money" should be a guiding principle in the management of Structural Funds, through benchmarking and incessant evaluation improvements. Therefore, a strong message should be sent to beneficiaries that there is a precious pool of EU "best practice" that they can turn to in pursuing value-for-money results.

- Much as it might seem self-evident that stress should be laid on less developed regions, this has to be reflected in very practical terms in the distribution of funds. Thus, two-thirds of Structural Funds allocations should be earmarked for the poorest EU regions currently covered under Objective 1, both before and after the next enlargement. Another practical imperative is that Objective 1 regions should continue to receive EU funding to the tune of 75% of relevant expenditure.

- On the other hand, we should bear in mind the "tricky" fact that the accession of new Member States will lower the average EU socio-economic indicators and many of the current Member States' poor regions will seemingly find themselves in a better position, but only nominally. Therefore, poor regions in the current Member States should continue to be examined on the EU-15 scale even after enlargement, at least over the next programming period, and any region of EU-15 with a per capita income below 75% of the current Union's 2006 average should remain entitled to an Objective 1 status beyond 2006.

– Apart from Objective 1 areas, which are more geographically located, the EU should undertake large-scale "horizontal" action, along three main axes: i) the environment, ii) Information Society developments, and iii) innovation. Environmental protection and sustainable economic development are an utmost priority, both in current Member States and in the candidate countries. The Information Society should become a powerful engine for job creation all across the board if Europe is to live up to the challenges of the 21st century. Last but not least, innovative measures should be designed for *specific beneficiaries*, such as mountainous regions, islands, and rural and urban areas in decline. Given the current concentration of high-tech businesses in certain parts of the Union, innovation can greatly help the EU in coming up with a visible added-value, particularly in its peripheral regions.

– This leads us to the point that the Union's political leadership should, in fact, make sure that all Structural Funds investment has a high degree of *visibility*, for only that way will regional policies enjoy the acceptance of European citizens. Irish fishermen and Spanish farmers may – or may not – be familiar with the *jargon communautaire*, riddled with incomprehensible technical terms (e.g. "Objectives", "additionality", etc), but they have to see the tangible results of Structural Funds intervention, be it in the form of modern equipment on their ships or improvements in the healthcare system in rural areas, to pick two random examples.

– Trans-border co-operation, all across the EU, is also essential. Not only will it boost trade flows and labour mobility, thus bringing Europeans ever closer, but it will stimulate the technological exchange as well as the transfer of know-how and the unification of administrative practices among Member States and regions. This, in turn, will greatly contribute to the integration of less developed regions in the overall economic "tissue" of the EU.

– A final remark, with regard specifically to the candidate states, tomorrow's newcomers on board the EU. It is obvious that they will have to put considerable effort into economic restructuring and towards greater social cohesion, in order to meet the accession requirements. What may be less well understood – but is just as important – is that accession is neither a "pain-killer" nor a panacea. Once the candidates become Member States, they will have to remain on the track of continuous self-improvement, with necessary reforms in their administrative and socio-economic structures. Of course, they will not be alone in tackling these issues, as they are already being assisted through the ISPA and SAPARD instruments and, no doubt, will be beneficiaries of the Structural Funds upon accession. It would be expedient to point out that the EU should invest in the new Member States both in large-scale infrastructure projects as well as in the improvement of their know-how and labour-force skills.

To wind up a huge topic, so briefly outlined here, let me finish by stressing the significance of cohesion and regional policies in relation to the global challenges of the new century. A reference to these challenges is highly timely, only a few months into the third millennium. Few doubt that globalised economy and Information Society developments will pose a number of new opportunities for Europe. However, these opportunities can only be utilised by a Europe which is cohesive from within. The more divided Europe is, the more introverted it will be. The more cohesive, the more open it will be to the outer world in the 21st century.

3.2.2 Improving the quality of transport for our citizens

Loyola de PALACIO
Vice-President of the European Commission
responsible for relations with the European
Parliament, energy and transport

I am grateful to the EPP-ED Group in the European Parliament for having given me this opportunity to set out my ideas on how efforts to improve the quality of transport will bring benefits for Europe's citizens.

Introduction: The key role of transport in the European economy

Today, when transport is increasingly under critical review because of its negative effects, it is essential to recall that it is a basic service essential for business and everyday life. It is abundantly clear that such is the importance of transport to every sector of the European economy that very careful thought has to be given to measures that will affect the future transport system's capacity to serve people and industry as it does currently.

Transport and economic growth have gone hand in hand to ensure that the EU continues to expand its economy and reduce the disparities between the most favoured and the least well-off as well as between the regions. The question now is how will this partnership continue? Before examining the difficulties that transport has created, I believe it is important to make it clear that improving living standards will require economic growth to be strong and consistent. The benefits that have been enjoyed from the long upward trend in the EU economy are clearly linked to continuous improvement of the transport system. To ensure continued economic progress it is vital that the relationship between economic growth and transport is properly assessed when evaluating policy initiatives.

Transport in the EU is in some ways a victim of its own success. Due to the concentration on road transport – responsible for a substantial part of CO_2 emissions – the environmental spotlight is being increasingly turned on the transport sector. A further problem concerns safety: the number of casualties due to transport accidents has thankfully come down but the number of people killed in road accidents – by far the most serious problem – remains stubbornly over 40,000 per year. In addition to this very tangible human problem, there is also the more insidious risk of long-term ecological damage by chemical and other incidents that concerns the maritime sector notably.

Even in the transport sector itself congestion is becoming an everyday phenomenon of our major cities and even some of the main road and rail inter-city links. Similar problems are experienced at key airports where delays at peak times are the norm rather than the exception. The future growth of traffic will worsen these problems unless action is taken.

Transport then presents something of a paradox for the policy-maker. It has made a major contribution to underpinning the economic success of the EU. But transport is widely seen as a long-term problem for the environment. How to resolve these questions, to balance sustainable growth and the enhancement of the quality of the world around us, is the challenge for the Common Transport Policy of the Union. In the following pages I will try to set down how this might be achieved.

The Common Transport Policy and its revision to meet new challenges

The Common Transport Policy (CTP) was subject to a complete re-think in 1992. The principal objective of the policy was to provide for a 'Single Market' of the transport sector that would advance in parallel with the Single Market overall. To that end, the policy proposals set out a far-reaching objective that aimed to remove the many bureaucratic rules that imposed unjustified burdens. The 1992 White Paper recognised the possibility that negative 'external' effects could develop from some of the proposals – particularly in relation to the expansion of road transport. However, with the advantage of hindsight, it can now be seen that too little attention was paid to ensuring that the 'liberalisation' legislation had effective provisions against negative side-effects. The task for the 2001 revision of the Common Transport Policy is to build on the best of the 1992 policies to stop and then reverse the negative impacts from transport. I will go on to provide a brief general review of transport in the EU today and then pass quickly on to outline the potential for change in each mode of transport.

EU transport in 2010

In the past ten to fifteen years transport has grown at a faster rate than the economy as a whole. Will this trend continue? My view, taking account of the studies and forecasts that are available, is that for freight transport the trend will continue but for passengers there is likely to be some change. Let me explain this in more detail. For freight transport growth has been due to a combination of economic factors – adhesion of new members to the EU, industrial restructuring and so on, combined with the increased efficiency and lower prices in the transport sector. For the period up to 2010 economic growth forecasts are good and there is also the likelihood that new Member States will enter. Against this background it is predicted that overall freight traffic in the period 1998-2010 will rise by almost forty per cent. Passenger traffic shows a somewhat different picture. The average age of Europe's population is rising, car ownership is already high and congestion is starting to have an effect: these factors, taken together, lead to the prediction that there will be a slow-down in passenger growth and the likely figure for the period is around 20%.

These then are the trends in traffic. As regards the distribution of the growth, the continuation of existing policies will lead to most of the increased traffic being concentrated on the roads. For this reason I believe it important to develop new policies that will initially stop the reduction in the share of total traffic being handled by the railways, public transport and other environmentally-friendly modes. In addition this period of stability should be used to launch the new and radical alternative technologies that are becoming available – new motors, new fuels and new systems of management. An example of the new possibilities is the GALILEO programme: this ambitious plan aims to create a European system for navigation and management that will have many applications in fields outside transport also. With new technologies in place by around 2010 there should be a real possibility of reducing pollution, accidents and congestion. This is the target I would like to set.

What policies would need to change to arrive at the target scenario? A presentation by mode follows.

Passenger transport: There is a temptation to look upon the *private car* as the villain of the piece; such thinking is as unrealistic as it is partial in its diagnosis. The private car is certainly the direct cause of much of the congestion and pollution that we experience – especially in the major conurbations. But, rather than focus upon the car as an enemy, the aim should be to adapt it to a more sustainable lifestyle in the future. This will certainly require that a number of car trips are replaced by other means of transport or other organisational forms concerning workplace, entertainment etc. However, such trip replacement on the margin will only concern a relatively small number of peak-hour trips and will be in corridors where a good and reliable alternative service exists.

The Commission will seek to follow up the progress that has already been made through the voluntary agreements with car manufacturers to reduce emissions. Further progress can also be made in a better control of vehicle movements through the fitting of new devices developed in the framework of the Commission's programme on Intelligent Transport Systems (ITS). This emphasises the importance of *public transport* and it is clear that in many cities in the EU there has been inadequate attention paid to public transport. It is not for the EU as such to become directly involved in the details of the policies. The CTP should be seen as a tool that regional and city authorities could call on for assistance, as they need it. The Framework Programme for Research in the EU has undertaken studies of best practice in city transport planning: this could well be expanded to make available some financial assistance to those cities that are contemplating innovative, multimodal transport strategies. Indeed, the success of public transport operations in the cities will largely depend on multimodal solutions. The new CIVITAS programme will in 2001 start to make a major contribution to new, innovative urban development projects.

As for *infrastructure, the transeuropean networks (TEN-T)* will be revised to ensure that the available financial support is concentrated on projects of clear European interest. Funding of transport improvements is a problem in the large cities. There could be some increase in general taxation to raise revenue but a more efficient solution would be to revise the current systems of taxation, based largely on excise duties on fuel, on licences etc. to move towards a pricing policy for road use in congested areas at peak periods. There is now a considerable body of evidence to demonstrate how such systems can radically improve flows and cut down congestion. It is also apparent that the acceptability of such an approach would be considerably enhanced if a certain percentage of the revenue raised were to be devoted to providing transport improvements in the areas concerned. Studies undertaken by various cities show that this approach would swing many of those concerned over to favour the adoption of pricing policies. These measures should provide the breathing-space needed – up to 2010 – for radically new solutions such as fuel cell vehicles to be commercialised.

A particular question is posed concerning middle to long distance travel where the forecast growth by *air* is exceptionally high – up to 90% in twelve years. Many of these trips are for holiday or tourist purposes and arguably are vital for the continued development of the peripheral areas of the EU. Unfortunately, this rate of growth will worsen the quality of service in the sector where air traffic control is under increasing strain. Once again, the political response to this situation has to be attentive to the needs of all concerned. The long-term objective has to be to offer extra seats but fewer aircraft movements and hence less congestion and emissions. This objective can be achieved by policies that combine:

First, the role of the high-speed train and the plane as service providers in the main corridors has to be re-thought. The railways and the airlines on many routes should be seen as complementary. The advancing pace of development of the high-speed transeuropean rail network and the need to make the best use of capacity at airlines requires reassessment of the potential. The future has, to lie with the railways being much more integrated into the air companies networks for air trips of up to four hours and even longer on busy routes. This will require a more open structure for rail passenger services with solutions being found for baggage handling, through ticketing etc. On a number of potentially rail-served corridors in the EU there are up to fifty flights each way on peak days: to replace just ten per cent of these by 2010 will be a significant step forward.

Second, the development of liberalised air services has led in its turn to the opening up of many more 'hub and spoke' operations that rely on lower-capacity aircraft than previously used. For the future, it will be important to ensure that charges fully reflect the costs incurred by aircraft including the use of scarce capacity. This logical development could result in the setting up of more direct services between lesser-used airports also – another positive move for society and the user.

Third, the encouragement of movements involving higher-capacity aircraft. This comes at a suitable moment when manufactures are working on new, larger, wide-bodied planes. Manufacturers should also be given a further stimulus to more designs by appropriate charging and taxation regimes.

To sum up, for *passenger transport*, we need to:

– Develop policies to integrate the car more closely into multimodal urban transport systems.
– Encourage the development of 'clever ITS' systems to control traffic and cars, using the results to build up effective long-term policies for cars and transport in cities.
– Push for further measures to develop more economic instruments (pricing) and new fuels in the medium term.
– Stimulate better co-ordination of high-speed trains and aircraft on middle distance, high-traffic corridors.
– Develop economic and technical measures to encourage higher-capacity planes and more efficient engines.

Freight transport: In relation to freight transport, it is once again easy to come up with wonder solutions to quickly resolve the problem – transfer all heavy lorries to the railways is frequently recommended. Although as Transport Commissioner I am anxious to encourage the railways – not to forget coastal shipping and all environmentally-friendly modes – one has to be practical. I should make it clear that the target strategy to maintain modal split at its 1998 level will require the railways to carry forty per cent more traffic by 2010. Against this ambitious objective, it is clear that the key to success of measures for freight traffic must aim at the market leader: the road freight sector itself.

Analysing the road freight business, it becomes rapidly clear that its apparent success conceals a failure to achieve a stable, profitable structure. Many road haulage firms are small and although this is no problem in itself, their numbers in this sector and the absence of a counterbalance to powerful freight forwarders means that the rewards of increased efficiency accrue mainly to the shipper. Moreover, the predominance of road transport is now such that other modes of freight transport are required to price their services at the going rate in the road haulage market. The final result of this is that freight rates in the EU have constantly been reduced in real terms in the last decade. This has been to the benefit of industry but at the cost of the environment and other social concerns: clearly, the current situation where many road hauliers are required to work excessive hours and may be tempted to ignore safety measures are grounds for concern. This has to be coupled with the fact that the other, non-road, freight operators suffer from unsustainable road freight rates as well and receive significant amounts of public support to continue in business. Against this background, the European citizen has every right to expect action to be taken and obviously measures at the EU level are called for.

On the basis of the analysis I have made, the first problem to tackle has to be the profitability of road haulage. Although the principle of the freedom of access to the profession has to be vigorously defended, action has to be taken to ensure that newcomers are qualified and have sufficient resources to be expected to be profitable. Allied to reviewing the rules on the access to the profession, the authorities concerned have to be encouraged to improve the enforcement of existing rules that are widely flouted. Such measures should rapidly improve the situation of the average firm and also enhance the position of other modes. Action on appropriate levels needs to be taken to integrate transport operators better into the freight logistics chain where significant economies can be made. Notably for the railways, a decision has to be made as to whether they should continue to be general hauliers or limit themselves increasingly to those sectors where their greatest advantages lie. In view of the inertia of the railways to date, under overly attentive 'management' by national authorities, the process of opening up the rail sector to new types of pan-European operation has to be accelerated. The contribution of the European Parliament at the end of 2000 to the success of the first 'rail package' was vital: I plan to put forward a package of further measures in the course of this year and count on the continued support of Parliament. My vision of the EU freight sector in 2010 is of a much more successful industry than today providing a high level of service and requiring little in the way of public resources. Clearly, if this is to be achieved, rail infrastructure should be accessible to all operators in all markets. Already there are movements in the right direction and a number of Member States have opened their networks, but unified action on accessibility and infrastructure pricing is essential for the railways to flourish in the expanding international market. The EU must keep in the van of such movements with early changes in the 'Eurovignette' system for heavy lorries in particular. On the theme of infrastructure, the railways will need extra freight capacity on the key long-distance routes. The prioritisation of the TEN-T guidelines in favour of clear projects of European interest has to be accelerated to provide support for the creation of a dedicated European rail freight network and links to ports with the potential to develop short sea shipping.

Transport and the citizen: the safety issue

Although I have not touched upon safety, it is universally agreed to be a key issue. The principal, immediate problem is the level of casualties in the road sector. Although the situation has improved, it still gives grounds for deep concern, particularly due to the number of young people affected. The large differences between Member States suggests that major improvements are possible if safety measures are better applied. It is tempting to consider establishing quantified targets for improvement but the problem is that the means for success do not lie with the Community as such. All the authorities concerned have to enforce existing rules and agree on new practical measures to be applied if success is to be achieved. In the other modes of transport considerable progress can come through the creation of well-staffed agencies dependent upon EU institutions to focus upon safety issues and provide appropriate guidance for policy making. While discussing safety matters I also have to mention the subject of maritime safety. Following the series of recent disasters the EU is now beginning to act in a unified manner and progress has been made in the gradual eradication of unsafe vessels. Once again I have a programme planned that will involve a series of measures to radically change the way in which the maritime community treats safety and I intend to pursue this vigorously.

Conclusions: Bringing together the various objectives

The EU made up of 15 members needs an efficient, profitable transport system: an EU of 28 members will need this even more. Transport has to contribute to the improvement of the environment if it is to be sustainable in the long run. I have tried to explain what I think are the principal obstacles that have to be overcome to develop an effective long-term policy. Essentially, the first challenge to be tackled is to reverse the current negative trend whilst maintaining the capacity and efficiency of the sector. This should be the goal for the year 2010 using a series of measures drawing upon the regulatory, economic and research mechanisms and ideas that are already available. No single measure will succeed on its own; rather packages of measures put together by all the actors involved will have to be devised and fine-tuned to the specific nature of the problem. If the goal of reversing the trend by 2010 is achieved, phase two of the plan can be launched: attention should be concentrated on the rapid inception of radically new technical approaches to transport that have been developed but that still need technical and commercial work. These new techniques should be set into a much better organised planning framework that brings together the citizens' need for a pleasant and efficient living space and optimises the use of transport and other resources far more effectively than today. My goal during my time as Transport Commissioner is to set in motion the new policies needed to achieve these objectives.

3.2.3 The Nordic regions will not be forgotten: Integration begins at the periphery

Eija-Riitta KORHOLA
Member of the EPP-ED Group in the
European Parliament

The four biggest Scandinavian countries base their solid economic growth on highly international industries. It appears that the three Baltic States will follow with accelerating speed. That will draw the Nordic countries ever closer to the heart of Europe in coming years. But what would draw the hearts of citizens in these countries to Europe?

This will probably happen as soon as they realise they are an essential and irreplaceable part of Europe, and as soon as they can see that: there are structures of solidarity, providing welfare to areas others than those of the fastest economic growth; that those structures exist to serve the larger entity, for the balanced development of the whole continent, as well as for relations with all its neighbouring areas; and that citizens in fact are needed in those structures.

This is how I understand regional policy – in contrast to the common image of regional policy, usually manifested as petty details called for by provincial petty politicians. The latter is, if not to be condemned, then at least ridiculous and has no role to play in the EU. Supporting balanced development is designed to ensure that the European Community is organised in a constructive way in all the regions of the EU while promoting Europe-wide partnership rather than antagonism. Therefore regional policy is part of a larger structure for stability and security in Europe.

The origins of the Northern dimension

It is not at all clear and unambiguous what actually is meant by "Northern". My own hometown Helsinki represents to most Finns the "South" with all southern vice and potential. Looking from Helsinki, though, the "South" begins on the other side of the Baltic Sea. From the EU view, all States round the Baltic Sea, Germany included, are Northern. This definition of "Northern" depends on who and where the observer is; it could be called

Local North. Then, no matter who is observing and where, there is the Arctic North beginning at the Polar Circle; the Arctic North has been part of the EU since 1995.

The Northern dimension of Finland and Sweden was addressed in accession talks, especially in relation to the structural funds: an Objective 6 was created. Otherwise large areas of those two countries would have been left without subsidies because the original criteria for structural aid in the EU did not apply. The new criteria for Objective 6 were remoteness and extremely low density of population. Arctic agriculture was exempted from some of the common EU rules. This was of benefit to Finland especially because all its agriculture is north of the 61st parallel – further north than any other agriculture in the world!

The challenge Finland offered to the EU was not only one of agriculture or regional development but also of a geopolitical nature: on accession in 1995, the eastern border of Finland became a new border for the EU, shared with Russia along 1200 kilometres (750 miles).

Later, in a proposal from the Finnish Prime Minister Paavo Lipponen in 1997, the Northern dimension was transformed from a Finnish-Swedish matter into an EU approach to regional and cross-border co-operation with north-western Russia and the Baltic States – in an area stretching from the Baltic to the Barents Sea. It covers fields such as energy, communications, research, environment, nuclear safety, public health and even the fight against international crime and drugs. A separate part of Russia, Kaliningrad, between Poland and Germany on the shore of the Baltic Sea, is mentioned in particular. An action programme for the Northern dimension was adopted at the Feira Summit in June 2000.

The Northern dimension benefits the whole EU

Although it might not look like it, the Northern dimension is above all EU foreign policy. In the spirit of Schuman and the EU itself, the Northern dimension is in practice based on trade, regional development and direct contacts at the grass roots level. This approach enabled TACIS funds, for example, to be granted to finance a hazardous waste management project in Krasnyi Bor. Slowly, the EU and Russia are becoming tied together in co-operation as France and Germany were in the dawn of the European Communities. This time, the challenge is not only to overcome the memories of the war and post-war division of Europe, but also to find a way to build bridges between the EU states, with well-developed civil societies, and Russia, with practically no civil society at all. If the Northern dimension is able to facilitate the emergence of civil society in Russia, this will promote stability and security in the North-east and indeed the whole of Europe.

The so-called Barcelona process (created in 1995) is in the end very similar to the Northern dimension while it strives for stability and development on the southern borders of the EU. The idea in both is to integrate a range of highly varied Community instruments into one programme and thus increase output through co-ordination and synergy.

The rise of oil prices in 2000 made all Member States see the importance of the Northern dimension. This is of great value, as it could never have been developed in a balanced way with only Denmark, Finland, Germany and Sweden, who were committed to the idea from the start. The massive resources of oil and natural gas in the Barents region are believed to play an important role in future EU energy policy as the Union's dependence on imported resources is growing.

Togetherness in co-operation

In the Barents region, there has been co-operation for more than a decade now. This co-operation has faced many difficulties and obstacles due to quite different cultural infrastructure, but yet there is great motivation to improve it. One of the most important practical results has been bringing tuberculosis under control in the frontier region of Russia and preventing it spreading over the border.

The Barents Regional Council has also proved to be an important channel for humanitarian aid. This has been a reality ever since the governor of Murmansk – encouraged by personal contacts established earlier – could simply pick up the phone and call for help from his colleagues in Finland, Norway and Sweden in 1998 after the economic crash in Russia.

Most citizens living in regions surrounding the Baltic Sea can with ease accept co-operating with each other around the Sea. Perhaps this stems from the old Hanseatic traditions. Now, co-operation is widening from traditional fields like trade, environment, research and education to areas such as social and health care. The Baltic Sea region will soon be a dynamic economic zone.

After enlargement has reached Poland and the Baltic States, the Baltic Sea will be almost totally surrounded by the EU. This may well lead to a situation where Baltic Sea co-operation becomes less exceptional and becomes part of everyday life. Simultaneously, the weight of the Baltic Sea region decreases in the Northern dimension – and the Arctic North increases. Local North in the EU comes closer to the Arctic North as enlargement, once again, moves northwards. Even then the Northern dimension will be more than just part of the EU's Russian strategy; it will also strengthen the EU's contacts to the West. In the Far North, West is close to East.

The Northern dimension could link the EU to the Arctic Council

Experience gained so far is helping the EU to make a good start. Arctic conditions have united Canada, Denmark, Finland, Iceland, Norway, the Russian Federation, Sweden, and the United States since the Arctic Council was finally founded in 1996. Two of the eight countries are EU Member States, and several other EU Member States are observers. The EU, however, is not participating in the Council even as an observer. The main part of the Council's work is aimed at promoting sustainable use of resources and projects favouring indigenous populations, including the development of a virtual Arctic University.

The indigenous people – the Saami Council, the Inuit, the Aleut, and the federation of the indigenous people in Russia – are "permanent participants" in the Council, which represents the best status that any indigenous people has in an international body. Saami people are not represented in the Barents Euro-Arctic Council even though they live in all four countries of the Barents. Even in the Nordic Council the initiative to improve the status of Saami representatives has been extremely slow to lead to anything concrete.

The situation of the only indigenous people in the whole EU, the Saami, should be taken into careful consideration in the Northern dimension. The Nenets, for example, a small sub-population of the Saami, which barely survived the Soviet regime, are again threatened as market forces rush to rich reserves of oil and natural gas in the zone where the Nenets live.

Nordic regions cover a vast geological area: the Baltic states, all the Scandinavian countries, a slice of Russia and a strip of North America: from cherry trees on the southern banks of the Baltic Sea to ice-cold winds of the Barents and Kara Sea. The area is so vast that it does not really form a "Nordic" identity, nor does it give rise to a "unified Nordic front" inside the EU. Instead, there is a lack of European identity. This could easily be improved if the EU were involved in the work of the Arctic Council. Years of co-operation have contributed to a clear vision of the region, the people living in it and the essence of sustainable development in the Arctic. This vision would benefit the EU.

The Nordic Council – pioneer in integration

Nordic co-operation began in 1907 with unofficial meetings between parliamentarians and ministers. Today, it is still a unique intergovernmental form of co-operation since it is firmly anchored in the people's activities and support. Back in the 1950s – before the EU/EEC started building the European internal market – the Nordic Passport Union was launched together with a common labour market, municipal voting rights, Nordic language convention, social convention, cultural agreement and transport agreement. Today, the Nordic countries are similar as far as most features of society are concerned.

The Nordic Council is above all a policy-making body. Its working tools are however "soft law" in nature. The Council has stressed questions like social welfare, children and young people, democracy and human rights, and regional co-operation. Some results of its work include the Nordic prohibition of tobacco advertising in 1972, or the swan label, launched in 1989 as the Nordic eco-label, covering more than 1500 products.

Open to the winds of the world

For some 500 years, Nordic countries were easily able to develop as even very radical social reforms were quite manageable with such small populations. Thus Scandinavians were in the front line in forging modern civil liberties, reforming religion, forming a monetary union, organising basic education, or granting universal suffrage. The foundations were laid a long time back in history in medieval provincial law, which was the starting-point for a gradual and harmonious process for legal unity. This also gave the economy a boost and the power to compete despite its small size.

The situation changed totally with increasingly dominant globalisation – being small became a handicap for reformers. Competition in world-wide markets meant that the smallest ones could not make reforms that their competitors would not make, or reforms that could not be agreed inter- nationally – even if all would have liked to have them. This meant that the Nordic countries had to widen the scope of integration from Scandinavian to European, but today there are many who have not realised this, and Scandi- navian co-operation is sometimes proposed as an alternative – rather than an addition – to European integration.

Nordic co-operation – today involving eight countries as the three Baltic States are in fact participating actively – is facing many challenges. Accord- ing to polls, more than 70 per cent of Nordic citizens wish to increase Nordic co-operation. A panel of wise men has recently submitted proposals for the future development of Nordic co-operation, entitled "North 2000 – Open to the winds of the world". They point to a need for comprehensive reform, as concerns both institutional and substantial aspects of Nordic co-operation. This co-operation would function more effectively through closer co-ordina- tion and by focusing on fewer and politically important areas in response to real needs and where acting together is of real benefit.

In the intergovernmental conference in 2004 the EU is expected to draw up catalogues of competences. Even though there would not be any actual change in competences there is a need to clarify responsibilities. As soon as

Member States know more precisely what fields are left to their competence and at which level, they will be able to reconsider mandating regional organisations more precisely. For small and peripheral areas of the North this would be a good way of achieving secondary integration at the regional level – without competition with the EU. This would mean deepening co-operation in e.g. the Nordic Council and in other regional structures. The EU would also benefit from this. Its Member States would be more committed to working at each level if there was less fear of overlapping, and if there were local representatives working across borders in areas where it would be difficult or at least less economical for the EU itself to reach.

Only the EU makes foreign policy at the grass roots level

Finns are used to seeing themselves on the edge of any map: for many decades in the Nordic Council it was the eastern edge of Scandinavia; in Europe, it clearly is the northern fringe; now in the Northern dimension, it shows the model of western societies; and in Arctic co-operation it is the bridge to southern Europe. Surprisingly, by putting these maps one on top of the other, Finland now finds herself at the centre point. This has sparked an unseen determination to benefit from opportunities, to be active and to participate. Despite the unchanged geographical facts, Finland is positioning herself in the virtual core of Europe.

This is how regional policies should work: giving a new view, not placing a region on the fringes but rather at the centre of opportunities. In finding this kind of wider perspective, the vast amount of experience from all over Europe to be found in the EU institutions can be of great value.

Like circles in water, integration starts at the local level, grows to regional co-operation and unifies states. At all levels regional policies are needed to create cohesion, but they are extremely important at the contact points between the EU and its neighbouring regions, in the South, in the North and in the East. There the EU, the legacy of Schuman and other founding fathers, will be an exceptional actor in history conducting foreign policy at the grass roots level.

This will make many more hearts beat for Europe.

3.2.4   Europe, take heart:
the Mediterranean is European

Francesco FIORI
Vice-Chairman of the EPP-ED Group in the
European Parliament

A strategy of small steps, taking care to avoid the pitfalls, to ensure the future of the Mediterranean free exchange area. The ambitious goal set by the European Union in Barcelona in 1995 made this strategy necessary. Now, the finishing post of 2010 is actually just around the corner. But there is still, unfortunately, a lot of distance left to cover in spite of the efforts that have been made so far. I refer in particular to the positive conclusion of the recent Athens agreement, in which the European Union, together with the 12 Mediterranean Partners, has decided to give a fresh impetus to the role of training and information, with a view to fostering an improvement in the quality (and not purely in financial terms) of the well-being of the Mediterranean basin through interchange. This is undoubtedly a political attitude which demonstrates a desire to pursue the Barcelona objectives and which will undoubtedly assist in developing future regional cooperation projects between countries in the southern European basin. A new departure must not be made along this route: the unwarranted delays and indecision which Europe is so often prey to when it ought to be taking action in the international political arena must be overcome. The truth is, unfortunately, that the European Union has often run away from taking any initiative, as an economic power of its size ought to do, but has been a victim of its own weakness and has left others to take on the role of spokesman for political involvement which millions of people are pressing it to undertake. UN demographic studies tell us, in addition, that by the end of 2025 the population of the Mediterranean area will be 500 million, distributed unevenly: over 300 million in the south and fewer than 200 million in the north. Combined with the current state of affairs, these facts make it necessary for us to reflect on growing problems: mass migration, meeting food needs, communication, transport, energy, the environment, resources and security. On this last point I mean, clearly, active participation in finding a definitive peaceful solution to the problems of the Middle East.

The European Union is staking its own international political credibility here. The European government must, from Brussels, take on greater responsibility for foreign policy, whether or not this includes enlargement to the east, as this is an essential prerequisite for establishing, at last, a free trade area for the Mediterranean as a whole, not only in economic and financial terms but also in social and cultural terms. The situation we are currently faced with makes this necessary. And economic assessments also argue in favour of it. Current European growth is steady at about 3%, while in the USA it is 5%, and investment by European firms over the last seven years has been less than half the amount invested by American firms.

There are bilateral and regional cooperation instruments in the Mediterranean area, based on Association Agreements and financial instruments from the MEDA regulation and from the European Investment Bank (EIB). It will fall to the EIB to provide financial support for the choices which the European Union decides to make in those countries which share the same 'geographic destinies' (meaning social, political and economic destinies) in an international market shaped by the GATT, WTO, Mercosur and NAFTA agreements. And above all by the birth of the euro. It may seem risky and rather ambitious to conceive of the euro replacing the dollar as the basic currency used in governing trade in the Mediterranean basin countries, but if we bear in mind that in the end it is man's determination and actions that count, it can easily be achieved. This historic goal would meet all the targets which were set for 2010 at Barcelona: establishing a solid Mediterranean political and economic bloc within a new international system made up of fragile financial balances. And after all, since the dawn of civilisation the Mediterranean has been the centre of cultural and commercial trade for all of mankind. The Mediterranean culture's vitality is enabling universities and chambers of commerce to become more and more like intercultural centres, giving a central role once again to training, technology and know-how, which provide essential support for the effort needed to promote economic cooperation in the Mediterranean basin, transforming it into an integrated system of networks of permanent trade flows. Above all, Europe must become deeply involved in the vital sector of training, not only in order to support efforts to promote cooperation in the social field, particularly as regards equal opportunities for men and women, but also to encourage efforts to improve professional training, particularly for young people and women. Regional cooperation in this field must be improved by exchanging information, transferring experience and boosting capacity. But an end to the deafening European silence on the Mediterranean involves resolving situations of war and poverty on our doorstep, and dealing with paradoxes such as the fact that even though 95% of traffic from the Far East to Europe comes through the Suez canal, less than 50% of ships put into a Mediterranean port.

This state of affairs results from, on the one hand, the weakness of the transport and communication network provided by southern Europe's road system as compared to its northern European partners and, on the other hand, the many problems which the Mediterranean area must still solve in order to achieve a standard that can compete with the globalisation of international trade. The efficiency of each country's system, together with the cost and quality of its services and infrastructure, will become more and more important.

It will thus be vital for the Mediterranean economic sectors not to be solely concerned with improving their own internal efficiency, but, above all, to do their utmost to improve the efficiency of the entire pan-Mediterranean logistical system, overcoming national infrastructure delays and promoting efficient integration of the various ways of moving goods. The need to improve production efficiency, and to improve control over the cost of increasing sales, will be essential factors in increasing southern Europe's competitiveness. But this area can make progress, and can do so quickly, closing up any gaps there may be with the rest of the continent. In fact, it is reckoned that of 180 million tons of goods imported by ship within the Mediterranean by Italy, France, Spain, Greece and Turkey, a third represents trade between those countries. As far as trends in world trade are concerned, solid growth is forecast up until 2004 in maritime traffic in the Mediterranean. Specifically, over the next six years growth in internal Mediterranean trade is expected to be 25%. From this information we can deduce that maritime traffic not only brings the northern and southern shores closer together, but also brings the Mediterranean closer to the rest of the world by making it into a strategic crossroads, above all for the new East-West routes.

In 1998, goods exported by the Mediterranean basin amounted to slightly over 100 million tons in total, and the forecast for 2004 is approximately 135 million tons. As far as imports are concerned, on the other hand, in 1998 255 million tons came in, and the forecast for 2004 is over 320 million tons. For the period from 1998 to 2004 imports should therefore increase by 26% while exports should rise by 31%. Thanks to its geographical position and sociocultural situation, Italy has the pre-eminence necessary to enable it to take on a fundamental role in mediating between the northern and southern shores of the Mediterranean basin in the development of this area. Italy therefore forms a natural link between the southern shore of the Mediterranean and central and eastern Europe, and also with the Balkan coast. The main Adriatic route can in fact be seen as a junction, using combined road-sea-road transport, in view of the trans-European and pan-European networks, which are expanding the East-West road infrastructure. The development of the trans-European transport networks system is a reflection of the direction that new Community policy is taking, following decisions at the 1994 Essen summit: providing the single market with an infrastructure network which is focused on the development of economic and commercial relations and regional cohesion. Now plans must be made for extending the trans-European networks to countries which are not in the Community economic area, creating a network of pan-European connections. The development of these 'corridors' will increase trade between the European Union, Russia and Ukraine. But in assessing these scenarios we must not leave out of consideration the deficit in the EU's current account, caused by the high price of oil and the strong dollar, which in 2000 was approximately € 49 million. In 1999 the resulting deficit in the balance of payments with countries outside Europe was € 4.7 billion. If tax incentives were allowed, with a percentage of investments made by firms in the Mediterranean Mezzogiorno areas deducted from taxes, this would incentivise trade dynamics between three different areas of the same market. In order to complement a financial strategy of this kind, a specific cultural programme should be established providing for the creation of study grants targeted at the exchange of economic, social, cultural and educational experiences, with the aim of broadening professional horizons.

Cooperation between the States will thus be the point of departure on which to focus efforts to combat internal conflicts and the brutality which is a part of the human condition. I refer to civil wars, violence – not only physical violence, but violence in all its forms – poverty and exploitation, which cannot be reconciled with any form of civilisation which is founded on respect for human life. In order to move in this direction, within the framework of multilateral and bilateral relations between the European Union and our Mediterranean partners a whole series of measures will have to be taken to strengthen democratic institutions and the rule of law, giving significant support to judicial reform, freedom of expression and sound management of public affairs, and it will also be necessary to urge that more emphasis is placed on the protection of human rights and fundamental freedoms, through supporting those in government and the NGOs.

The European Commission must therefore promote a Mediterranean area of freedom, security and justice, and study joint approaches and measures for all the States to deal with the influx of refugees and illegal immigrants from countries close to the European Union's borders. The creation of an Immigration Monitoring Centre to carry out tasks of this kind will be crucially important in setting up permanent information exchange arrangements between the authorities of the various countries in the Mediterranean area, with a view to repairing the religious and social divisions which in the past have cut across the Mediterranean, and it should become a vital tool for reconciliation between different peoples. However, a whole series of measures would need to be taken as quickly as possible: creating effective cooperation arrangements to combat the illegal immigration networks, and in particular trafficking in human beings; establishing programmes to put in place effective monitoring systems at the borders, especially by offering opportunities to take training courses and participate in exchanges of officials; embarking, together with the Mediterranean partners, on a search for solutions to immigration which take account of the economic, social and cultural realities which these countries have to face. This initiative implies the need to fight against poverty, to improve living and working conditions and to ensure that human rights are respected.

Cultural diversity and human rights are the principles on which the European Union bases its dialogue with the opposite shore of the Mediterranean, since these are the prerequisites for guaranteeing peace, stability and prosperity for the whole Mediterranean region. It is worth bearing in mind that, according to the International Office for Migration in Geneva, every year 400 000 illegal immigrants enter the European Union, 100 000 more than enter the United States. And, in spite of the Schengen rules, the major point of entry in recent times has been Italy itself. Because of this, pressure should be applied for the Euro-Mediterranean charter for cooperation on mutual security to be adopted soon. In the environmental field, too, cooperation between the States should not be overlooked, particularly with regard to setting up regional programmes for integrated management of water resources, waste disposal and problems connected with desertification.

But the capacity for civil and military intervention in a joint defence and security policy will also have to be developed. The European Union must develop its own role to the full by making a political contribution instead of just giving technical support to the peace process in the Mediterranean area. This presupposes, specifically, the creation of a crisis prevention and crisis management system which is integrated into Community instruments, and the creation of a rapid reaction fund for non-military crises. At the same time, the Mediterranean Member States should step up their close partnership with the countries of the southern shores of the Mediterranean, helping them to reorientate their activities, focusing them on the fight against poverty, and this should be demonstrated through strong solidarity, supported by a trade policy which ensures that the common interests of the Mediterranean States are protected. As well as development cooperation, the goal should be integration into the economy and the promotion of valid national strategies. In order to achieve this goal, the impact of all Community policies must be made more coherent, partly through more coordination and more complementarity with action taken by the Member States.

In each case it will therefore be necessary to take care over safeguarding the CAP and the Marrakech agreements, and over fisheries policy. The approach taken should not, however, be an exclusive one, setting out to achieve one objective at the expense of another. The Mediterranean area is a homogeneous region sharing a common area, which is the same for all the residents who make up the various nations bordering this sea.

On the other hand, it cannot be denied that there is a structural need to increase production, in view of demographic trends, and to ensure a clear improvement in the quality and safety of food products. This means that there is a growing need for countries outside Europe to introduce new organisational methods, overhaul the operational machinery used and achieve a new capacity for growth. Within this field, the European Union should promote initiatives and contacts with a view to establishing active cooperation in the agricultural sector. In fact, we must move from the concept of confrontation towards partnership, identifying joint strategies through comparison and experience. An integrated analysis of production, processing, research and training using joint methods of working for improvement is the route to take in order to get rid of competition as an end in itself in the agricultural field, as in others. This is especially true because the production at stake is delicate and vulnerable, and a common vision of the market is needed so that Mediterranean producers can be protected in a transparent fashion. I say this, in particular, because of the Mediterranean agricultural production data.

At present, the agricultural population accounts for about 40% of the total labour force in the Mediterranean countries (25 million jobs in 1991), as compared with 6% in the EU. What's more, agriculture contributes significantly to the gross domestic product of these countries, representing roughly 9%. Over the last 20 years, only Turkey and Morocco have maintained a positive agricultural balance. In the majority of the Mediterranean partners, though, the agricultural sector has become less significant in Euro-Mediterranean trade, and food dependency has increased, partly because their concentration on high added-value production has hit cereals hard. Another restricting factor which has made it necessary for crops to be adjusted to local resources is the water consumption of intensive agriculture in some regions. Finally, there are various aspects which combine to put agriculture in an even weaker commercial position: population growth, variations in technological development, and deficiencies in the development and transfer of technology. If this trend worsens, it will have a serious effect on the economy of the Mediterranean countries, with possible social and political repercussions.

The success of a Mediterranean free trade area also depends on the willingness of all the partners, including the EU Member States, to reform their trade policies in order to avoid imbalances which penalise the weaker partners. Take the experience of NAFTA – the North American Free Trade Agreement. Here, the removal of tariff barriers to agricultural trade has increased imports of low-cost food from the United States to Mexico, damaging small farmers who are not in a position to compete with foreign products or to buy them. Similarly, the drop in world cereal prices, caused by the subsidies given by developed countries, has driven many South

American countries to replace part of their cereal production with fruit and vegetables for export. In many countries in the continent there is a growing demand for cereals, which is directed abroad, while local crops of fruit and vegetables increase, with harmful consequences for the environment, since these crops are concentrated in arid or semi-arid valleys which depend on artificial irrigation, to the detriment of the soil and water resources. In this area the primary role of the Mediterranean Committee is to ensure that the guidelines set out by ministers are translated into concrete action.

In order to lessen the tendency for initiatives to become dissipated, and to make them as effective as possible, they should be set out in a list of priorities drawn up at the beginning of each year or within the framework cooperation programmes that already exist. This would encourage the partners and restrict the initiatives to projects of a sufficient scale and with a real impact on the partnership's progress. Rationalising the initiatives in this way might also allow the Euro-Mediterranean Committee to promote the visibility of the Euro-Mediterranean Partnership. Some key sectors, such as transport, water, energy and telecommunications deserve special attention. If the initiative clearly contributes to the market's economic development and integration, it should receive the label of 'measure of regional interest', regardless of the amount of MEDA funding allotted to it.

The Euro-Mediterranean Committee ought to carry out regular overall assessments of the other activities in the process (reports on meetings and seminars) and of the framework cooperation programmes currently being implemented, apart from the actual cooperation projects, in cooperation with the MED Committee, the Commission and the Mediterranean part-ners. Although in the short term it may not be possible to change current meetings practices (where the responsibility for chairing meetings and organ-ising the work belongs solely to the European section in Brussels), the nature of these procedures, on the face of it rather one-sided and incompatible with the spirit of the Euro-Mediterranean Partnership, seems in need of change. This could be given concrete expression, in particular, through proper consultation of the partners in the south over the drafting of the agenda. Finally, the next reform of the Euro-Mediterranean Partnership should reconcile the need for greater involvement of the Barcelona Committee in the decision-making process with greater procedural flexibility. Integration and the achievement of the goals set for 2010 are what is at stake.

3.2.5 The influence of the Committee of the Regions

Jos CHABERT
President of the Committee of the Regions

In moving from the second to the third millennium, Europe is now going through a transitional period during which certain phenomena no longer exist whilst others have yet to emerge. At the same time, some phenomena which were regarded as being still on the horizon have turned out to be already upon us. Earlier commitments which brought stability to the EU in the past and certainties on which we could rely have faded away. For nearly half a century European politics were dominated by the threat of Communism in Central and Eastern Europe and indeed in the Soviet Union. After the cold war period Europe is now in the throes of change. Indeed, changes are taking place in a whole range of fields – cultural, technological, economic and political. New challenges demand new structures.

Three major trends are in evidence in Europe:

1. "Integration" is the order of the day. The Latin word "integratio" implies restoration of a whole or a unity. Integration is the opposite of stagnation and decay. Integration, in the sense of "renewal" and "recreation of a whole", becomes vital if, in the absence of integration, the various parts of an entity are either no longer able to exist or cannot exist in a meaningful way. Everything was set in train here by the Schuman Declaration of 9 May 1950, just five years after the end of the Second World War. Europeans wanted at long last to be able to enjoy peace.

The organisation now known as the "European Union" evolved from the European Coal and Steel Community. The organisation thus moved from being a purely economic community to a political community, the form of which now falls somewhere between that of a confederation of states and a federal state. Europe had to embark upon this step as national states and national economies no longer had sufficient room for manoeuvre to enable them to find solutions to many of the problems facing Europe. A number of examples of such problems spring to mind, namely:

– problems of such a magnitude that they cannot be tackled by individual states using the possibilities and resources available to them;

- problems which are of a cross-border nature;
- problems involving the joint interests of several states; in such cases joint solutions offer the only prudent approach and the only approach which is likely to be successful.

We are facing an increasing trend towards "Europeanisation".

2. The process of change in eastern Europe began in Poland in the early 1980s. The Solidarnosc trade union – which was founded 20 years ago – demanded civil rights and liberties and political change and it also urged Poland to adopt a more self-confident approach in its relations with the communist superpower to the east. The Hungarian government, for its part, took steps – tentative at first and subsequently increasingly bolder – towards closer relations with the west and, in the summer of 1989, it finally opened up its borders with Austria. The dam had been breached. The Berlin Wall, in turn, was breached on 9 November 1989. We are all familiar with the rest of the story. The break-up of the "Cold War" eastern and western blocs will lead to the establishment of a much larger European Union in the next few years. This development has become clearer since the Nice Summit of December 2000.

3. The collapse of ideological bloc policy in eastern Europe, backed up by increasing Europeanisation, have however also brought about an additional phenomenon.

A large variety of campaigns have been launched, particularly in eastern Europe, to achieve ethnic and regional sovereignty and autonomy. This represented, and continues to represent, a swing from one extreme to another. It is a move away from a large-scale, common ideological identity to small separate identities.

In western Europe, too, there is a growing awareness of regional origins; such an awareness serves as a counterbalance to the ever-present globalisation of both the economy and communication systems. People are rediscovering their own regional cultures and regional linguistic differences. An awareness of individual, particular, different and unique identities and a consciousness of homeland and origin leads, directly or indirectly, to a renunciation of large-scale structures.

We are therefore also facing an increasing trend towards regionalisation!

We must not merely seek to understand these developments. We also have to take up the new challenges. We have to recognise that *regionalisation* and *Europeanisation* are the new reference points in Europe; they represent the new political criteria for defining identity and loyalty.

What I am referring to here is identity with one's own region, backed up by a loyalty towards Europe.

We are moving increasingly towards a "Europe of the Regions". This is not merely a vision – it is a reality. In this new Europe all levels of governments (Europe, Member States, Regions, Municipalities) should have their fields of competence clearly defined: the citizen should know precisely who is responsible for what.

The very clear trend towards greater decentralisation, regionalisation and federalisation in most EU Member States has made it imperative for regional authorities, too, to be more closely involved in EU decision-making. The demand for this course of action has come in particular from those EU Member States which have traditionally had a strong federal structure (Germany, Austria and Belgium); this course of action is, however, increasingly being advocated by those Member States which have hitherto been characterised by a highly centralised administration.

Although Europe's regions and local authorities were already represented by the Council of European Municipalities and Regions (established in 1984) and the Assembly of European Regions (established in 1985), it was not until the Treaty of Maastricht was adopted in 1992 that the Committee of the Regions was set up as an advisory body for the EU. The Committee of the Regions held its first plenary session in the spring of 1994.

The composition of the Committee of the Regions

The Committee of the Regions has 222 members who, under the provisions of the EC Treaty, "may not be bound by any mandatory instructions". The number of members may be increased to 344 following enlargement of the EU.

The Committee's members are appointed by the Council, acting on proposals from the respective Member States, for a four-year term of office. CoR members are thus not directly elected to serve on the Committee by a popular vote; they do, however, under the newly-adopted Treaty of Nice, have to be elected representatives in their own regions or local entities. EU Member States employ their own criteria when deciding on the composition of their national delegations to the Committee of the Regions.

Many CoR members represent large area authorities, such as the Spanish and Italian regions or the German Länder. A large number of members are also drawn from smaller area authorities, such as provinces or districts. The remainder of the Committee's members – who constitute the largest group – represent local authorities. These members include both the mayors of major European cities, such as Turin and Barcelona, and also councillors representing small local authorities. The distribution of members within the respective national delegations varies considerably. The German and Spanish members of the Committee are drawn primarily from representatives of the German Länder and the Spanish autonomous communities. In the case of the UK, however, the members of the Committee of the Regions have, up to now, been drawn from representatives of counties and local authorities.

As one will appreciate, therefore, the composition of the Committee of the Regions is far from being uniform. The very heterogeneous nature of its membership does, however, give the Committee its own particular attraction. The Committee represents the combined experience gained at all political levels below that of national states. A point which has to be borne in mind is that it is precisely the members of the Committee of the Regions who have both the task of explaining to the public at local level the regulations and directives drawn up by the EU and subsequently, the task of implementing these provisions. CoR members thus have their fingers on the local pulse when it comes to assessing whether given measures can really be implemented in practice.

As long as the Committee of the Regions does not directly take decisions in respect of EU legislation, but remains rather an advisory body, this lack of a homogeneous composition does not necessarily represent a disadvantage. A more homogeneous membership will only be an important consideration if in the future the CoR actually receives joint-decision making powers under the EU Treaty.

The influence of the Committee of the Regions

The Committee of the Regions, which is an advisory body, seeks to influence the main players in the EU legislative process through its opinions and resolutions, which reflect the views and experience of regional and local authorities in policy areas with a strong regional and/or local content.

The CoR issues opinions in respect of all of the fields on which it is to be consulted under the EU Treaty. The Treaty makes provision for mandatory consultation of the Committee in ten areas which typically come under the responsibility of the regions and local authorities, such as culture, education, regional development, employment, environment. The Committee may also be asked to give its views on any other policy area if the Commission, Council or the European Parliament deems it necessary to consult the Committee (optional consultation). The Committee of the Regions also has the right to issue own-initiative opinions with a view to convincing the Commission of the need to amend existing provisions or to submit new provisions. The CoR focuses on those political issues where it can give an added value and enhance the Union's decision-making process.

The Committee places new issues, which are of particular importance at local and regional level, on the political agenda of the EU.

The Committee is also the guardian of the principle of subsidiarity and the principle of ensuring that legislation is "people-oriented".

The Committee faces a major challenge in issuing its opinions in good time in the course of the legislative process. The Committee receives the Commission's legislative proposals at the same time as do all the other bodies involved, i.e. the European Parliament and the Council. If the Committee is to bring an influence to bear, however, it has to draw up and adopt its opinions as soon as possible. No purpose is served by the Committee drawing attention to particular problems facing the regions and local authorities, and putting forward proposals for improvement, if the European Parliament has already endorsed the Commission's proposal in its first reading, under the codecision procedure. We need to adopt our opinions before members of the European Parliament's committees put forward their proposals for amendments. The Committee is therefore constantly involved in a race against time with the European Parliament. In most cases – but not all – we are able to make known our views to the Parliament and its respective committees in good time. This gives you some idea of the pressures of time which the Committee frequently has to face when drawing up its opinions.

It should be borne in mind that the Committee of the Regions' eight committees, which prepare the opinions to be submitted to the Committee at its plenary session, hold meetings just five times a year, matching the number of plenary sessions. New CoR opinions can therefore be issued only every two months, at the earliest.

The European Parliament, for its part, meets 11 times a year (not including the extraordinary sessions) and its respective committees also meet much more often, thereby enabling the Parliament to carry out its work much more quickly.

The decisions taken by the EU legislative bodies, namely the European Parliament, the Council and the Commission, have an influence on even the most far-flung regions of Europe.

We, the representatives of the EU's regions and local authorities, for our part, will only be able to exert an influence if we are able to convince the legislative bodies of the validity of our arguments and if we are able to back up our opinions, our demands and our rejections – reflecting the views of the regions and local authorities – by first-rate, well-informed arguments and to present our views in a readily comprehensible form.

I do not pretend that the Committee of the Regions has been a perfect institution from the outset. What I will say, however, is that the Committee is becoming ever more effective in exploiting the niche provided for it under the Treaty. All our powers are conferred by grass-roots opinion. We need to make use of these powers in our dealings with the European Parliament, the Council and the Commission.

The aforementioned EU institutions represent the unity of the European Community; the members of the Committee of the Regions – representing, as they do, the diversity of the European Union – constitute a counter-balance to these institutions. The interplay between unity, on the one hand, and diversity, on the other, does, however, serve to enrich policy-making in the EU to a large extent and this aspect will become ever more important in the future.

The responsibility given to the regions and local authorities through the establishment of the Committee of the Regions does of course also mean that it is no longer possible for them to put forward the excuse that they are unaware of everything that is decided in Brussels. Local and regional politicians can no longer easily wriggle out of their responsibilities by main-taining that decisions are being imposed upon them from on high. This is a welcome development!

The Committee of the Regions therefore provides, so to speak, the platform for a dynamic public dialogue with the European Union which gives the EU public the opportunity to bring an influence to bear on what is decided in Brussels. The Committee thus represents the institutional link between the processes of regionalisation and Europeanisation.

An image may help illustrate the need for Europeanisation and regional-isation to proceed in tandem. I like to compare Europe to a large park having wonderful gardens and vistas (Europeanisation) in which, however, there are many different kinds of plants growing which have very different require-ments as regards location, soil and microclimate but which do bring mutual benefit to each other and thereby represent an inseparable entity.

Staying with this image, the task of looking after the variety of flora in the aforementioned park is assumed by the Committee of the Regions in the context of EU policy.

We are constructing a Europe in which respect for our fellow human beings and the environment constitutes the natural basis for everything that we are seeking to do. We have to remember constantly that we are working to promote the interests of people and to enhance the living conditions of everyone living in all the regions of the EU. We are seeking to build a Europe which is aware of its responsibilities for promoting development in the other regions in the world, a Europe which is imbued with humanitarian and democratic ideals and a Europe whose new generation is growing up with the certainty of having common roots, a common heritage and a common future.

3.3 Achievements and prospects of the European People's Party: 1976-2001

3.3.1 Shaping Europe: 25 years of the European People's Party

Wilfried MARTENS
President of the European People's Party and
former Prime Minister of Belgium

Looking back over the past fifty years, European integration has clearly been a success, bringing citizens a range of benefits and providing the nation states and political protagonists with completely novel forms of aligning supranational and inter-state mechanisms. After the repeated failures of 19th century foreign policy instruments, this new form of institutionalised cooperation was a logical – if not self-evident – consequence of two disastrous world wars in Europe. In the Fifties, people's vivid memories of the suffering in the first half of this century allowed steps to be taken that were previously thought impossible.

However, it must also be acknowledged that the success of previous decades and the everyday business of running Europe has lost some of the trademark verve and idealism of the generation that helped found and build the Union. There can be no doubt: times have changed. Generally speaking, war and peace is no longer a burning issue for Europe as it was in the Fifties and Sixties where it was the leitmotif of international and European politics. The fact that people are less concerned with this topic, however, does not mean that it no longer matters. The recent events in the Balkans have reminded us – not for the first time – of the triumph that European integration represents in terms of people living together in peace.

European unification – a Christian Democratic concept

The Christian Democrat politicians of the post-war period contributed greatly to this positive development as they took bold, groundbreaking decisions – and because they had visions for Europe's peoples and nations. The European People's Party is heir to the tradition of those great, visionary statesmen such as Robert Schuman, Alcide De Gasperi and Konrad Adenauer. Personal experiences during two World Wars drove this generation to strive for peaceful coexistence. It was, above all, Robert Schuman's sensational proposals that instigated the giant steps towards integration in the Fifties. Coming from the Lorraine, he was particularly interested in Franco-German relations. His personal efforts and the firm conviction with which he defended his proposals for a Paris Treaty in 1950, thus laying the foundation for European integration, shall never be forgotten. Personal friendships and shared political convictions were the very life-blood of this endeavour. At its heart lay the united struggle for a federal, peaceful Europe.

Institutionalised cooperation between Christian Democrats in Europe goes back a long way, to the Twenties and the founding of the Secrétariat International des Partis Démocratiques d'Inspiration Chrétienne (SIPDIC). In contrast to the Socialist International, which preceded national parties and in many cases provided the impetus for their establishment, it was the national parties who called for an international Christian Democratic movement. Don Luigi Sturzo, the founder of the Italian *Partito Popolare Italiano* (PPI), launched the first initiative. At the time, the members were chiefly Catholic political parties, such as the French *Parti Démocrate Populaire* (PDP) or the German centrist parties. The last SIPDIC Congress chaired by Konrad Adenauer was held in October 1932 in Cologne. The final communiqué adopted by the Congress demanded the gradual dismantling of trade barriers, and raised the ideal of a wholly unified Europe.

After the Second World War, the European Christian Democrats found it relatively easy to return to the international stage. The cast, including such figures as Konrad Adenauer, was unchanged, and the need for cooperation was greater than ever. In 1947 the constituent congress of the *Nouvelles Equipes Internationales* (NEI) was held in Chaudfontaine, Belgium. The NEI was the first international organisation to admit a German delegation as a member with equal rights. The Christian Democratic Union attended the second Congress in Luxembourg, under the impressive leadership of Konrad Adenauer. Cooperation between the Germans and the other Christian Democrats grew into trust. During the years 1955-1965 the NEI continued to facilitate an exchange of views between the Christian Democrat parties. However, its unwieldy structure stifled the euphoria of the early years.

In May 1965, the Bureau decided to transform the NEI into the *European Union of Christian Democrats* (EUCD); the Congress endorsed the decision that same year. The focus of EUCD cooperation was reaching agreement on the Christian Democrat doctrine for joint action with the aim of uniting Europe. However, traditions and approaches differed greatly between the member parties. Therefore, it was necessary to follow a programme and to define common positions.

Foundation and organisation of the EPP

Over the past 25 years, organised cooperation between parties at the European level has become increasingly significant. While the Fifties and Sixties were particularly defined by individual leading politicians' personal contacts and initiatives, integration was spurred on in the mid-Seventies by the establishment of supranational parties. These developed out of preparations for the first direct elections to the European Parliament in 1979. The European People's Party was always to be found at the forefront. Once established, it was to outdo all previous forms of integration and cooperation.

After the Heads of State and Government of the 1974 EC decided to hold the first direct elections to the European Parliament in 1979, many Christian Democrats called for the founding of a European party. The EUCD structure with its pan-European remit did not fit the bill. The new organisation was to be bound closely to the structures of the European Parliament. The necessary steps were taken swiftly: in September 1975 an ad-hoc *European Party* working party was established, and, through close cooperation between myself and Hans-August Luecker, a draft EPP Statute was submitted to the EUCD *Political Committee* on 20 January 1976.

The EPP was formally established during a constituent meeting of the *Political Bureau* on 8 July 1976 in Luxembourg. The following parties participated: *Christelijke Volkspartij* (CVP) and *Parti Social Chrétien* (PSC) from Belgium, *Christlich Demokratische Union* (CDU) and *Christlich-Soziale Union* (CSU) from the Federal Republic of Germany, *Centre des Démocrates Sociaux* (CDS) from France, *Fine Gael* (FG) from Ireland, *Democrazia Cristiana* (DC) from Italy, *Christlich-Soziale Volkspartei* (CSV) from Luxembourg, *Katholieke Volkspartij* (KVP), *Christelijk Historische Unie* (CHU) and the *Antirevolutionaire Partij* (ARP) from the Netherlands. The Belgian Prime Minister Leo Tindemans was elected President by universal suffrage. In February 1978, the Christian Democrat EP Group decided to rename itself the *Group of the European People's Party*. A few weeks later, the EPP presented its debut political programme at its first Congress in Brussels.

The Eighties were defined by ongoing efforts to develop the EPP's programmatic basis with the intent of furthering European integration. At that time, the generation most involved in reconstruction, personified by Helmut Kohl, was deeply influenced by Second World War experiences and saw European unification as the antidote to war. The German CDU, under its longstanding chairman Helmut Kohl, was a chief driving force behind this process and had considerable say owing to its position as the largest party in the EPP. In fact, Kohl was the only member among the group of Heads of Government to be present from the outset in his dual capacity as Head of Government and party leader – his contribution was often of decisive importance.

Since 1989, the EPP has consistently pursued the occasionally controversial aim of integrating Conservative parties. The reasons for this are easily explained. Six-member Europe's landscape of political parties was no longer in tune with the realities of a Europe of twelve States or more. There is no significantly-sized Christian Democrat party in many of the new candidate countries. If the EPP did not want to be sidelined, its only option was to cooperate with other parties of the same political leaning. The concept of a people's party, inherent to the EPP name, increasingly gained significance. It reflects the fact that there are different political traditions in Europe's different countries, which no European party can afford to ignore.

By 1983, the Greek *Nea Demokratia* (ND), a party without a Christian Democratic tradition but with a clearly pro-European stance, had joined the EPP. The need for EPP action increased after 1988: after Spain's accession to the EC, the Spanish members of the Conservative *Alianza Popular* (AP) joined the European Democratic Group, composed of Danish and British Conservatives. Therefore, Spain was only represented in the EPP Group by a single member of the *Unió Democratica de Catalunya* (UDC). As the AP members did not feel particularly comfortable in the Conservative group, they expressed interest in joining the EPP Group. After the 1989 European elections – in the meantime, the AP had changed its name to *Partido Popular* (PP) – the PP members joined the EPP Group. The PP became a full member of the EPP in 1991 after winning over a number of sceptics, in particular the Catalans and Basques.

Immediately following the 1989 European elections, the British Conservative MEPs put in a request for EPP membership. The EPP Bureau decided to refuse membership due to Margaret Thatcher's policies on Europe. However, cooperation was to be intensified and a decision would be taken two years later. The British and Danish Conservative MEPs joined the EPP Group in May 1992.

Then, in March 1995, the Danish *Konservative Folkeparti* (KF), the Finnish *Kansallinen Kokoomus* (KOK), the Swedish *Moderata Samlingspartiet* and the *Österreichische Volkspartei* (ÖVP) became full members of the EPP. Thus there are already a large number of Conservative parties who are full members of the EPP. Moreover, the Norwegian *Høyre* is an allied member of the EPP, and the members of the British *Conservative Party* and the French *Rassemblement pour la République* are allied members of the Group of the

European People's Party (Christian Democrats) and European Democrats (EPP-ED Group) in the European Parliament. *Forza Italia* were allied members of the EPP-ED Group until December 1999, when Forza Italia became a full member of the EPP. We have also welcomed many of our Central and Eastern European sister parties to the EPP as associate members. Most of these parties are the governing political forces in their countries.

It is difficult to adopt final positions on European policies due to the categorical divide between 'Conservative' and 'Christian Democrat'. The Scandinavian Conservatives have nothing in common with the British Conservatives' socio-political visions or their attitude towards Europe. Furthermore, it would be misleading to describe the Christian Democrats as a homogeneous group. Each national party draws on different traditions – that is true in all political camps (with the exception of the Communists until 1989). Therefore, there was more at stake for the EPP during this process than admitting a small number of parties and expanding the EPP spectrum. For the EPP had finally reached a crossroads by the end of the Eighties. The Christian Democrats could continue to 'keep to themselves' and thus risk becoming insignificant, failing to meet the demand for a people's party from small Christian Democrat parties, particularly in Scandinavia. However, the EPP wanted to attain a strong programmatic consensus that would also enable political organisation. Today's documents, forged after heated rounds of debate – the Statute, the manifesto and the action programme for the European Parliament 1999-2004 election period – show that the EPP did not lose substance by widening its scope. Quite the contrary: the EPP's unanimously developed strategy, backed by a broad consensus among a wide spectrum of member parties, is unique in Europe. It is the basis for our political endeavours and guarantees the majorities needed to implement our policy concepts for the European citizens. The XIV EPP Congress in Berlin (January 2001) showed that the EPP could develop far-reaching political programmes in an atmosphere of harmony and intense political debate. Expanding the EPP base has not undermined this increasingly vital approach. The EPP itself is a unique construction in European terms; it has surpassed any known models of integration or cooperation. The EPP is a party in the true sense of the word. Of course, the EPP cannot and does not want to be a party in the national mould, but sees itself as a federative party, drawing together its national member parties, for the purpose of organising them into an active unit at the European level. Thus, it allows member parties to acquire a supranational dimension beyond the reach of a national party, beyond the scope of the nation state. What is truly remarkable is the development of supranational opinion-making, decision-taking and actions. This supranationalism is chiefly manifested in the way that elections and votes, as a rule, are carried out by an absolute majority. The EPP never accorded great importance to the principle of unanimity as practised by various other existing party coalitions. The composition of the bodies also reinforces the supranational aspect: firstly, weighting is carried out in relation to the number of EP Group members, secondly, the bodies are composed of European parliamentary members and officials.

It is instantly clear from the EPP's structure that it is not a run-of-the-mill party, but a federation of various national member parties. For some years, individuals have also been able to attain membership but do not generally have any great influence. Party leaders and the international secretaries of the member parties are the main protagonists in the activity of a supranational party such as the EPP. The revised Statute, however, will ensure greater grassroots participation – the *executive committee* composed of *ex officio* members has been dissolved; instead, the Bureau has been allocated further powers. It is composed of delegated members of the national member parties, (ex officio) *Presidency* members, the heads of the national EPP-ED Group delegations, the Presidents of the member parties and unions, European Commissioners (if they belong to a member party) and the EP President and Vice-Presidents (if they belong to a member party).

In reality, the *Bureau* is the chief party body as it decides, among other things, which new members are to be admitted and maintains an even keel between party and group. The EPP *Presidency*'s main function is to ensure the party's constant, political presence, to guarantee the implementation of the Bureau's decisions and to monitor the work of the General Secretariat. The Congress elects the *Presidency* members for a three-year period. The EPP Congress is held at least every two years and consists of elected or designated delegates of the member parties. While previously the Congress could only make proposals for documents or petitions, since 1988 it has also been able to table amendments to Congress documents with a majority.

For some years now, the EPP has held '*summits*', where EPP members who are Heads of Government, for example, members in coalition governments or opposition leaders, participate in an exchange of views. The EPP Presidency, the President of the EU Commission and the President of the European Parliament also attend this debate if they belong to EPP member parties. These informal meetings – generally held just before the meetings of the European Council – allow the EPP to identify an early common position on current political issues.

One EPP particularity, compared to other European parties, is the marked distinction made between party and group, which is underlined by having a physically separate General Secretariat. The EPP is the only party to have a Secretariat located outside the European Parliament; this is a major step that other European party coalitions have not yet taken.

Like national parties, the EPP also encompasses a range of organisations, such as *the Youth of the EPP*, the *European Democratic Students*, the *European*

Union of Christian Democrat Workers, the *EPP/EUCD Women's Section*, the *European Local and Regional Government Association*, the *European Independent Business Association* and the *European Senior Citizens' Union*.

The Christian Democrats found it easier to broach real, supranational cooperation than other political groupings, due to their federalist political approach. Federalism and subsidiarity have always played a key role in Christian Democratic history.

Indeed, it was the shared political view of federalist subsidiarity that fostered a significant consensus in many areas of European politics, enabling the EPP to present a united front. Over the past 25 years or so of its existence – together with the EPP Group in the European Parliament – it has continually breathed fresh life into the process of European integration. The EPP does not shy away from intense programmatic debates. It has never limited itself to superficial election campaigning but to this very day continues to boldly tackle socio-political topics.

The European People's Party must develop visions for Europe's future.

The younger generations have never experienced the horrors of war – even if they are aware that savage, barbaric wars are still being waged in Europe outside the European Union. This generation's different experiences means that Europe must be created anew for young people. Today, especially, Europe needs to take new, brave steps and keep its eyes on the goal, amid the distractions of everyday politics.

But what is the goal? What is our future concept of Europe? Should we continue developing the institutions or do we need a new overall concept for Europe? A concept that will not only safeguard the efficiency of the institutions but also provide solutions for the essential tasks of the future: shaping a Europe of democracy, transparency and subsidiarity.

The European parties are a vital forum for discussing and answering these questions. Compared to national parties, their scope for action is still limited and they have less influence on constitutional and legislative development due to the Union's institutional structures. At the same time, however, the European Parliament's powers and confidence have increased appreciably over the past years. This extension of powers has clearly opened up new possibilities for the European parties and brought new challenges. There are more opportunities to intervene than ever – due to the new majorities in the European Parliament. It should be clear, however, that the European parties are not competing against the national parties – on the contrary: they broaden the scope of the latter and represent their interests at the European level. In view of the European Parliament's growing powers, one might even refer to the 'Europeanisation' of the democratic party system. This process is slow to gather momentum. The European parties must shoulder new responsibilities and take action. The EU Nice summit, however, has added fresh fuel to the process by expanding Article 191 ECT on European parties. The new wording has made it possible to develop a statute for European parties, providing them with a legal framework and financial resources. This will have a lasting effect on the politicisation of European decision-taking processes.

It is time to engage in open discussion about Europe's future once more. The imminent enlargement will need more than the reform of the Union's current institutions. We must also answer the question of the extent to which the Union can be enlarged, which necessarily begs the question of where Europe's borders will be. And we must also ask whether there will be further possibilities for cooperation in Europe outside of the context of the Union. In this way, Europe could eventually consider the possibilities of institutionalised cooperation with Russia, the Ukraine and possibly even Belarus.

At the turn of the 21st century, Europe faces many new challenges – all the protagonists are aware of this. The stakes are nothing less than ensuring peace for Europe and finding common answers to our societies' problems. All this is to be enabled by a decision-taking mechanism that will provide faster, more flexible solutions, closer to the citizens and the problems of our times. It is a formidable task. We must join forces to accomplish it.

That is precisely why the process of European integration cannot afford to run out of steam and why now is the time to discuss and implement future reform proposals. The European People's Party will play its part.

3.3.2   The future of the European People's Party

Alejandro AGAG LONGO
Secretary-General of the European People's Party
and Member of the EPP-ED Group in
the European Parliament

Paul Claudel once said that in order to discover how something ends, we must look at how it began. If we go back to the beginnings of European integration, it is clear that the spirit of the European People's Party (EPP) and that of its founding fathers played a key role in inspiring and driving what, today, is the most ambitious attempt yet to pool values, ideals and shared objectives.

Throughout its fifty-year history, the EPP has left its mark on each and every crucial stage of this shared project. Our founding fathers, Schuman, Adenauer and De Gasperi, showed that it was possible to deal with the problems of others without renouncing one's own. Out of such a sentiment was born a logical desire to build peace and prosperity in Europe. Again, it was a majority of leaders from our political family who, meeting in Maastricht, decided to sow the seeds of what is now our single currency, to give the European project the stability that an undertaking of this magnitude requires.

But if we had to single out one area in which our political family has particularly distinguished itself in this lengthy process, it would have to be its trailblazing role in the process of European integration.

At the XIVth Congress, held in Berlin recently, we imbued this role and this spirit with new vitality. At this Congress, the EPP confirmed its dominance in the European political arena by anticipating and interpreting the approaching new reality. Drawing on the traditional values that have inspired our political actions from the outset, we have been able to adapt them to a New Europe that, now more than ever before, needs new ideas and new answers to the challenges thrown up by the new century.

In Berlin, then, the EPP began a process of profound ideological renewal designed to ensure that it remains at the forefront of European integration. Today we can boast that we are the European party *par excellence*, because we have always been able to adapt to change and to see it as an opportunity for the advancement of our ideas and of society as a whole. Such was the spirit that informed our approach to a Congress that was a showcase for our project for the twenty-first century. President Martens summed this up brilliantly when he stated that the European People's Party must reclaim the middle ground and shape the New Europe, as it had successfully shaped the old one.

The Congress saw a consensus, indeed almost unanimous support, in favour of embracing the core principles of the 'reformist centre' as the guide for our political action over the coming decades. Prosperity, solidarity, liberty and justice: these are the values that shape our vision of Europe. They are the values that we share and which, by adopting the document, 'A Union of Values', with unprecedented levels of support, we have embraced as our own.

This document advocates a revitalised centrism, and claims this political space as our own. It was conceived not just with a view to the next few years, but to addressing issues such as biotechnology and electronic democracy, to hand over to the youth of today the baton of responsibility for building a European Union worthy of the name – a Europe that is united, free and prosperous.

It is our responsibility to ensure that European integration continues and that it is not watered down. For this reason, we support competitive federalism as a flexible structure within which Europe may advance. It is our responsibility to ensure that the information society becomes the opportunity society, and for this reason we support the reform and modernisation of economic structures and an open and competitive approach to the knowledge society.

But above all, it is our responsibility to ensure that Europe is built on the values and principles in which we believe: people, above all, economic freedom, solidarity and subsidiarity.

Europe, today, is at a crucial juncture in its history. Nice marked a decisive step towards the united Europe we all want. It is certainly true that this is a step towards the unknown, but it would be a terrible mistake to look to the future with apprehension or fear.

The dream for which the founders of our party fought, of a Europe of peace, prosperous and united in the respect for the dignity of all human beings, cannot be confined to a limited number of countries. Covering half of the continent will allow Europe to be reunited with itself. A wider Europe, more diverse and, probably, more difficult to manage, but a Europe capable of leading the new globalised project that the twenty-first century needs.

Today, our enlargement strategy has reached fruition. Ours was an innovative strategy – from the mid-90s we began to integrate into our structure our sister parties in Central and Eastern Europe. We can affirm, with legitimate pride, that we are the party of enlargement, and that we now have the opportunity and the responsibility to reaffirm ourselves as the first and true European party.

In this new context, the European Union must provide itself with the structural elements necessary to serve as a backbone and to give it the cohesion necessary to look to the future on the basis of shared objectives. In the future, the European political parties will be called on to carry out this important work, as was finally recognised at the Nice European Council. The European political parties' statute, which will shortly become a reality, marks the culmination of our hopes for formal acknowledgement in the Union's institutional framework, and will transform completely our capacity for political action and give us real opportunities to carry out our political project.

This project, which takes into account the increasing obligations of the European People's Party in an open world, and its growing responsibility in the new world order that is starting to emerge, strengthens the international dimension of our political family. In a global world, political parties must have global ties, global partners and global answers to humanity's problems. In this respect, our gradual integration with the European Democrat Union and our active involvement in the Christian Democratic International will allow us to develop and enhance our presence and our cooperation with centrist, Christian Democratic and popular parties in other parts of the world, especially Latin America, showing that the message of the reformist and humanist centre is and must be universal.

Our task, now, is to set ourselves ambitious objectives that will allow us to convert today's uncertainties into tomorrow's opportunities. The EPP's vision for a Europe for the next decade is one that is open, dynamic and optimistic – a Europe that offers more opportunities for all, and that allows us to reclaim the tradition of change, innovation and progress that has been an integral part of Europe's history.

With the confidence gained from the last European elections in June 1999, and the security of observing how many of the proposals embodying our values have become part of the Community *acquis*, the EPP is facing the new century, with the centre as the point of reference, with the information society as a tool for creating opportunities, and with people as the ultimate focus of political action.

We are aware, however, that the only way to move forward and capitalise on the opportunities provided by the New Europe is through being in government in the Member States. We must be capable of transferring to the European Council the majority so brilliantly obtained in the European Parliament. For this reason, we believe that the centre is the natural political space from which we can use our ideas and our programme to end the Socialist majority in the governments of the European Union before the next European elections in 2004.

The political centre is the natural space to which we must look for the answers and solutions to citizens' new concerns and demands. In the last analysis, the political centre, together with dialogue and moderation as tools of political action, is the only means of achieving large majorities in government.

Somebody once said that failure is proof not of the rashness of the desire, but of its weakness. Our strength to date has been none other than the strongest possible belief that it is possible to attain and extend the dream of peace and prosperity that is the European Union. This has been and remains the key to our success and, in the future, will continue to be what defines us and supports us in our function as an instrument at the service of all the citizens of Europe.

3.3.3 The European People's Party – a political family reinvents itself

Klaus WELLE
Secretary-General of the EPP-ED Group in the
European Parliament

From fringe group to the strongest force

The European elections in June 1999 made the Group of the European People's Party into the strongest force for the first time since direct elections were introduced. Many observers were surprised. This little political bombshell exploded in the midst of the newspaper leaders about the new Social Democratic era, the triumph of the Third Way and the end of Christian Democracy.

A few weeks before the elections, the *Financial Times* made the resounding announcement that the EPP would become marginalised while the Party of European Socialists would achieve a surprise victory. Instead, the reverse is now true: the European People's Party and the Liberals have formed an alliance that is proving a brilliant success with the election in the first round of Nicole Fontaine as the new President of the European Parliament.

The story behind this story has not really been told yet. The outcome of the European elections is not purely accidental. It shows that after ten years spent working towards integration the EPP is now able to achieve a structural majority, thanks to tenaciously applying a long-term political strategy and resolving considerable internal conflicts.

The 1980s

In the 1980s, the Social Democrats increasingly established themselves as the strongest force in the European Parliament, managing to increase their number of seats from 112 to 180, giving a percentage increase from 27.6% to 34.8%. Meanwhile the EPP had to face a further relative decline, hitting rock bottom in 1989 with 121 seats and a percentage share of only 23%.

Even in the days before the Assembly was directly elected, the share of the Christian Democratic Group had been declining systematically and continuously from the nearly 50% it had reached in the 1950s. The EPP was heading towards marginalisation. It had no partner in the United Kingdom and until 1989 it did not have many representatives in Spain and was not a strong force in France either.

The 1990s

In the 1990s, this downhill trend did not just stop, it actually reversed.

In the space of just ten years, the share of the European People's Party rose from 23% to 37%. This is even more evident if we look at the trend in the absolute number of seats. Between 1989 and 1999 the Social Democrats' share stood still at 180 seats, while the European People's Party increased its number of seats from 121 to 233, i.e. almost doubled it.

How do we explain this dramatic increase? After all, it was in the 1990s that Democrazia Cristiana (DCI), one of the pillars of European Christian Democracy together with the Benelux Christian Democrats and the German parties, collapsed. The Christian Democrats of the Netherlands and Belgium were in a state of acute crisis and had been defeated, as had the German government. So this increase needs explaining.

If the European People's Party had kept to the same membership as before 1989, it would now account for fewer than 100 Members of the European Parliament. More than half of these (53) would have come from the German parties. Sixty per cent of members of the EPP-ED Group come from parties that did not belong to the family before 1 January 1989.

Only 19 of these 135 members come from parties from the new EU Member States of Austria, Sweden and Finland. Less than 10% represent traditionally Christian Democratic parties. In short, the EPP-ED has become the strongest force not because its traditional member parties have become stronger or because it has found itself highly successful partners in the new Member States, but because it has managed to bring together the civic forces of the European Union in a large people's party.

More and more parties have joined the group: Partido Popular (Spain, 89), the Conservative Party (UK, 92), Det Konservative Folkeparti (Denmark, 92), Parti Républicain (France, 94, now Démocratie Libérale), Österreichische Volkspartei (Austria, 95), Moderaterna (Sweden, 95), Kristdemokraterna (Sweden, 95), Kansallinen Kokoomus (Finland, 95), Partido Social Democrata (Portugal, 96), Forza Italia (Italy, 98), and, finally, Rassemblement pour la République (France, 99).

That has not only removed but more than made up for the weaknesses in the large Member States. In Germany, Spain, the United Kingdom and Italy, the number of members of the EPP-ED Group now actually exceeds the already very high group average of 37.2%. In Italy, the collapse of Democrazia Cristiana has been offset in full.

Reasons for this process

Christian Democratic people's parties were born under very specific histori-cal circumstances. They came into being only when the church and the state were engaged in deep conflict and when the church also took the offensive.

The predecessors of the Christian Democratic people's parties of Belgium and the Netherlands came into being in reaction to Liberal governments' attempts in the 1880s and 1890s drastically to reduce the role of the church in education. The German Centre party emerged and gained strength as a collective Catholic movement opposed to the Protestant state.

Faced with the same situation and while awaiting the rapid restoration of the monarchy, the French Catholic church decided not to enter into conflict with the state. With the brief exception of the MRP, the Christian Demo-cratic movement always remained numerically weak there.

Christian Democratic people's parties in the true sense of the term could never become established in the state-church countries of northern Europe, where religious and secular leadership were combined in the person of the ruler. The Christian-denomination parties of northern Europe emerged from the conflicts between small religious minorities and the state, which is why they remained marginal for a long time. Yet the very recent Bondevik gov-ernment in Norway, and especially the Swedish Kristdemokraterna led by Alf Svensson, are making it more and more clear that it is possible to gain markedly broader support.

For all these reasons the Christian Democratic EPP was faced with the alter-native of either opening its doors to like-minded political parties or becoming a 'regional party' in the six founding Member States of the Euro-pean Union.

Had it chosen the second option, we would have had a Scandinavian party model in the European Union. There would have been a dominant Social Democratic party, supplemented by Green and left-wing parties, with a civic camp split into Christian Democrats, Conservatives and Liberals, and in which differences could always have been exploited by the Social Democrats on specific issues.

Furthermore, the EPP parties would not, of course, have been able to con-tinue being the prime movers in the process of European integration, as they had always been since the days of Adenauer, De Gasperi and Schuman.

So there certainly were reasons for this strategy of openness; but how did it become able to gain majority support? Earlier attempts at rapprochement, for example by the British Conservatives, had been rejected, such as their request for membership of the European Union of Christian Democrats in 1965 or the attempt in the early and mid-1970s to found a European Democratic Party open to Christian Democratic and Conservative parties.

Without attempting to explain the process in full here, we can certainly say that the acceptance of the Partido Popular in the group and then in the party had a bandwagon effect. The internal majority view shifted in favour of the German concept of what the European People's Party should stand for, namely bringing together Christian Social and free-liberal traditions as well as conservative values in a single party. The fact that the DCI became weaker at the same time doubled this effect.

It is certainly not by chance that this EPP model corresponds in every respect to the story of the foundation of the Partido Popular and the CDU/CSU.

After the war, the Germans had to bring these different traditions together in order to form a Union party of Catholics and Protestants. Between the wars, the non-socialist Protestants had been organised in Liberal and Conservative parties, which they now disavowed where possible. The Partido Popular was formed from the Conservative Alianza Popular and small Liberal and Christian Democratic splinter parties.

Every time a party that was not traditionally Christian Democratic was incorporated, this increased the majority for that political line and drove opponents of it further into the minority.

Is the new EPP stable?

Pauline Green, Chairman of the PES Group during the last legislative term, said after the European elections that in fact the EPP Group was not a group at all but consisted of two groups, a Conservative majority (!) and a Christian Democratic minority, and that it was bound to fall apart. Her press spokesman distributed diagrams based on the same compelling logic to show that the Group of the Party of European Socialists remained the strongest force in spite of its disastrous electoral defeat.

Although it is easy enough to regard this as both a psychological and a political strategy to come to terms with electoral defeat, yet the underlying question remains a real one: how stable is a political force that has recreated itself over the past 10 years, that is part of a family to which 60% of MEPs did not even belong just over ten years ago? Will the group prove unstable and eventually disintegrate?

One first yardstick can be the extent to which the new partners have also become integrated in the EPP party. Membership of the EPP party demands not only recognition of the 1992 Athens Basic Programme and the Statutes, but also acceptance of majority decisions. In the EPP party, all issues except amendments to the Statutes are decided by a simple majority, including the comprehensive electoral programmes for the European elections.

Of the 135 members from parties that only joined the EPP Group after 1 January 1989, 82 now also belong to the EPP party through their national parties. Of them, 53, basically the British Conservatives and the French Démocratie Libérale and Gaullists, are only allies under Article 5(b) of the group's Rules of Procedure. If the EPP-ED Group is to be stable despite its size, a key factor will be the consolidation of these alliances.

Group members under Article 5(b)

In this respect, William Hague's participation in summits of EPP party leaders since June 1998 is an important event. It means that without formally becoming a member, the leader of the British Conservatives has broken with a major taboo. The picture painted for many years of the British as being allied with the group but having nothing in common with the 'transnational party' is no longer accurate. That means, however, that the EPP party itself is also questioning this taboo.

William Hague has also played a most constructive role in the rapprochement between the European People's Party and the European Democratic Union, which have been cooperating very extensively since 1 April 2000. The most visible result of this cooperation is the closure of the EDU office in its Vienna headquarters and its move into the offices of the European People's Party.

All the signs suggest, therefore, that the Conservatives are not just in favour of the existing alliance but are even trying to deepen it.

When they joined the group in summer 1999, the French Gaullists broke with a more than 35-year-long tradition of having their own group in the European Parliament. President Chirac's European policy, no doubt also inspired to a considerable extent by Michel Barnier, the French EU Commissioner responsible for institutional questions, is pro-Europe, dynamic and entirely compatible with EPP policy. The French Gaullists' clearly defined stance on social policy also makes them more acceptable to Christian Democratic traditionalists.

In the European Parliament, the Démocratie Libérale Members opted for the EPP again in spite of vigorous Liberal canvassing. They have proposed a key figure, Françoise Grossetête, as Vice-Chairman of the group and are feeling much better politically since the end of their coalition with the Socialists.

There seems little danger, therefore, of any falling off of support on this side of the group.

Athens Group / Schuman Group

The inclusion of the Forza Italia members in June 1998 produced heated reactions, not least among the public. The most tangible result of the emergence of an outnumbered minority was the creation of the 'Athens Group' headed by the Irish party leader John Bruton (Fine Gael). The Athens Group wanted to help uphold the tradition of the Athens Basic Programme.

The fierce internal debates about the attitude towards the new Austrian government and the ÖVP, a member party of the EPP, led to the formation of a new group headed by François Bayrou (UDF), which basically differs little from the Athens Group. Curiously enough that group's leader, John Bruton, together with prominent Benelux Christian Democrats such as Wim van Velzen, Vice-Chairman of the group and Vice-President of the party, had been among those seeking understanding for the line taken by Chancellor Schüssel.

Basically, this group is made up of members of national parties that have a strong democratic competitor on their right and are therefore sceptical about the acceptance of 'Conservative' parties: the CDA in the Netherlands, the CVP and PSC in Belgium, the CSV in Luxembourg, Fine Gael in Ireland, Kristdemokraterna in Sweden, PPI and others in Italy and the Nouvelle UDF in France. Together these parties account for 41 Members of the European Parliament.

These parties, especially the Christian Democrats from Benelux, but also the Italians, dominated the EPP for a long time; today, however, they represent the left wing of the EPP on economic and social issues. All EPP presidents from its creation to the present day have been Benelux Christian Democrats. Representatives of these parties feel they have been driven out of the centre of the party onto the left fringe.

A symptom of this was the Belgian CVP's refusal to allow Wilfried Martens, President of the EPP party and Chairman of the group, to be placed top of the CVP list of candidates for the European elections. Even though there were no doubt internal Belgian reasons for this decision, it was also an unmistakable move away from the policy of openness and enlargement in which Wilfried Martens had played a key role for ten years.

However, these tensions are easing too, and not just because the issue of Austria has been resolved within the party.

In the early 1990s all the Benelux Christian Democrats were still in coalition governments with Socialists. While the Christian Democrats in the Netherlands had to move into opposition as early as 1994, the same fate did not befall the Belgian Christian Democrats until 1999. The Luxembourg Christian Democrats changed to a coalition with the Liberals. This means that all the Benelux Christian Democrats are now the political opponents of Social

Democratic parties.

The election of Jaap de Hoop Scheffer as Chairman of the CDA in the Lower House of the Dutch Parliament, and Stefaan de Clerck as President of the CVP, has given leadership responsibility to representatives of the right wing of these parties who view the trend within the EPP with more composure.

The parties that have moved into opposition have also become more keenly aware that perhaps they need to give deeper thought to the strategic direction of their own policy. The Walloon PSC, on the other hand, is currently torn by internal strife that raises serious questions about the future of the party following the defection of prominent younger members to the Liberals.

Moreover, many leading Benelux Christian Democrats have meanwhile realised that Forza Italia has integrated extremely well in the EPP family. The latest surveys have shown that in its voting pattern the national delegation of Forza Italia is the most loyal of all to the group.

Nordic Conservatives

A few months after their countries joined the European Union in early 1995, the Nordic Conservatives became full members of the EPP. The Danish Conservatives seized the opportunity and joined their friends from Sweden and Finland. That meant a parting of the ways with the British Conservatives, who continued to prefer simply remaining allied members of the group.

For the Nordic Conservatives, accession to the EPP was a cultural shock in several respects. Accustomed to the principle of unanimity that applied in the EDU, they were suddenly confronted with the guillotine of majority voting during the EPP Congress in Madrid at the end of the year. Even the parties in these countries that were most in favour of integration found it difficult to fully join in the euphoria the EPP showed in that respect during the run-up to Amsterdam.

Furthermore, they discovered that they are fairly small parties by European standards, which translates into correspondingly small numbers of delegates, and that their German friends also have other friends of whom they had not even been aware in their EDU activities, such as the Benelux Christian Democrats.

By the time of the 1997 Toulouse Congress they were much better armed. Thanks to taking an active part in the preparatory working groups and forums, they became one of the key actors in the debate on the Christian Democrats' and Conservatives' answer to globalisation, under the heading of 'We are all part of one world', and especially the decisions on the future of the social state.

In the action programme for the 1999-2004 legislative term, which the EPP Congress adopted in Brussels in February 1999, they even saw themselves as clear political winners. Whether this reflected the true situation or was simply the expression of learning processes on both sides is hard to say. However, by the time the EDU office was moved to Brussels, they too felt at home in the EPP.

The dominant centre

Over the past ten years or more, the EPP has brought together parties with the most varied traditions. At times this has given rise to considerable tension and to the formation of a right and a left wing. The assumption that there had been no political tensions prior to that time and that the Christian Democrats had been united must, however, be relegated to political mythology. There are European Parliament statistics to show that in fact it is often the smallest groups that are most deeply split from within.

Within the EPP there are large people's parties situated between the two wings, which are faced nationally with the challenge of bringing 40% of the electorate together. They are the CDU/CSU, the Partido Popular, the PSD, Nea Demokratia and, potentially, Forza Italia. So long as they do not feel bound to support integration, the wings will remain wings, which means they could take flight. The Austrian crisis was so dangerous precisely because it could have been a threat to its cohesion.

Enlargement eastward and EUCD integration

Our analysis so far has concentrated on the EPP as an organisation within the European Union. That is still its main focus. Nevertheless, while it has opened its doors to parties with other traditions, we must not forget that for equally important strategic reasons it is now open to parties from countries that are not yet members of the European Union.

The European Union of Christian Democrats had led a shadowy existence since the founding of the EPP – some would say scornfully since even before that date. At any rate, by the time the EPP was founded in 1976 at the latest, the EUCD had come to take second place in the eyes of the EPP members, while to non-EPP members it must have seemed like a consolation prize for the refusal to grant them EPP membership.

Towards the end of the 1980s, therefore, a broad consensus emerged on putting an end to separate EUCD activities. It was only with the fall of the Iron Curtain that the EUCD acquired a new purpose in life. It became the forum for organising cooperation with the new Central and Eastern European parties, which meant that the EPP did not have to commit itself immediately to parties many of which were still short-lived, threatened with collapse and whose political content was difficult to evaluate precisely.

For example, the EUCD also granted the right of membership to the Croatian HDZ and the Albanian Democratic Party, had to exclude the KDNP and the Smallholders' Party of Hungary because of their right-wing nationalism and embarked on a few adventures in Poland. The first EUCD Congress in Eastern Europe took place in Warsaw, in cooperation with the Centre Alliance shortly before it decided to stop cooperating.

During those years, the EUCD accomplished a great deal, by holding seminars and conferences and by serving as a forum for exchanges of information and, above all, as a seal of quality for Central and Eastern European parties, which helped them compete in their own countries. For those Central and Eastern European countries that hoped to join the European Union, however, the split into two organisations, the EUCD and the EPP – and in many cases even into three organisations if we include the EDU – became an artificial one and the old arguments in favour of merging them gained the upper hand again.

This renewed attempt at a merger was largely initiated by Dr Helmut Kohl, the former CDU party leader and German Chancellor. During 'bungalow talks' at a supper with leading representatives of the European People's Party held in the Chancellery in Bonn in September 1995, it was proposed that the European Union of Christian Democrats should be integrated in the European People's Party.

In face of considerable resistance, in early 1996 the EPP officially submitted a first proposal on integration in a joint strategy paper by Wim van Velzen, the elected President of the EUCD, and the EUCD secretary-general. The commitment towards integration of the Benelux Christian Democrat Wim van Velzen was very much a deciding factor here.

Reservations were expressed not only by traditional Christian Democrats, who still saw the EUCD as a purely Christian Democratic organisation, unlike the EPP. The CSU representatives also expressed strong reservations, as did a number of vice-presidents, such as Ludwig Steiner of the ÖVP who had grown fond of the organisation after decades of working with it.

The matter was finally decided when the EPP offered to put the member parties of non-EU countries on virtually the same footing as EU parties. The last EUCD Congress held in Ljubljana in Slovenia in autumn 1996 adopted a list of demands to that effect agreed with the EPP. The deadline for implementing these demands was fixed for the end of 1998, the date originally planned for the EPP Congress.

Under the amended EPP Statutes, parties from countries involved in accession negotiations can now become Associate Members. Although the nominal differentiation remains, they are now granted all the rights of ordinary member parties, including the right to vote, differentiated by party. The election of Bulgarian Foreign Minister Nadezhda Mihajlova as EPP Vice-

President at the EPP Congress in February 1999 made this clear to all concerned.

Parties from countries that are only at the stage of applying for accession can become observers. The only parties that did not make the leap from the EUCD to the EPP are the Croatian HDZ and the Albanian Democratic Party.

Furthermore, it was agreed to hold a number of EPP conferences to show how much importance the EPP attached to the activities in Central and Eastern Europe: an annual East-West forum in Berlin with the group chairmen from the applicant countries and leading EU politicians concerned with the accession process; an annual conference in the CIS states targeted at parties from these countries and at establishing or deepening contacts with them; and, lastly, a conference for the Balkans. The working group on Central and Eastern Europe continued its activities under the EPP banner.

In summer 2000 the European People's Party had seven heads of government in its family in the 12 applicant states: Estonia, Poland, Slovakia, Slovenia, Bulgaria, Malta and Cyprus. The cooperation established with the heads of government of two other countries, Lithuania and Hungary, is so close that they can be counted as extended family members and it looks as though it is only a question of time before their parties formally join the EPP.

In Latvia and Romania, EPP parties form part of the government. Only in the Czech Republic are they in the opposition. Although the situation can change rapidly, the EPP remains in a good position in relation to EU enlargement.

Rapprochement between the EPP and the European Democrat Union

To understand the creation of the European Democrat Union in 1978 we have to know the background to the foundation of the EPP in 1976. In 1976 the EPP decided to say 'no' on two counts: 'no' to accepting like-minded parties outside the Christian Democratic tradition and 'no' to parties outside the Community. Two years later, the excluded parties joined the CDU/CSU to form the EDU.

When the EPP decided to admit parties from other traditions and parties outside the European Union, the EDU lost its *raison d'être*. All the European Union's EDU parties now belong to the EPP-ED Group in the European Parliament; much the same applies to the Central and Eastern European EDU member parties.

This led to ever closer cooperation during the 1990s.

In October 1994 the leader of the DEMYC, the EDU youth organisation, was elected secretary-general of the EPP. In late 1995 the European Union of

Seniors was formed as a joint EPP and EDU organisation. The EDU student organisation EDS was also recognised as an EPP student organisation. The youth organisations of the EDU and EPP, DEMYC and EJCD, agreed to form a new joint youth association, YEPP, or Youth of the EPP (although in the end the DEMYC decided against because it feared dissolution).

This process also involved joint parliamentary conferences between national EPP and EDU members and MEPs, the most recent of which was held in Luxembourg in summer 1996.

The first joint meeting between the EPP and EDU Presidencies in September 1998 in Caddenabbia was certainly another milestone. Both confirmed that their aim was to have a single organisation to cover the political spectrum in Europe currently covered by the two organisations.

The merger of the secretariats in the EPP secretariat in Brussels on 1 April 2000 should be seen in the same context. Henceforth the EDU executive secretary will also be the EPP deputy secretary-general. The EPP and EDU statutory organs hold their meetings in succession at the same location in order to minimise travel expenses and make it easier for members to participate.

Whether and if so at what pace it will be possible to deepen this integration even further remains an open question, but no doubt the answer will largely be determined by future political developments in the United Kingdom.

Programme

Thomas Jansen, EPP Secretary-General until 1994, first suggested that programme work means working towards integration. This is particularly true of the European People's Party. Since the EPP parties cannot fall back on a single, common ideological tradition and only share a very short common history, it is crucial for them to agree on common basic programmes.

The EPP has done far more advanced programme work than its rivals, perhaps partly for the reasons mentioned above. The EPP not only has a basic programme that was drawn up jointly over a very long period of time, in the form of the 1992 Athens Programme, but is also engaged in a continuous process of programme work.

Joint working groups have drawn up comprehensive programmes for every congress held in the past legislative term: 1995 in Madrid, 1997 in Toulouse and 1999 in Brussels. Each of these programmes took at least a year to prepare and is far more detailed and specific than most of the national parties' programmes.

At each congress, the member parties and associations may table hundreds of amendments. A special committee then recommends their adoption or rejection and the congress takes the final decision by a simple majority vote. In the case of the PES, the preliminary texts are carefully adjusted before being adopted under a consensus procedure. That could be an indication that although its member parties come from the most varied backgrounds, the EPP's internal working capacity certainly matches that of the PES.

Nor has the EPP shied away from thorny issues. The 1995 Madrid Congress, in the run-up to Amsterdam, adopted a programme on the reform of the European institutions that lives up to the best federalist traditions. The 1997 Toulouse Congress entitled 'We are all part of one world' considered questions related to globalisation, deliberately not confining itself to economic aspects but including such issues as the environment, immigration and asylum, combating crime and preventing regional conflicts. These preparatory activities did much to shape the 1999-2004 action programme adopted in Brussels in February 1999.

Conclusions and prospects

It is not possible in the context of a paper of this kind to consider or analyse all the major developments in any real detail. Yet it should have become clear that European parties are highly dynamic organisations in full spate of development. For many years now, much of the research work on parties has tended to classify European political parties as insignificant because their functions do not match those of the national parties; it is to be hoped this will soon be a thing of the past.

In a federal system, European political parties perform their tasks on the basis of the principle of subsidiarity. They should do only that which the national parties cannot in fact do. Any attempt to measure European political parties by the same criterion as national parties is, therefore, bound to be systematically misleading.

So what are the functions of European political parties?

First of all, European parties offer legitimation. National parties acquire greater legitimacy if they are incorporated in a group of recognised parties. The acceptance of the Spanish Partido Popular in the group of European Christian Democratic parties marked a big step away from the old right to the centre, which is where elections are won. Forza Italia's acceptance is an important step for Silvio Berlusconi, in terms of establishing his party as an acceptable partner in Italy and Europe in the long term.

Second: European parties are a form of entrance ticket. They provide access to the most important political personalities in Europe. It is precisely the informal nature of the cooperation, which does not involve political protocol or scores of colleagues, that makes it possible to develop a personal relationship and build up trust. Parties that no longer have to rely on foreign ministries have a decisive advantage in political competition.

Third: European parties reduce transaction costs. Multilateral cooperation is infinitely cheaper than attempts to build up bilateral cooperation. In a Union of 15 and potentially of 25, it is vital to take a multilateral approach. This is crucially important for the summit meetings of party and government leaders and for preparing the agenda of the EU summits.

Fourth: European parties decide the majorities and minorities. Majorities are won not only in elections but also as a result of gains and acquisitions between the elections. In the final analysis, even if they are not always formal these decisions are the party's decisions. In Central and Eastern Europe, the decision which parties will or will not have majorities in the European Union tomorrow will depend on whether they have been accepted in the European families of parties today.

Fifth: European parties offer a common programme, which parliamentary groups simply cannot manage. This is crucially important in an increasingly large European Union with increasingly varied cultural backgrounds.

This list of functions could easily be extended. This is an area on which it would be worth carrying out research, instead of once again uselessly attempting to measure European parties by Duverger's typology. Analyses of that kind say more about the observers and their restricted, national approach than about the object under observation.